British Columbia Legislative Assembly

Papers in Connection with the Construction of the Canadian Pacific Railway

Between the Dominion, Imperial, and Provincial Governments

British Columbia Legislative Assembly

Papers in Connection with the Construction of the Canadian Pacific Railway
Between the Dominion, Imperial, and Provincial Governments

ISBN/EAN: 9783337208998

Printed in Europe, USA, Canada, Australia, Japan

Cover: Foto ©ninafisch / pixelio.de

More available books at **www.hansebooks.com**

IN

CONNECTION WITH THE CONSTRUCTION

OF THE

CANADIAN PACIFIC RAILWAY,

BETWEEN THE

DOMINION, IMPERIAL, AND PROVINCIAL GOVERNMENTS.

𝔓𝔲𝔟𝔩𝔦𝔰𝔥𝔢𝔡 𝔟𝔶 𝔬𝔯𝔡𝔢𝔯 𝔬𝔣 𝔱𝔥𝔢 𝔏𝔢𝔤𝔦𝔰𝔩𝔞𝔱𝔦𝔳𝔢 𝔄𝔰𝔰𝔢𝔪𝔟𝔩𝔶.

VICTORIA : Printed by RICHARD WOLFENDEN, Government Printer,
at the Government Printing Office, James' Bay.
1880.

PAPERS

IN

CONNECTION WITH THE CONSTRUCTION

OF THE

CANADIAN PACIFIC RAILWAY.

Extract from Journals of the Legislative Assembly of 5th May, 1880.

"On the motion of Mr. Galbraith, seconded by Mr. Smithe, it was Resolved,—

"That all the papers in connection with the construction of the Canadian Pacific Railway, between the Dominion, Imperial, and Provincial Governments, be printed in pamphlet form for circulation."

No. 1.

Despatch from Earl Granville to the Governor of British Columbia on Confederation.

BRITISH COLUMBIA.   DOWNING STREET,
   No. 84.   14th August, 1869.
   DUPLICATE.

SIR,

    In my Despatch of 17th of June, in which I communicated to you your appointment to the Government of British Columbia, I informed you that I should probably have occasion to address you on the question then in agitation of the incorporation of that Colony with the Dominion of Canada.

    You are aware that Her Majesty's Government have hitherto declined to entertain this question, mainly because it could not arise practically till the Territory of the Hudson's Bay Company was annexed to the Dominion, but also, perhaps, in the expectation that the public opinion of British Columbia might have opportunity to form and declare itself.

    I have now to inform you that the terms on which Rupert's Land and the North West Territory are to be united to Canada have been agreed to by the parties concerned and that the Queen will probably be advised before long to issue an Order in Council which will incorporate in the Dominion of Canada the whole of the British Possessions on the North American Continent, except the then conterminous Colony of British Columbia.

    The question therefore presents itself, whether this single Colony should be excluded from the great body politic which is thus forming itself?

    On this question the Colony itself does not appear to be unanimous. But as far as I can judge from the Despatches which have reached me, I should conjecture that the prevailing opinion was in favour of union. I have no hesitation in stating that such is also the opinion of Her Majesty's Government.

    They believe that a Legislature selected from an extended area, and representing a diversity of interests, is likely to deal more comprehensively with large questions, more impartially with small questions, and more conclusively with both than is possible when controversies are carried on and decided upon in the comparatively narrow circle in which they arise. Questions of purely local interest will be more carefully and dispassionately considered when disengaged from the larger politics of the country, and at the same time will be more sagaciously considered by persons who have had this larger political education.

Finally, they anticipate that the interests of every Province of British North America will be more advanced by enabling the wealth, credit, and intelligence of the whole to be brought to bear on every part, than by encouraging each in the contracted policy of taking care of itself, possibly at the expense of its neighbour.

Most especially is this true in the case of internal transit. It is evident that the establishment of a British line of communication between the Atlantic and Pacific oceans is far more feasible by the operations of a single Government responsible for the progress of both shores of the Continent than by a bargain negotiated between separate, perhaps in some respects rival, Governments and Legislatures. The San Francisco of British North America would under these circumstances hold a greater commercial and political position than would be attainable by the capital of the isolated Colony of British Columbia.

Her Majesty's Government are aware that the distance between Ottawa and Victoria presents a real difficulty in the way of immediate union. But that very difficulty will not be without its advantages if it renders easy communication indispensable and forces onwards the operations which are to complete it. In any case it is an understood inconvenience and a diminishing one, and it appears far better to accept it as a temporary drawback on the advantages of union than to wait for those obstacles, often more intractable, which are sure to spring up after a neglected opportunity.

The constitutional connection of Her Majesty's Government with the Colony of British Columbia is as yet closer than with any other part of North America, and they are bound on an occasion like the present to give, for the consideration of the community and the guidance of Her Majesty's servants, a more unreserved expression of their wishes and judgment than might be elsewhere fitting.

You will, therefore, give publicity to this dispatch, a copy of which I have communicated to the Governor-General of Canada, and you will hold yourself authorized, either in communication with Sir John Young or otherwise, to take such steps as you properly and constitutionally can for promoting the favourable consideration of this question.

It will not escape you that in acquainting you with the general views of the Government I have avoided all matters of detail on which the wishes of the people and the Legislature will of course be declared in due time. I think it necessary, however, to observe that the constitution of British Columbia will oblige the Governor to enter personally upon many questions, as the condition of Indian tribes and the future position of Government servants, with which, in the case of negotiation between two Responsible Governments, he would not be bound to concern himself.

         I have, &c.,

Governor Musgrave,   (Signed)   GRANVILLE.
 &c., &c., &c.

No. 2.

"PROPOSED TERMS."

1. Canada shall be liable for the Debts and Liabilities of British Columbia existing at the time of Union.

2. The population of British Columbia shall, for the purpose of financial arrangements, be estimated at 120,000. British Columbia not having incurred debts equal to those of other Provinces now constituting the Dominion, shall be entitled to receive, by half-yearly payments in advance from the General Government, interest at the rate of five per centum per annum on the difference between the actual amount of its indebtedness at the date of Union and the proportion of the Public Debt of Canada for 120,000 of the population of Canada at the time of Union.

3. The following sums shall be annually paid by Canada to British Columbia for the support of the Local Government and Legislature, to wit:—

No. 3.

"ACCEPTED TERMS."

1. Canada shall be liable for the debts and liabilities of British Columbia existing at the time of Union.

2. British Columbia not having incurred debts equal to those of the other Provinces now constituting the Dominion, shall be entitled to receive, by half-yearly payments in advance from the General Government interest at the rate of five per cent. per annum on the difference between the actual amount of its indebtedness at the date of the Union, and the indebtedness per head of the population of Nova Scotia and New Brunswick (27.77 dollars), the population of British Columbia being taken at 60,000.

3. The following sums shall be paid by Canada to British Columbia for the support of its Government and Legislature, to wit: an annual subsidy of 35,000 dollars, and an annual grant equal to 80 cents per head of the said population of 60,000, both half-

No. 2.
"PROPOSED TERMS."—*Continued.*

An Annual Grant of $35,000, and a further sum equal to 80 cents a head per annum of the population, both payable half-yearly in advance, the population of British Columbia being estimated as aforesaid at 120,000. Such grant, equal to 80 cents a head, to be augmented in proportion to the increase of population, when such may be shown, until the population amounts to 400,000, at which rate such grant shall thereafter remain.

4. The Dominion shall guarantee interest at the rate of five per centum per annum on such sum, not exceeding £100,000, as may be required for the construction of a first-class Graving Dock at Esquimalt.

5. In addition to the other provisions of this Resolution, Canada shall assume and defray the charges of the following Services:—
a. Salary and allowances of the Lieutenant-Governor;
b. Salaries and allowances of the Judges and Officers of the Supreme Court and of County Courts;
c. The charges in respect of the Department of Customs;
d. The Postal Department;
e. Lighthouses, Buoys, Beacons, and Lightship, and such further charges as may be incident to and connected with the Services which by the "British North America Act, 1867," appertain to the General Government, and as are or may be allowed to the other Provinces.

6. Suitable pensions, such as shall be approved of by Her Majesty's Government, shall be provided by the Government of the Dominion for those of Her Majesty's servants in the Colony whose position and emoluments derived therefrom would be affected by political changes on the admission of this Colony into the Dominion of Canada.

7. The Dominion Government shall supply an efficient and regular fortnightly steam communication between Victoria and San Francisco by steamers adapted and giving facilities for the conveyance of passengers and cargo.

8. Inasmuch as no real union can subsist between this Colony and Canada without the speedy establishment of communication across the Rocky Mountains by Coach Road and Railway, the Dominion shall, within three years from the date of union, construct and open for traffic such Coach Road from some point on the line of the Main Trunk Road of this Colony to Fort Garry, of similar character to the said Main Trunk Road; and shall further engage to use all means in her power to complete such Railway communication at the earliest practicable date, and that Surveys to determine the proper line for such Railway shall be at once commenced; and that a sum of not less than One Million Dollars shall be expended in every year, from and after three years from the date of union, in actually constructing the initial sections of such Railway from the Seaboard of British Columbia, to connect with the Railway system of Canada.

9. The Dominion shall erect and maintain, at Victoria, a Marine Hospital and a Lunatic Asylum, either attached to the Hospital or separate, as may be considered most convenient.

The Dominion shall also erect and maintain a Penitentiary, or other Principal Prison, at such place in the Colony as she may consider most suitable for that purpose.

No. 3.
"ACCEPTED TERMS."—*Continued.*

yearly in advance, such grant of 80 cents per head to be augmented in proportion to the increase of population as may be shown by each subsequent decennial census, until the population amounts to 400,000, at which rate such grant shall thereafter remain, it being understood that the first census be taken in the year 1881.

4. The Dominion will provide an efficient mail service, fortnightly, by steam communication between Victoria and San Francisco, and twice a week between Victoria and Olympia; the vessels to be adapted for the conveyance of freight and passengers.

5. Canada will assume and defray the charges for the following Services:—
A. Salary of the Lieutenant-Governor;
B. Salaries and allowances of the Judges of the Superior Courts and the County or District Courts;
C. The charges in respect to the Department of Customs;
D. The Postal and Telegraphic Services;
E. Protection and Encouragement of Fisheries;
F. Provision for the Militia;
G. Lighthouses, Buoys and Beacons, Shipwrecked crews, Quarantine and Marine Hospitals, including a Marine Hospital at Victoria;
H. The Geological Survey;
I. The Penitentiary;
And such further charges as may be incident to and connected with the services which by the "British North America Act, 1867," appertain to the General Government, and as are or may be allowed to the other Provinces.

6. Suitable pensions, such as shall be approved of by Her Majesty's Government, shall be provided by the Government of the Dominion for those of Her Majesty's servants in the Colony whose position and emoluments derived therefrom would be affected by political changes on the admission of British Columbia into the Dominion of Canada.

7. It is agreed that the existing Customs tariff and excise duties shall continue in force in British Columbia until the railway from the Pacific coast and the system of railways in Canada are connected, unless the Legislature of British Columbia should sooner decide to accept the tariff and excise laws of Canada. When customs and excise duties are, at the time of the union of British Columbia with Canada, leviable on any goods, wares, or merchandizes in British Columbia, or in the other Provinces of the Dominion, those goods, wares, and merchandizes may, from and after the Union, be imported into British Columbia from the Provinces now composing the Dominion, or from either of those Provinces into British Columbia, on proof of payment of the customs or excise duties leviable thereon in the Province of exportation, and on payment of such further amount (if any) of customs or excise duties as are leviable thereon in the Province of importation. This arrangement to have no force or effect after the assimilation of the tariff and excise dutics of British Columbia with those of the Dominion.

8. British Columbia shall be entitled to be represented in the Senate by three members, and by six members in the House of Commons. The representation to be increased under the provisions of the "British North America Act, 1867."

9. The influence of the Dominion Government will

No. 2.

"PROPOSED TERMS."—*Continued.*

10. Efficient Coast Mail Steam Service, in connection with the Post Office, shall be established and maintained by the Government of the Dominion, between Victoria and New Westminster, Nanaimo, and such other places as may require such Services.

11. Whatever encouragement, advantages, and protection are afforded by the Dominion Government to the Fisheries of any of its Provinces shall be extended in similar proportion to British Columbia, according to its requirements for the time being.

12. British Columbia shall participate, in fair proportion in any measures which may be adopted and Funds which may be appropriated by the Dominion for the encouragement of Immigration.

13. British Columbia shall be entitled to be represented in the Senate by Four Members, and by Eight Members in the House of Commons, until the year 18 , and thereafter the Representation in the Senate and the House of Commons shall be increased, subject to the provisions of the "British North America Act, 1867."

14. The Union shall take effect on such day as Her Majesty by Order in Council (on an Address to that effect, in terms of the 146th Section of the "British North America Act, 1867,") may direct; and British Columbia may, in such Address, specify the Districts, Counties, or Divisions, if any, for which any of the Four Senators to whom the Colony shall be entitled shall be named—the Electoral Districts for which—and the time within which the first Election of Members to serve in the House of Commons shall take place.

15. The Constitution of the Executive authority and of the Legislature of British Columbia shall, subject to the provisions of the "British North America Act, 1867," continue as existing at the time of Union, until altered under the authority of the said Act.

16. The provisions in the "British North America Act, 1867," shall (except those parts thereof which are in terms made, or by reasonable intendment may be held to be specially applicable to and only affect one and not the whole of the Provinces now comprising the Dominion, and except so far as the same may be varied by this Resolution) be applicable to British Columbia in the same way and to the like extent as they apply to the other Provinces of the Dominion, and as if the Colony of British Columbia had been one of the Provinces originally united by the said Act.

With reference to Defences:—

a. That it shall be an understanding with the Dominion that their influence will be used to the fullest extent to procure the continued maintenance of the Naval Station at Esquimalt.

b. Encouragement to be given to develop the efficiency and organization of the Volunteer Force in British Columbia.

No. 3.

"ACCEPTED TERMS."—*Continued.*

be used to secure the continued maintenance of the naval station at Esquimalt.

10. The provisions of the "British North America Act, 1867," shall (except those parts thereof which are in terms made, or by reasonable intendment may be held to be specially applicable to and only affect one and not the whole of the Provinces now comprising the Dominion, and except so far as the same may be varied by this Minute) be applicable to British Columbia, in the same way and to the like extent as they apply to the other Provinces of the Dominion, and as if the Colony of British Columbia had been one of the Provinces originally united by the said Act.

11. The Government of the Dominion undertake to secure the commencement simultaneously, within two years from the date of Union, of the construction of a railway from the Pacific towards the Rocky Mountains, and from such point as may be selected, east of the Rocky Mountains, towards the Pacific, to connect the seaboard of British Columbia with the railway system of Canada; and further to secure the completion of such railway within ten years from the date of the Union.

And the Government of British Columbia agree to convey to the Dominion Government, in trust, to be appropriated in such manner as the Dominion Government may deem advisable in furtherance of the construction of the said railway, a similar extent of public lands along the line of railway throughout its entire length in British Columbia, not to exceed, however, twenty (20) miles on each side of the said line, as may be appropriated for the same purpose by the Dominion Government from the public lands in the North-West Territories and the Province of Manitoba. Provided, that the quantity of land which may be held under pre-emption right or by Crown Grant within the limits of the tract of land in British Columbia to be so conveyed to the Dominion Government shall be made good to the Dominion from contiguous public lands; and provided further, that until the commencement, within two years as aforesaid, from the date of the Union, of the construction of the said railway, the Government of British Columbia shall not sell or alienate any further portions of the public lands of British Columbia in any other way than under right of pre-emption, requiring actual residence of the pre-emptor on the land claimed by him. In consideration of the land to be so conveyed in aid of the construction of the said railway, the Dominion Government agree to pay to British Columbia from the date of the Union the sum of one hundred thousand dollars per annum, in half-yearly payments in advance.

12. The Dominion Government shall guarantee the interest for ten years from the date of the completing of the works at the rate of five per centum per annum on such sum, not exceeding £100,000 sterling, as may be required for the construction of a first-class Graving Dock at Esquimalt.

13. The charge of the Indians, and the trusteeship and management of the lands reserved for their use and benefit, shall be assumed by the Dominion Government, and a policy as liberal as that hitherto pursued by the British Columbia Government shall be continued by the Dominion Government after the Union.

To carry out such policy, tracts of land of such

No. 3.
"ACCEPTED TERMS."—*Concluded.*

extent as it has hitherto been the practice of the British Columbia Government to appropriate for that purpose shall from time to time be conveyed by the Local Government to the Dominion Government in trust for the use and benefit of the Indians on application of the Dominion Government; and in case of disagreement between the two Governments respecting the quantity of such tracts of land to be so granted, the matter shall be referred for the decision of the Secretary of State for the Colonies.

14. The constitution of the Executive Authority and of the Legislature of British Columbia shall, subject to the provisions of the "British North America Act, 1867," continue as existing at the time of the Union until altered under the authority of the said Act, it being at the same time understood that the Government of the Dominion will readily consent to the introduction of Responsible Government when desired by the inhabitants of British Columbia, and it being likewise understood that it is the intention of the Governor of British Columbia, under the authority of the Secretary of State for the Colonies, to amend the existing Constitution of the Legislature by providing that a majority of its members shall be elective.

The Union shall take effect according to the foregoing terms and conditions on such day as Her Majesty by and with the advice of Her Most Honourable Privy Council may appoint (on Addresses from the Legislature of the Colony of British Columbia and of the Houses of Parliament of Canada, in the terms of the 146th section of the "British North America Act, 1867,") and British Columbia may in its address specify the electoral districts for which the first election of members to serve in the House of Commons shall take place.

No. 4.

At the Court at Windsor, the 16th day of May, 1871.

PRESENT,

The QUEEN'S Most Excellent Majesty.
His Royal Highness Prince Arthur.
Lord Privy Seal.   Lord Chamberlain.
Earl Cowper.   Mr. Secretary Cardwell.
Earl of Kimberley.   Mr. Ayrton.

WHEREAS by the "British North America Act, 1867," provision was made for the Union of the Provinces of Canada, Nova Scotia, and New Brunswick into the Dominion of Canada, and it was (amongst other things) enacted that it should be lawful for the Queen, by and with the advice of Her Majesty's Most Honorable Privy Council, on Addresses from the Houses of the Parliament of Canada, and of the Legislature of the Colony of British Columbia, to admit that Colony into the said Union on such terms and conditions as should be in the Addresses expressed, and as the Queen should think fit to approve, subject to the provisions of the said Act. And it was further enacted that the provisions of any Order in Council on that behalf should have effect, as if they had been enacted by the Parliament of the United Kingdom of Great Britain and Ireland.

And whereas by Addresses from the Houses of the Parliament of Canada and from the Legislative Council of British Columbia respectively, of which Addresses copies are contained in the Schedule to this Order annexed, Her Majesty was prayed, by and with the advice of Her Most Honourable Privy Council, under the One hundred and forty-sixth Section of the hereinbefore recited Act, to admit British Columbia into the Dominion of Canada, on the terms and conditions set forth in the said Addresses.

And whereas Her Majesty has thought fit to approve of the said terms and conditions: It is hereby ordered and declared by Her Majesty, by and with the advice of Her Privy Council, in pursuance and exercise of the powers vested in Her Majesty by the said Act of Parliament, that from and after the Twentieth day of July, One thousand eight hundred and seventy one, the said Colony of British Columbia shall be admitted into and become part of the Dominion of Canada, upon the terms and conditions set forth in the hereinbefore recited Addresses. And, in accordance with the terms of the said Addresses relating to the Electoral Districts in British Columbia, for which the first election of members to serve in the House of Commons of the said Dominion shall take place, it is hereby further ordered and declared that such Electoral Districts shall be as follows:—

* * * * * * * *

And the Right Honourable Earl of Kimberley, one of Her Majesty's Principal Secretaries of State, is to give the necessary directions herein accordingly.

(Signed) ARTHUR HELPS.

No. 5.

The Secretary of State to the Lieutenant-Governor.

COPY.
No. 58.
OTTAWA, 10th June, 1873.

SIR,—I have the honour to enclose, for the information of your Government, a copy of an Order of His Excellency the Governor-General in Council, fixing Esquimalt, in Vancouver Island, as the Terminus of the Canadian Pacific Railway, and further deciding that a line of Railway be located between the Harbour of Esquimalt and Seymour Narrows on the said Island.

I have further the honour to apply to you to bring the subject under the notice of your Government, with a view to the conveyance, in the manner and for the purposes stated in the said Order, of a strip of land Twenty Miles in width, along the Eastern Coast of Vancouver Island, between Seymour Narrows and the Harbour of Esquimalt.

I have, &c.,
(Signed) E. A. MEREDITH,
Under Secretary of State.

No. 6.

Report of the Privy Council, approved by the Governor-General on the 7th June, 1873.

The Committee of Council having had before them the memorandum of the 29th May last, from the Chief Engineer of the Canadian Pacific Railway, and the Minute of Council thereupon of the 30th May, beg leave to recommend to Your Excellency that Esquimalt, in Vancouver Island, be fixed as the Terminus of the Canadian Pacific Railway; and that a line of Railway be located between the Harbour of Esquimalt and Seymour Narrows on the said Island.

The Committee further recommend that application immediately be made, by despatch to the Lieutenant-Governor of British Columbia, for the conveyance to the Dominion Government, in trust, according to the 11th paragraph of the Terms of Agreement of Union, of a strip of land, Twenty Miles in width, along the Eastern Coast of Vancouver Island, between Seymour Narrows and the Harbour of Esquimalt.

An Order of the Lieutenant-Governor of British Columbia in Council appropriating this tract of land, in furtherance of the construction of the said Railway, will be necessary, in order to operate as a sufficient conveyance and reservation of the said land to and for the Dominion Government.

(Certified) W. A. HIMSWORTH,
Clerk, Privy Council.

No. 7.

The Lieutenant-Governor to the Secretary of State for Canada.

Copy,
No. 67.

GOVERNMENT HOUSE,
26th July, 1873.

Sir,—I have the honour to state that the Under Secretary of State for the Provinces' Despatch No. 58, of the 10th ultimo, and the copy therewith enclosed of an Order of His Excellency the Governor-General in Council, fixing Esquimalt, on Vancouver Island, as the Terminus of the Canadian Pacific Railway, and further deciding that a line of Railway be located between Esquimalt Harbour and Seymour Narrows, was duly received and submitted by me for consideration in my Executive Council, and that the strip of land Twenty Miles in width along the Eastern Coast of Vancouver Island, between Seymour Narrows and the Harbour of Esquimalt, specified in the said Order in Council, was accordingly reserved on the 1st July instant, under the powers and provisions of the 42nd Section of the Land Ordinance of 1870 of British Columbia, and notice of such reservation duly published in the Government Gazette, as appears in the copy thereof herewith enclosed.

With further reference to the Under Secretary of the Provinces' Despatch, I have also the honour to enclose herewith, and to request that you will lay before His Excellency the Governor-General, a Minute of my Executive Council conveying the conclusion of this Government that it is not advisable to make, at present, the conveyance applied for in the said Despatch and accompanying Order in Council of the land therein specified and now held under reservation, and setting forth the grounds upon which that conclusion is based.

I have, &c.,
(Signed) JOSEPH W. TRUTCH.

No. 8.

Report of the Executive Council, approved by the Lieutenant-Governor on the 30th day of June, 1873.

On a Memorandum dated 30th June, 1873, from the Honourable the Attorney-General, recommending that, for the present, a bare reservation of the Twenty Mile belt lying between Esquimalt Harbour and Seymour Narrows be made, to protect the Government of the Dominion, until the question raised by the Order in Council of the Privy Council of Canada, dated the 7th instant, with its covering Despatch on the subject of the 10th instant, be more fully discussed and determined, and that the conveyance, in trust, of the said land asked for by the Ottawa Government be for the present deferred, and that the enclosed notice of reservation be adopted and published in a Gazette Extraordinary.

(Certified) W. J. ARMSTRONG,
Clerk of the Executive Council.

No. 9.

Notice.

Whereas by an Order in Council dated the 7th day of June, 1873, of the Honourable the Privy Council of Canada, it has been decided "that Esquimalt, in Vancouver Island, "be fixed as the Terminus of the Canadian Pacific Railway, and that a line of Railway "be located between the Harbour of Esquimalt and Seymour Narrows, on the the said "Island;" and whereas, in accordance with the terms of the said Order in Council, application has been made to His Excellency "the Lieutenant-Governor of British "Columbia, for a reservation and for the conveyance to the Dominion Government, in "trust, according to the 11th Paragraph of the Terms of the Agreement of Union, of a "strip of land Twenty Miles in width along the Eastern Coast of Vancouver Island, "between Seymour Narrows and the Harbour of Esquimalt, in furtherance of the con- "struction of the said Railway."

And whereas it has been deemed advisable that the land within the limits aforesaid should be Reserved, prior to any conveyance aforesaid being made thereof. Public notice is therefore hereby given that from and after this date a strip of Land Twenty Miles in width along the Eastern Coast of Vancouver Island, between Seymour Narrows and the Harbour of Esquimalt, is hereby Reserved.

By Command.

Provincial Secretary's Office,
1st July, 1873.

JOHN ASH,
Provincial Secretary.

No. 10.

The Lieutenant-Governor to the Secretary of State.

COPY.
No. 68.

GOVERNMENT HOUSE,
26th July, 1873.

SIR,—I have the honour to enclose at the request of my Ministers, for submission to His Excellency the Governor-General, a Minute of my Executive Council, representing the non-fulfilment by the Dominion of the 11th Section of the Terms of Union of British Columbia with Canada, expressing regret that the Railway has not been commenced, and strongly protesting against the breach of a condition of the Terms so highly important to this Province.

I have, &c.,
(Signed) JOSEPH W. TRUTCH.

No. 11.

Order in Council of this Province, dated July 25th, 1873.

The Committee of Council have had under consideration the non-fulfilment by the Dominion Government of the 11th Section of the Terms of Union.

The Committee regret that the construction of the Railway has not been commenced, and therefore strongly protest against the breach by the Dominion Government of a condition of the Terms so highly important to the Province.

The Committee recommend the above for the approval of Your Excellency, and, if sanctioned, respectfully request that a copy thereof be at once forwarded to the Dominion Government.

(Certified) W. J. ARMSTRONG,
Clerk, Executive Council.

No. 12.

Report approved by the Lieutenant-Governor on the 25th July, 1873.

The Committee of Council have had under consideration a memorandum of the 23rd July, 1873, from the Honourable the Attorney-General, reporting upon a Despatch, dated the 16th June last, from the Honourable the Secretary of State for the Provinces to Your Excellency, covering an Order of the Honourable the Privy Council of Canada, of the 7th of the same month, which states that the Privy Council had decided as follows:—"That Esquimalt, in Vancouver Island, be fixed as the Terminus of the "Canadian Pacific Railway, and that a line of Railway be located between the Harbour "of Esquimalt and Seymour Narrows on the said Island."

In pursuance of this decision, Your Excellency is requested to convey by Order in "Council" to the Dominion Government, in trust, according to the 11th paragraph of "the Terms of the Agreement of Union, a strip of land Twenty Miles in width along "the Eastern Coast of Vancouver Island, between Seymour Narrows and the Harbour "of Esquimalt."

Upon the Despatch and Order in Council the Honourable the Attorney-General reports as follows:—

"The agreement of Union is embodied in a Statute. Its language must therefore be measured by the ordinary and well known rules of interpretation as applied to Statutes. The language must not be construed too narrowly, but a fair and liberal construction—and one in accordance with the spirit and true meaning of the agreement—should be placed upon the wording of the 'Terms.' Allowing, however, the greatest latitude of interpretation, and applying the broadest and most liberal construction to the eleventh Section of the Agreement, nothing appears which would seem to warrant the Dominion Government in claiming, or justify Your Excellency in granting, a conveyance of the Twenty Mile belt of land mentioned, until the line of Railway be defined.

"It is admitted that the Dominion Government is entitled to the greatest consideration for the energy it has hitherto displayed in its desire to faithfully carry out the Railway provisions contained in the Agreement.

"Hence the Government of this Province, holding these views and anxious to render all the assistance in its power to the Dominion Government, assumed the responsibility of reserving the belt of land mentioned almost immediately after the receipt of the Despatch, which is the subject of this report. It was, however, expressly understood that the Order in Council creating the reserve should *not operate as a conveyance of the lands* within its limits, and that the reserve itself should not be of a *permanent character.*

"The 11th Section of the Terms of Union reads as follows :

'The Government of the Dominion undertake to secure the commencement, * * 'within two years from the date of the Union, of the construction of a Railway from 'the Pacific towards the Rocky Mountains,' thence Eastward, &c.

'The Government of British Columbia agree to convey to the Dominion Govern-'ment in trust, to be appropriated in such manner as the Dominion Government may 'deem advisable, in furtherance of the construction of the *said Railway*, an extent of 'public lands *along the line of Railway* throughout its entire length in British Columbia, 'not to exceed, however, Twenty Miles on *each side of said line* * * * and 'provided further that until the commencement, within two years, as aforesaid, from 'the date of the Union, of the construction of the said Railway, the Government of 'British Columbia shall not sell or alienate any further portion of the public lands of 'British Columbia in any other way than under right of pre-emption requiring actual 'residence of the pre-emptor on the land claimed by him.'

"Under this agreement the Dominion Government undertook 'to secure the commencement of the construction of a Railway from the Pacific' eastward on the 20th July, 1873, and the Province in consideration thereof agreed to convey to the Dominion Government 'in furtherance of the construction of the *said Railway*,' certain 'public lands *along the line of Railway*' not exceeding in extent Twenty Miles 'on *each side of said line*.'

"As far as the Government of this Province has been informed, no line of Railway has been surveyed between Esquimalt and Seymour Narrows. A conveyance cannot therefore be made of public lands 'along a line of Railway' and 'on each side of said line' where no such 'line of Railway' exists. The demand made is for a conveyance of 'a strip of land' Twenty Miles in width along the 'Eastern Coast of Vancouver Island,' or in other words in the absence of a survey for a strip of the public lands along the sea coast, but not along any defined line of Railway.

"It is respectfully submitted that had a 'line of Railway' been defined by a location survey, the Government of this Province would have been notified thereof, and the language of the Despatch and of the Order of the Privy Council would have been materially different from that used in the present instance. Instead of asking for a conveyance of land along a sea coast, a demand would have been made for a conveyance of certain lands 'along a line of Railway' adopted and laid out according to an accompanying plan, such a demand, it is humbly conceived, would have been in accordance with the spirit and language of the 11th Section.

"The term of two years mentioned in the first and second paragraphs of the section was inserted by the framers of the terms as a period amply sufficient to enable the Dominion Government to complete the preliminary surveys necessary to determine 'the line of Railway,' and the Provincial Government agreed to withdraw all its public lands from sale for the like period in order that the first opportunity should be afforded to the Dominion Government of acquiring *within the two years* and before the work of construction should commence, the land contiguous to its line of Railway, as defined from time to time.

"The two years have expired, and as the claim for the reserve mentioned is not established, it becomes the duty of the Government of British Columbia in the interests of the Province, to respectfully press upon the Dominion Government, the necessity of some immediate action being taken to render the valuable belt of land containing an area of some 3,500 square miles of service to the Province.

"The undersigned therefore suggests that, as no line of Railway has been defined, Your Excellency be respectfully recommended, for the above reasons, to withhold the conveyance to the Dominion Government of the land mentioned in the Despatch; and that the Reserve of the said land be continued until a fair opportunity shall have been afforded to the Dominion Government to consider the subject, and inform the Government of this Province of its views thereon.

(Signed)   "GEO. A. WALKEM,
                              "*Attorney-General.*"

The Committee concur in the above Report of the Attorney-General, and submit the same for Your Excellency's approval, and if sanctioned, they suggest that a copy of this Order in Council be transmitted to His Excellency the Governor-General.

(Certified)   W. J. ARMSTRONG,
                           Clerk, Executive Council.

No. 13.

Secretary of State to the Lieutenant-Governor.

COPY.   OTTAWA,
No. 72.   23rd August, 1873.

SIR,—I have the honour to acknowledge the receipt of your Despatch, No. 68, 26th ultimo, covering a copy of a Minute of your Executive Council, complaining of the non-fulfilment by the Dominion Government of the 11th Section of the Terms of Union of British Columbia with Canada.

Your Despatch and its enclosures will be at once laid before His Excellency the Governor-General in Council.

I have, &c.,
(Signed)   E. J. LANGEVIN,
                            Under Secretary of State.

No. 14.

Secretary of State to the Lieutenant-Governor.

COPY.   OTTAWA,
No. 74.   26th August, 1873.

SIR,—I have the honour to acknowledge the receipt of your Despatch, No. 67, of the 26th ultimo, referring to the Order of His Excellency the Governor-General in Council, communicated to you on the 10th June last, applying for the conveyance to the Dominion Government of a strip of land Twenty Miles in width along the Eastern Coast of Vancouver Island, between Seymour Narrows and the Harbour of Esquimalt, and enclosing a copy of a Minute of your Executive Council on the subject of the said application.

Your Despatch and its enclosures will be laid before His Excellency the Governor-General in Council.

I have, &c.,
(Signed)   E. J. LANGEVIN,
                            Under Secretary of State.

No. 15.

The Secretary of State to the Lieutenant-Governor.

DEPARTMENT OF THE SECRETARY OF STATE FOR CANADA,
OTTAWA, 11th September, 1873.

SIR,—I have the honour to transmit to you herewith, for the information of your Government, a copy of an Order of His Excellency the Governor-General in Council, on your Despatch, No. 67, of the 26th July last, enclosing a Minute of your Executive Council, conveying their conclusion that it is not advisable to make, at present, the conveyance applied for in the letter to you of the 10th of June last.

I have, &c.,
(Signed) J. C. AIKINS,
Secretary of State for Canada.

No. 16.

Report of the Privy Council approved by the Governor-General on the 3rd *September,* 1873.

The Committee of the Privy Council have had under consideration a Despatch from the Lieutenant-Governor of British Columbia, of the 26th July, 1873, enclosing a Minute of his Executive Council, conveying the conclusion of the Government of British Columbia, that it is not advisable to make at present the conveyance applied for in a Despatch of the Under Secretary of State for the Provinces, of the 10th of June.

The Committee of the Privy Council have read with great attention, the report of the Executive Council of British Columbia, enclosed in the Lieutenant-Governor's Despatch, and beg to submit, that so long as the land which is referred to is not alienated from the Crown, but held under reservation, as stated in the Lieutenant-Governor's Despatch, the object of the Government of the Dominion will be obtained, that object being simply that when the Railway shall come to be constructed, the land in question shall be at the disposition of the Government of the Dominion, for the purposes laid down in the 11th Section of the Terms of Union with British Columbia.

(Certified) W. A. HIMSWORTH,
Clerk Executive Council.

No. 17.

The Lieutenant-Governor to the Secretary of State.

COPY.
No. 80.

GOVERNMENT HOUSE,
22nd September, 1873.

SIR,—With reference to my Despatch, No. 67, of the 26th July last, I have the honour to enclose for the information of His Excellency the Governor-General, a Minute of my Executive Council, urging that the boundaries of the land on Vancouver Island, proposed to be claimed by the Government of the Dominion in trust, to aid the construction of the Railroad, under the Terms of Union of British Columbia with Canada, may be at once defined, and that a competent person in this Province may be appointed to dispose of said lands, on such terms as will admit of settlement, and authorizing the Honourable A. DeCosmos, President of the Executive Council and Premier of my Ministry, to confer with the Government of Canada on this subject.

A duplicate of this Despatch and enclosure will be handed to you by Mr. DeCosmos, who starts to-morrow for Ottawa.

I have, &c.,
(Signed) JOSEPH W. TRUTCH.

No. 18.

Report of the Honorable the Executive Council, approved by the Lieutenant-Governor on the 20th day of September, 1873.

On a Memorandum, dated 18th September, 1873, from the Honorable Chief Commissioner of Lands and Works, reporting that the Order in Council of the 30th June, 1873, reserving Crown Lands of the East Coast of Vancouver Island, is seriously retarding the settlement of that portion of the Province; and recommending that, in view of the fact that the Despatch from His Excellency the Lieutenant-Governor to the Secretary of State, transmitting the Minute of this Executive Council, dated 25th July, 1873, upon the subject of this reservation, has not as yet been replied to, and as the matter requires immediate settlement, that the Dominion Government be respectfully urged to at once define, by survey, the land they propose claiming on the East Coast of Vancouver Island; and that they appoint, also, a competent person in this Province to dispose of said lands on such terms as will admit of settlement; and that the Honourable Amor DeCosmos, as Special Delegate, about to proceed to Ottawa, be authorized to confer with the Dominion Government upon the subject.

(Certified)   W. J. ARMSTRONG,
Clerk, Executive Council.

No. 19.

The Secretary of State to the Lieutenant-Governor.

COPY.   OTTAWA, 8th October, 1873.

SIR,—I have the honour to acknowledge the receipt of your Despatch of the 22nd ultimo, on the subject of the occupation of lands reserved by the Dominion Government, and to state that the same will receive due consideration.

I have, &c.,
(Signed)   EDOUARD J. LANGEVIN,
Under Secretary of State.

No. 20.

The Lieutenant-Governor to the Secretary of State.

COPY.   GOVERNMENT HOUSE,
No. 96.   24th November, 1873.

SIR,—I have the honour to enclose a further Minute of my Executive Council, referring to the non-fulfilment by the Dominion Government of the 11th Article of the Terms of Union of this Province with Canada.

In accordance with the advice of my Ministers, expressed in this Minute, I beg you to be pleased to lay before His Excellency the Governor-General, and to be good enough to bring to His Excellency's attention the previous Minutes of my Executive Council on the same subject, which were forwarded for his consideration in my Despatches, Nos. 67 and 68, 26th July last, the latter of which conveying a protest from this Government on the failure of the Dominion Government to secure the commencement, within two years from the date of Union, of the construction of a Railroad from the Pacific towards the Rocky Mountains, as provided in the 11th Article of the Terms of Union, is yet unanswered; and to move His Excellency to communicate to this Government, in whatever manner he may deem advisable, in time to meet the requirement of the desire indicated by my Ministers, the course intended to be taken by the Dominion in fulfilment of the 11th Article of the Terms of Union of this Province with Canada.

I have, &c.,
(Signed)   JOSEPH W. TRUTCH.

No. 21.

Report of the Executive Council, approved by the Lieutenant-Governor on the 22nd day of November, 1873.

The Committee of Council having had under consideration a memorandum from the Honourable the Provincial Secretary, dated 19th November, 1873, setting forth the facts—

That the Government of British Columbia has protested against the non-fulfilment by the Dominion Government of the 11th Article of the Terms of Union.

That beyond the acknowledgment of the receipt, no reply has been made by the Dominion Government to the Despatch conveying the protest.

That the Government of British Columbia looking at the actual condition of affairs felt compelled to await the action of the Parliament of Canada, expected shortly to meet, and which did meet at Ottawa on the 23rd of October last past.

That the Parliament of Canada has been prorogued not to meet until February next, without making provision for the construction of the Pacific Railway.

That the Legislative Assembly of the Province stands called to meet at Victoria on the 18th day of December next, and

That the non-fulfilment by the Dominion Government of the Terms of Union has caused a strong feeling of anxiety and discouragement to exist throughout the Province.

The Committee advise your Honour to ask the Dominion Government through the proper channel, for a decided expression of its policy with regard to the fulfilment of the 11th Article of the Terms of Union, in order that the information may be given to the Legislature at the opening of the coming Session.

And they request that the decision arrived at be communicated to Your Honour by telegram at the earliest moment possible; and the Committee respectfully suggest that, if the present report be sanctioned, Your Honour will be pleased to forward the same to His Excellency the Governor-General; and also to draw his attention to the Minutes of Council, each bearing date the 25th day of July last, on the same subject, one being a protest against the breach of Article 11, and the other a denial of the right of the Dominion Government to a conveyance or reserve of any of the public lands for Railway purposes until the line of Railway should be defined.

(Certified) W. J. ARMSTRONG,
Clerk, Executive Council.

No. 22.

The Secretary of State for Canada to Lieutenant-Governor.

SIR,—I have the honour to acknowledge the receipt of your despatch, No. 96, of the 24th ultimo, enclosing, with reference to your previous despatches on the subject, a further minute of your Executive Council respecting the non-fulfilment by the Dominion Government of the 11th Article of the "Terms" of the Union of British Columbia with Canada.

In reply, I have to inform you that the subject will receive the consideration of the Government.

I have, &c.,

No. 23.

Telegram.

OTTAWA, December 22nd, 1873.

The Hon. G. A. Walkem.

The Dominion Government scheme for the construction of Pacific Railway was outlined in my speech at Sarnia, Ontario, on the 25th November, which you have no doubt seen.

We are giving earnest consideration to the details of the scheme, which we believe will be acceptable to the whole of the Dominion including British Columbia. We hope to communicate with you shortly, probably, by special agent. I will telegraph you again in a week or so.

(Signed) A. MACKENZIE.

No. 24.

The Secretary of State for Canada to the Lieutenant-Governor.

(590–246.)
DEPARTMENT, SECRETARY OF STATE,
20th December, 1873.

22nd December, 1873.

SIR,—Adverting to your Despatches, Nos. 68 and 96, of the 26th July and 24th November last, respectively, I have the honour to transmit to you herewith, for the information of your Government, a copy of an Order of His Excellency the Governor-General in Council, on the subject of the alleged non-fulfilment by the Dominion Government of the 11th Article of the Terms of Union of the Province of British Columbia with Canada.

I have, &c.,

No. 25.

Report of the Privy Council, approved by the Governor-General in Council on the 23rd December, 1873.

The Committee have had under consideration the despatch dated 24th November, 1873, from the Lieutenant-Governor of British Columbia, enclosing a further minute of his Executive Council, referring to the non-fulfilment by the Dominion Government of the 11th Article of the Terms of Union of this Province with Canada, and stating that in accordance with the advice of his Ministers expressed in this Minute, he requests that this despatch, and its enclosure, be laid before Your Excellency, together with the previous minutes of his Executive Council on the same subject, which were forwarded for consideration in his despatches, No. 67 and No. 68, of the 26th of July last, the latter of which, conveying a protest from that Government on the failure of the Dominion Government to secure the commencement within two years from the date of Union, of the construction of a railroad from the Pacific towards the Rocky Mountains, as provided in the 11th Article of the Terms of Union, he states is yet unanswered, and requesting Your Excellency to communicate to that Government, in whatever manner may be deemed advisable, in time to meet the requirement of the desire indicated by his Ministers, the course intended to be taken by the Dominion Government in fulfilment of the 11th Article of the Terms of Union of that Province with Canada.

The Committee of Council respectfully recommend that the Lieutenant-Governor of British Columbia be informed that this Government is giving its most earnest consideration to the project for the construction of the Pacific Railway, an outline of which was given in the speech delivered by Mr. Mackenzie at Sarnia, on the 25th November, a scheme which they believe will be acceptable to the whole Dominion, including British Columbia, and that they hope to be able, within a short time, to communicate more definitely with that Province on the subject.

Certified,
(Signed)   W. A. HIMSWORTH,
Clerk Privy Council.

No. 26.

The Lieutenant-Governor to the Secretary of State for Canada.

(No. 4.)
BRITISH COLUMBIA,
Government House, 21st January, 1874.

SIR,—I have the honour to acquaint you that I have duly received and laid before my Executive Council your despatch of the 30th ultimo, and the copy therewith enclosed of an Order of His Excellency the Governor-General in Council, on the subject of the non-fulfilment by the Dominion Government of the 11th Article of the Terms of Union of this Province with Canada.

I have, &c.,
(Signed)   JOSEPH W. TRUTCH.

No. 27.

The Governor-General to the Earl of Kimberley.

(No. 301.)   OTTAWA, December 26th, 1873.

MY LORD,—I have the honour to enclose, for your information a copy of a despatch from the Lieutenant-Governor of British Columbia to the Secretary of State of Canada, forwarding a minute of his Executive Council referring to the non-fulfilment on the part of the Government of the Dominion, of the 11th Article of the Terms of Union with that Province, in respect to the construction of the Canada Pacific Railway.

24th March.

I also beg to transmit copy of a report of a Committee of the Privy Council of the Dominion, on the above mentioned despatch, stating that my Government is giving its most earnest consideration to the project for the construction of a Railway to the Pacific.

23rd December.

I have, &c.,
(Signed)   DUFFERIN.

No. 28.

The Earl of Kimberley to the Earl of Dufferin.

DOWNING STREET,
15th January, 1874.

MY LORD,—I have the honour to acknowledge the receipt of your despatch No. 301, of the 26th December, enclosing a copy of a despatch from the Lieutenant-Governor of British Columbia, with a copy of a minute of his Executive Council, referring to the non-fulfilment, on the part of the Canadian Government, of the 11th Article of the Terms of Union between that Province and Canada in respect to the construction of the Pacific Railway.

I have, &c.,
(Signed)   KIMBERLEY.

No. 29.

Extract from Journals of Legislative Assembly.

MONDAY, 9th February, 1874.

On the motion of the Honourable Mr. *Beaven*, seconded by Mr. *Duck*, it was *Resolved*,—

That whereas, on the 20th July, 1871, the Colony of *British Columbia* was united to and became part of the Dominion of *Canada*, in accordance with certain Terms; and whereas by Section Eleven of the said Terms, the Government of the Dominion undertook to secure the commencement, simultaneously, within two years from the date of Union, of the construction of a Railway from the *Pacific* towards the *Rocky Mountains*, and from such point as may be selected East of the *Rocky Mountains* towards the *Pacific*; and whereas, the two years therein referred to expired on the 20th July last, and the construction of the said Railway was not then, and has not since been, commenced, causing thereby serious loss and injury to the people of this Province, be it, therefore, Resolved—

That an humble Address be presented to His Honour the Lieutenant-Governor, respectfully requesting him to protest, on behalf of the Legislature and people of this Province, against the infraction of this most important clause of the Terms of Union, and to impress upon the present Administration in *Canada* the absolute necessity of commencing the actual construction of the Railway from the seaboard of *British Columbia* early in the present year.

No. 30.

The Lieutenant-Governor to the Secretary of State.

Victoria, 25th February, 1874.

Sir,—I have the honour to enclose herewith, a copy of an Address to me from the Legislative Assembly of this Province, requesting me to protest on behalf of the Legislature and people of British Columbia, against the infraction of the 11th Article of the Terms of Union of British Columbia with Canada, by which the Dominion undertook to secure the commencement simultaneously within two years from the date of Union of the construction of a Railway from the Pacific towards the Rocky Mountains, and from such point as may be selected East of the Rocky Mountains towards the Pacific, to connect the seaboard of British Columbia with the Railway system of Canada, and to urge the absolute necessity for the commencement of the actual construction of such Railway, from the seaboard of British Columbia, early in the present year.

I also enclose a Minute of my Executive Council concurring in the prayer of this Address to me, and recommending that a copy be forwarded by me to His Excellency the Governor General, with a request that he will be pleased to order immediate action to be taken thereon.

In accordance, therefore, with the advice of my Ministers, I beg that you will be good enough to lay this Despatch and its Enclosure before His Excellency the Governor-General, and to recommend to His Excellency's favourable consideration, the representations and urgent requests of the Government and Legislature of British Columbia herein set forth.

I have, &c.,
(Signed)   Joseph W. Trutch.

No. 31.

Report of the Executive Council, approved by the Lieutenant-Governor on the 23rd February, 1874.

The Committee of Council have had under consideration an Address of the Legislative Assembly of the 9th instant, respecting the breach of the railway clause contained in the Terms of Union.

On the 25th of July last, and again on the 24th November last, strong protests and representations on the subject of the Address were forwarded to the Dominion Government, but no reply of an assuring character has yet been received by the Province. The result of this silence has been one of painful and growing dissatisfaction.

The Committee feel that a strong but respectful protest against the course pursued by the Dominion Government should be once more forwarded to His Excellency the Governor-General.

The Committee recommend that should this their report be approved of His Honour the Lieutenant-Governor be respectfully requested to cause a copy of the Address to be forwarded to His Excellency the Governor-General, with a request that he will be pleased to order immediate action to be taken thereon.

The Committee advise that their recommendation be approved of.

Certified.
(Signed)   W. J. Armstrong.
Clerk Executive Council.

No. 32.

Address of the Legislative Assembly of British Columbia to the Lieutenant-Governor.

To His Honour the Honourable Joseph William Trutch, *Lieutenant-Governor of the Province of British Columbia.*

"May it please Your Honour:— We, Her Majesty's dutiful and loyal subjects, the "Legislative Assembly of the Province of British Columbia, in Parliament assembled, "beg leave to approach Your Honour with our respectful request that Your Honour "will be pleased to take into consideration the following Resolution of the House:—

"Whereas, on the 20th July 1871, the Colony of British Columbia was united to and became part of the Dominion of Canada, in accordance with certain terms; and whereas by Section 11 of the said Terms, the Government of the Dominion undertook to secure the commencement, simultaneously within two years from the date of Union, of the construction of a railway from the Pacific towards the Rocky Mountains, and from such point as may be selected east of the Rocky Mountains towards the Pacific; and whereas the two years therein referred to expired on the 20th July last, and the construction of the said railway was not then, and has not since been, commenced, causing thereby serious loss and injury to the people of this Province, be it therefore *Resolved*, That an humble Address be presented to His Excellency the Lieutenant-Governor, respectfully requesting him to protest on behalf of the Legislature and people of this Province against the infraction of this most important clause of the Terms of Union, and to impress upon the present administration the absolute necessity of commencing the actual construction of the railway from the seaboard of British Columbia early in the present year."

(Signed)   J. ROLAND HETT,
9th February, 1874.   *Clerk of the Assembly.*

No. 33.

The Secretary of State to the Lieutenant-Governor.

OTTAWA, 12th March, 1874.

SIR,—I have the honour to acknowledge the receipt of your Despatch No. 9 of the 25th ultimo, covering a copy of an Address of the Legislative Assembly of the Province of British Columbia, and of a Minute of your Executive Council founded thereon, on the subject of the non-fulfilment of the 11th Section of the Terms of Union of the Province to the Dominion.

Your Despatch, and its enclosures, will be submitted for the consideration of His Excellency the Governor-General.

I have, &c.,
(Signed)   E. J. LANGEVIN,
Under Secretary of State.

No. 34.

Mr. Mackenzie to Mr. Edgar (Confidential.)

OTTAWA, February 19th, 1874.

MY DEAR SIR,—In your conversations with leading men in and out of the Government in Columbia, it will be well to let them understand that in proposing to take longer time than is provided in constructing the railway, we are actuated solely by an urgent necessity. That we are as anxious as possible to reach the object sought by all—the early construction of the road.

We are, however, advised by our Engineers, that it is a physical impossibility to construct the road in that time—that is within the time provided in the Terms of the Union—and that any attempt to do so can only result in very great useless expense and financial disorder. You can point out that the surveys for the Intercolonial Railway were begun in 1864, and the work carried on uninterruptedly ever since, and although the utmost expedition was used, it will require still eighteen months to complete it. If it requires so much time in a settled country to build 500 miles of railway, with facilities everywhere for procuring all supplies, one may conceive the time and labour required to construct a line five times the length through a country all but totally unsettled.

You will point out that it is because we desire to act in good faith towards Columbia, that we at once avow our inability to carry out the exact conditions of the Terms of Union. That it would have been an easy matter for us to have said nothing about it, or carelessly to have assumed the task of finishing the road before the month of July, 1881. Acting from a desire to deal frankly and honestly with Columbia, we considered what we could do to afford, at the earliest possible date, some means of travel across the continent, preliminary to and in advance of a complete line of railway.

You will point out that, as part of the Dominion, it is as much in their interest as in ours to pursue a careful, judicious policy; also, that in assuming a disposition in spite of all reason to insist on impossibilities, they are only setting at defiance all the rest of the Dominion and the laws of nature.

That by insisting on the "pound of flesh," they will only stimulate a feeling on the part of people generally to avoid in the future giving anything but the "pound of flesh."

You will remember that the Dominion is bound to reach the seaboard of the Pacific only, not Victoria or Esquimalt, and you will convey an intimation to them that any further extension beyond the head waters of the Bute Inlet, or whatever other portion of the sea-waters may be reached, may depend entirely on the spirit shown by themselves in assenting to a reasonable extension of time or a modification of the terms originally agreed to.

You will also put them in remembrance of the terms they themselves proposed, which terms were assented to by their Local Legislature, and point out that it was only the insane act of the Administration here which gave such conditions of Union to Columbia; that it could only have been because that Administration sought additional means of procuring extensive patronage immediately before the general election, and saw in coming contests the means of carrying the elections, that the Province obtained on paper terms which at the time were known to be impossible of fulfilment.

If you find any favourable disposition among the leading men of the Province towards affording a generous consideration to the obvious necessity of giving a sufficient time for pushing the road through Columbia, you will endeavour to ascertain what value they attach to such consideration.

You will point out that the action of this Government in the matter of the Graving Dock, and the agreement to advance in cash the balance of the amount of debt with which Columbia was allowed to enter the Confederation, showed that it was not considering itself bound to the exact Terms of Union, but was willing to go beyond them when the necessities of the Province seemed to demand such action, and that we not unnaturally expect similar action on the part of the Province.

In the event of your finding that there is a willingness to accept a proposition to extend the time for building the road, you will endeavour to obtain some proposition from them, directly or indirectly, and communicate this to us by cipher telegraph at once.

If, on the other hand, they make or indicate no proposition, you will telegraph to us what you think would be acceptable, but wait a reply before making any proposition.

In the event of the leading men evincing a disposition to negotiate, you will endeavour to secure something like a combination of parties to sanction any proposition likely to be generally accepted.

It will be well that you should take some means of ascertaining the popular view of the Railway question. This may be done by mingling among the people and allowing them to speak freely while you listen, remembering, in taking impressions, that your audience may be impressed by special local considerations rather than the general question.

It will be well not to confine yourself to the vicinity of the Government offices or Victoria, but to cross to the mainland and meet with the people at Westminster and other towns and villages on the lower reaches of the Fraser.

It may be that you will find there is a disposition manifested to negotiate at Ottawa, in which case you will advise us of the existence of such a desire.

You will take special care not to admit in any way that we are bound to build the railway to Esquimalt or any other place on the Island; and while you do not at all threaten not to build there, to let them understand that this is wholly and purely a concession, and that its construction must be contingent on a reasonable course being pursued regarding other parts of the scheme.

It may be that the Local Government will desire to constitute the members for the Commons a delegation to discuss matters here; if this be the case, you will still remain until we shall communicate with you.

You will take every opportunity of noting the various matters connected with Dominion business, in accordance with instructions that will be sent.

I am, &c.,
(Signed) A. MACKENZIE.

No. 35.

Letter of Introduction from the Hon. A. Mackenzie to the Hon. G. A. Walkem.

OTTAWA, February 19th, 1874.

DEAR SIR,—Allow me introduce Mr. James D. Edgar, of Toronto, who visits your Province on public business for the Government. Mr. Edgar will confer with yourself and other members of the Government of Columbia on the questions lately agitating the public mind in Columbia, and will be glad to receive your views regarding the policy of the Government on the construction of the Railway.

But for the meeting of Parliament in four weeks, some member of the Government would have visited your Province, but Mr. Edgar, as a public man, is well known here, and fully understands the question he will discuss with you.

I need not, I am sure, assure you of my own sincere desire to do all I can to not only act justly but generously to Columbia.

It is in your interest, and in the interest of the Dominion, that we should both act with a reasonable appreciation of difficulties which are unavoidable, and to devise means to remove them or overcome them.

We have induced Mr. Edgar to go to Columbia, as we thought you would prefer a full conference with an agent to a tedious, and possibly unsatisfactory, correspondence.

I have, &c.,
(Signed) A. MACKENZIE.

No. 36.

Mr. Mackenzie to the Lieutenant-Governor.

February, 21st, 1874.

SIR,—The bearer is James D. Edgar, Esq., Barrister, Toronto, who visits Columbia as the Agent of the Dominion Government, to consult with your Government with reference to the late agitation concerning an extension of time for the construction of the Pacific Railway beyond that promised in the Terms of Union.

Mr. Edgar will explain to Your Excellency our anxiety to do everything in our power to meet the views of your people.

He will be glad to receive your suggestions concerning matters which may require attention.

I am, &c.,
(Signed) A. MACKENZIE.

No. 37.

PROVINCIAL SECRETARY'S OFFICE,
22nd March, 1875.

SIR,—I have the honour to draw Your Excellency's attention to a letter dated the 21st February, 1874, from the Honourable A. Mackenzie to yourself, a copy of which is printed amongst the papers laid before the Dominion Parliament, respecting the non-fulfilment of the Terms of Union, and to request you will inform the Committee of Council if the letter in question ever reached Your Excellency.

This request is made because the Committee has always understood that Mr. Edgar never presented you with any credentials other than letters from the Governor-General of Canada, which were marked "private and confidential."

I have, &c.,
(Signed) JOHN ASH.

His Excellency Lieutenant-Governor Trutch,
&c., &c., &c.

No. 38.

LIEUTENANT-GOVERNOR'S OFFICE,
22nd March, 1875.

SIR,—The Lieutenant-Governor directs me to state in reply to the letter of this day's date addressed by you to His Honour, that the letter dated 21st February, 1874, from the Honourable A. Mackenzie to the Lieutenant-Governor, a copy of which is printed amongst the papers laid before the Dominion Parliament respecting the non-fulfilment of the Terms of Union, has never reached His Honour, nor was he aware until he read the printed copy above referred to, that any such letter had been addressed to him.
I have, &c.,
(Signed) ARTHUR G. J. PINDER,
The Honourable the Provincial Secretary. Private Secretary.

No. 39.

OTTAWA, March 24th, 1875.

SIR,—I have just received your telegram, informing me that you had not received the letter I addressed you, by Mr. Edgar, of February 21st, 1874.

I was not aware, until I received your telegram, that the letter had not been delivered to you. Mr. Edgar has, to-day, informed me that he did not hand you the letter, as your Ministers objected to any communication being made except through them. Mr. Edgar did not previously make me aware of this objection. Had I been informed of it at the time, I would have directed him to deliver the letter, notwithstanding the objection.

I can only now express my regret that the letter was not delivered; and, that seeing it was not delivered, that it was published with the correspondence. I observe however, that there is nothing in the letter which could, apparently, affect the question to be discussed by Mr. Edgar, as similar assurances were conveyed in my letter by Mr. Edgar to Mr. Walkem.
I am, &c.,
His Honour (Signed) A. MACKENZIE.
Lieutenant-Governor Trutch,
Victoria, B. C.

No. 40.

Report of the Executive Council, approved by the Lieutenant-Governor on the 7th May, 1874.

On a memorandum dated 7th May, 1874, from the Honourable the Attorney-General, recommending that his Excellency the Lieutenant-Governor be requested to telegraph to His Excellency the Governor-General for a reply by telegram, containing full information of the Railway policy of the Dominion Government, especially as it affects British Columbia, and whether it is true that the Premier has publicly stated in the Commons that the Dominion Government do not intend to commence railway construction this year, in this Province.

The Committee advise that the recommendation be approved.
(Certified) W. J. ARMSTRONG,
Minister of Finance and Agriculture,
and Clerk of the Executive Council.

No. 41.
Telegram.

To the Secretary of State for Canada,
Ottawa, Canada. VICTORIA, May 7th, 1874.

It being reported here to-day that the Premier stated in the House of Commons, on the 4th inst., that construction of Railway in British Columbia would not be commenced this year, this Government urgently requests to be fully informed immediately, by telegraph, of particulars of policy adopted by Dominion Government respecting Railway Clause of Terms of Union.

(Signed) JOSEPH W. TRUTCH.
Lieutenant-Governor.

No. 42.

Telegram.

OTTAWA, ONTARIO, May 8th, 1874.

Lieutenant-Governor Trutch.

Mr. Mackenzie simply said, that until the location of the road was ascertained it was impossible to commence construction; that a large surveying force was now at work, and there was no reason to believe that it would be possible to complete the survey before the close of the year.

      (Signed) R. W. SCOTT,
              Secretary of State.

No. 43.

The Governor-General to the Earl of Carnarvon.

GOVERNMENT HOUSE, OTTAWA,
May 15th, 1874.

MY LORD,—I have the honour to enclose for Your Lordship's information a newspaper report of the speech delivered by Mr. Mackenzie on the 12th instant, when introducing Resolutions for a Bill to provide for the construction of the Pacific Railroad, together with a summary of this speech, and an article from the *Globe* newspaper of the 12th instant, explanatory of the Government project.

Globe, 13th and 14th May.
Globe, 12th May.
Globe, 13th May.

      I have, &c.,
       (Signed) DUFFERIN.

No. 44.

The Governor-General to the Earl of Carnarvon.

GOVERNMENT HOUSE, OTTAWA,
May 15th, 1874.

MY LORD,—In continuation of my despatch No. 130, of this day's date, I have the honour to enclose an extract from the Toronto *Mail*, an opposition paper, criticising the scheme of the Government.

May 14th. For article see Scrap Book, page 40.

      I have, &c.,
       (Signed) DUFFERIN.

No. 45.

Mr. J. D. Edgar's Letter to the Hon. G. A. Walkem.

VICTORIA, B.C., May 8th, 1874.

SIR,—I have the honour to inform you that I have been instructed, by the Premier of Canada, to make you aware of the views of his Administration upon the subject of the construction of the Canadian Pacific Railway, in order that British Columbia may have full opportunity of considering and deciding upon a question so closely affecting her material interests. The scheme originally adopted for the carrying out of this work has, for a variety of reasons, proved unsuccessful, and to devise a plan for its more certain accomplishment has been the aim of the Dominion Cabinet. The chief difficulty to be encountered in attempting to carry out the existing system of construction, is to be found in the stipulation as to the completion of the Railway by the month of July, 1881. In proposing to take a longer time for constructing the Railway, the Canadian Government are actuated solely by an urgent necessity. They are advised by their Engineers that the physical difficulties are so much greater than was expected, that it is an impossibility to construct the Railway within the time limited by the Terms of

Union, and that any attempt to do so can only result in wasteful expenditure and financial embarrassment. It is because they desire to act in good faith towards British Columbia that the Canadian Ministry at once avow the difficulty of carrying out the exact Terms of Union, whilst they have no desire to avoid the full responsibility of Canada to complete the Railway by all means in her power, and at the earliest practicable date.

The eleventh article of the Terms of Union embodies the bald proposition that the Railway should be commenced in two, and completed in ten years, from the date of Union, to connect the seaboard of British Columbia with the Railway system of Canada. Feeling the impossibility of complying with this time limit for completion, the Government is prepared to make new stipulations, and to enter into additional obligations of a definite character, for the benefit of the Province. They propose to commence construction from Esquimalt to Nanaimo immediately, and to push that portion of railway on to completion, with the utmost vigour, and in the shortest practicable time.

The engineering difficulties on the Mainland have unfortunately turned out to be so serious that further surveys must necessarily be made before the best route can be determined upon. The Government have already asked Parliament for a large sum for the purpose of carrying on these surveys, and no expenditure will be spared to achieve the most speedy and reliable selection of a permanent location of the line upon the Mainland. It is useless to propose an actual construction being undertaken before the location has been determined upon; but in order to afford as much benefit from the works of construction from the very first as can possibly be derived by the people of the interior, the Government would immediately open up a road, and build a telegraph line along the whole length of the railway in the Province, and carry the telegraph wire across the continent. It is believed that the mere commencement to build a railway at the seaboard, as stipulated for in the existing terms, would give but little satisfaction to the producers living upon the east side of the Cascade Mountains, who would be unable, without a road being first constructed, to find a market all along the whole extent of the railway wherever construction was progressing. It would then be the aim of the Government to strain every nerve to push forward the construction of the railway; and they would endeavour at the same time so to arrange the expenditure that the legitimate advantages derivable from it would as much as possible fall into the hands of our producers. In addition to constructing the road to facilitate transport along the located line, they are anxious to avail of the large supplies of all kinds of provisions now existing, or capable of being produced in the interior, and would proceed from the very first with all the works of construction in that portion of the country that their engineers could sanction.

It is to be observed that while the Terms of Union contemplated the completion of the whole railway within a certain number of years, they made no provision for any certainty of expenditure in any particular time, or on any particular portion of the line. To predicate the highest expenditure which in any one year might be warranted in a particular portion of a great work like this is certainly difficult; and it is still more difficult to arrive at the lowest fixed annual sum which, in every year, and under all circumstances, might be judiciously expended as a minimum in local construction. To a country like British Columbia, it is conceded, however, to be an important point that not only the prompt and vigorous commencement, but also the continuous prosecution, of the work of construction within the limits of the Province should be guaranteed. In order, therefore, to secure an absolute certainty in this direction, and although the length of the line falling within the Province is estimated at only about one-fifth of the whole length, the Dominion Government are disposed to concede to British Columbia that the moment the surveys and road on the Mainland can be completed there shall be in each and every year, and even under the most unfavourable circumstances, during the construction of the railway, a minimum expenditure upon works of construction within the Province of at least one million five hundred thousand dollars. That this will secure the continuous progress of the works in the Province, without any intermission, is quite apparent, and it must also be perfectly clear that so large an annual sum could not be expected by any Dominion Administration in a remote district without holding out to the country some early prospect of a return for it, and at the same time showing that they were proceeding with the works with sufficient rapidity to bring the investment into an early condition to earn something. In reference to this point, I may be permitted to refer to the fact that the Delegates from British Columbia, who negotiated the Terms of Union were instructed by the Provincial Legislature to accept an undertaking from Canada to build the railway, with a guaranteed annual expenditure in the Province upon construction of one million dollars, to begin at the end of three years after Union. We must assume that this guarantee of continuous construction was only abandoned by the Delegates upon a conviction of both the sincerity and feasibility of the offer of early completion that was made to them.

I trust that the proposals of the Dominion Cabinet, which I have sketched above, will be considered and accepted by British Columbia, as an earnest effort on the part of the former to carry out the spirit of the obligations to the Province.

The leader of the Canadian Government has instructed me to place these matters before you, as leader of the Provincial Administration, and at the same time to furnish a copy to His Excellency the Lieutenant-Governor. The substance of these proposals has been sent to me by telegraphic cipher, and based upon that, I have the honour of communicating them to you. The Dominion Government would be glad to have the consideration of this proposal entertained by your Administration, and to learn the conclusion of the Government of British Columbia upon the subject.

I have, &c.,
(Signed)   J. D. EDGAR.

No. 46.

Mr. Edgar to the Lieutenant-Governor.

VICTORIA, B. C., May 9th, 1874.

SIR,—I have the honour to inform Your Excellency that in accordance with instructions from Honourable Alexander Mackenzie, leader of the Canadian Government, I have submitted to the Honourable G. A. Walkem, leader of your Ministry, the views of the former upon the question of the Canada Pacific Railway, with a view to the relaxation of the Terms of Union so far as regards the time limited for the completion of the railway. I was at the same time instructed to furnish, for Your Excellency's information, a copy, which I now have the honour to enclose, of the communication addressed by me to your Minister upon that subject.

I have, &c.,
(Signed)   J. D. EDGAR.

No. 47.

Hon. G. A. Walkem to Mr. J. D. Edgar.

ATTORNEY-GENERAL'S DEPARTMENT,
VICTORIA, May 11th, 1874.

SIR,—I have the honour to acknowledge the receipt, on Saturday, the 9th instant, of your letter of the previous day's date.

In reply to your request, that I should submit your proposals for a change in the Railway Clause of the Terms of Union to the Local Administration, for their consideration and acceptance, I have the honour to inform you that I am not in a position to advise His Excellency the Lieutenant-Governor in Council to treat such proposals officially; nor can I tender such advice until I shall have been informed that you have been specially accredited to act in this matter as the Agent of the General Government, and that they will consider your acts or negotiations in the matter binding upon them.

I have, &c.,
(Signed)   G. A. WALKEM,
                        Attorney-General.

No. 48.

Report of the Executive Council approved by the Lieutenant-Governor on the 18th May, 1874.

On a memorandum, dated 16th May, 1874, from the Honourable the Attorney-General, recommending that His Excellency the Lieutenant-Governor be respectfully requested to ascertain by telegraph, from the Honourable the Secretary of State, whether any propositions purporting to be, or to have been, made by James D. Edgar, Esquire, on behalf of the Dominion Government, will be considered binding by them; and, further, whether he has any power to enter into any negotiations with this Government.

The Committee advise that the recommendation be approved.

(Certified) W. J. ARMSTRONG,
Minister of Finance and Agriculture,
and Clerk of the Executive Council.

No. 49.

Mr. J. D. Edgar to the Honourable G. A. Walkem.

VICTORIA, May 18th, 1874.

SIR,—I have the honour to acknowledge having received your letter of the 11th instant, just before leaving for the Mainland.

I am sure you cannot have forgotten that letters from the highest dignitaries at Ottawa which have been long ago delivered by me, both to His Excellency the Lieutenant-Governor and to yourself, have informed you that I came to this Province on behalf of the Dominion Government, and possessing their entire confidence. In my communication of the 8th instant, I stated most distinctly that I was making the proposals contained in it by the instructions and on behalf of the Canadian Ministry. You have, however, done me the honour of assuming that my statement was incorrect, and that I am acting without authority and without instructions. I can afford to pass over without notice the personal insinuations, but I must most strongly protest against such extraordinary treatment of a document which emanates from the Government of Canada, upon a subject of such deep and pressing moment to British Columbia.

I have, therefore, the honour to request that the proposals of the Dominion Government may receive the consideration at the hands of the Provincial Administration to which such communications are entitled, and which the extreme importance of the subject demands.

I have, &c.,
(Signed) J. D. EDGAR.

No. 50.

Hon. G. A. Walkem to Mr. J. D. Edgar.

VICTORIA, May 18th, 1874.

SIR,—In reply to your letter of this date, I must express my suprise and regret that you should have taken umbrage at the contents of my letter of the 11th instant.

Mr. Mackenzie in an unofficial—and in his only—letter to me, respecting your visit, has expressly narrowed and confined the object of your mission to the holding of a personal interview with my colleagues and myself, in order that our "views regarding "the policy of the Government on the construction of the Railway" should be ascertained without "tedious and possibly unsatisfactory correspondence"—I quote his words. These things having been done, the special aim desired, I may be permitted to think, has been attained by Mr. Mackenzie.

When, however, you proceed further, and propose changes to this Government of the gravest importance to the Province, I must be pardoned for considering it my duty, in my public capacity, to ask for your official authority for appearing in the *role* of an agent contracting for the Dominion of Canada. This information I have not yet received.

I have, &c.,
(Signed) GEO. A. WALKEM.

No. 51.

Telegram.

VICTORIA, 18th May, 1874.

The Hon. R. W. Scott, Secretary of State, Ottawa, Canada.

My Ministers request to be informed whether Mr. Edgar is empowered to negotiate with this Government, and whether propositions purporting to be made by him on behalf of the Dominion Government, will be considered binding by that Government.

(Signed) JOSEPH W. TRUTCH,
Lieutenant-Governor.

No. 52.

The Lieutenant-Governor to the Secretary of State for Canada.

BRITISH COLUMBIA, GOVERNMENT HOUSE,
18th May, 1874.

Minute of Executive Council.
Tel. Mess., May 18th, 1874.

SIR,—I have the honour to enclose herewith a Minute of the Executive Council of this Province to state that, in accordance with the advice of my Ministers therein expressed, I have this day addressed to you a message by telegraph, of which a copy is appended hereto.

I have, &c.,
(Signed) JOSEPH W. TRUTCH.

No. 53.

Telegram.

OTTAWA, May 20th, 1874.

To Lieutenant-Governor Trutch:—

I refer Ministry to my letter by Mr. Edgar, which sufficiently indicated his mission, and which they recognized.

He is now recalled, and I await his return and reports.

(Signed) A. MACKENZIE.

No. 54.

Telegram.

VICTORIA, May 21st, 1874.

Hon. A. Mackenzie, Ottawa.

Will you kindly answer Governor's telegram fully. Do Mr. Edgar's propositions to change railway terms bind your Government.

(Signed) GEO. A. WALKEM.

No. 55.

Report of the Executive Council, approved by the Lieutenant-Governor on the 21st day of May, 1874.

The Committee of Council have had under consideration the subject of the non-fulfilment, by the Dominion Government, of the 11th or Railway Clause of the Terms of Union; and in view of the importance of the question as affecting the whole Province, they recommend that a letter of Mr. J. D. Edgar, dated 8th May, 1874, addressed to the Honourable Attorney-General, and the Orders in Council, the Telegrams, and the correspondence relating thereto, be published for general information.

The Committee remark that the letter alluded to by Mr. Edgar as having been delivered by him to your Excellency, is the only document bearing on the subject which will not be published. This letter they have never seen, nor have they any further knowledge of it beyond the reference made to it by your Excellency as a letter received by you from His Excellency the Governor-General marked "private and confidential," and therefore not communicated to the Council.

(Certified) W. J. ARMSTRONG,
*Minister of Finance and Agriculture,
and Clerk of the Executive Council.*

No. 56.
Telegram.

OTTAWA, Ontario, June 8th, 1874.

To *Lieutenant-Governor Trutch.* *Received at Victoria June 8th.*

On May 8th Mr. Edgar, on behalf of the Dominion Government, made certain proposals to your Government respecting the construction of the Pacific Railway, which involved immediately heavy expenditure for purchases (purposes) not contemplated by the Terms of Union—in consideration of foregoing the limit of the time for the completion of the Railway.

I exceedingly regret that your Government have not replied to the proposals, or apparently considered them. I beg, therefore, that you will now inform your Ministers that the proposals are withdrawn.

(Signed) A. MACKENZIE.

No. 57.

Order in Council, approved by the Lieutenant-Governor 9th June, 1874.

On a memorandum of the 9th day of June, 1874, reporting on a Telegram, laid before this Council by His Excellency the Lieutenant-Governor, yesterday received by him, from the Honourable Alexander Mackenzie, Premier of the Dominion of Canada, copy of which is enclosed, respecting certain proposals in writing made on the 8th of May last by Mr. Edgar to Mr. Walkem, and recommending that His Excellency be respectfully requested to send the enclosed telegraphic message in reply thereto.

The Committee advise that the recommendation be approved.

(Signed) GEO. A. WALKEM,
President Executive Council.

No. 58.

The Lieutenant-Governor to the Secretary of State for Canada.

BRITISH COLUMBIA,
Government House, 9th June, 1874.

SIR,—With reference to my telegraphic despatch to you of to-day's date, I have the honour to enclose a minute of my Executive Council, in accordance with which that telegram was addressed to you, together with copies of the documents referred to in the said minute, being copy of a telegram to me from the Honourable A. Mackenzie, which, at his request, I communicated to my Ministers, and a draft of the telegraphic message to you in reference thereto sent by me at the instance of my Ministry.

I have, &c., (Signed) JOSEPH W. TRUTCH.

No. 59.
Telegram.

The Honourable R. W. Scott, *Secretary of State,* VICTORIA, June 9th, 1874.
   Ottawa, Canada.

My Ministers request me to state, in reference to a Telegram to me from Mr. Mackenzie, dated yesterday, that it conveys the first direct information to this Government, (although such information was formally applied for by Telegram to you of 18th May,) that the views on the Railway question, contained in a letter from Mr. Edgar to Mr. Walkem, were proposals to this Government from the Dominion Government, and that they consider it remarkable that the only communication to this Government which acknowledges such proposals authoritative should at the same time withdraw them.

(Signed) JOSEPH W. TRUTCH.
Lieutenant-Governor.

No. 60.

Extract from the Montreal Weekly Gazette, May 15th, 1874.

" They were quite aware that the difficulties to be surmounted were extensive, and they were quite aware that the terms of the agreement with British Columbia had been violated. Under these circumstances they thought that in the meantime the first step to be taken, was to confer with the Local Government of the Province of British Columbia, and endeavour to ascertain from them if any means could be arranged by which an extension of time could be procured for the prosecution of the work we were bound to undertake. With that view an agent was sent as a representative of this Government to visit that Province, and in the course of his communications with the Local Government, it became very apparent, as it had been made apparent in the House by several members from the Island of Vancouver, that it was an exceedingly important matter with them to have the road commenced at once. He, for one, was quite willing, if the Local Government were disposed to make some terms for the extension of time, that the Government should undertake the construction of the land portion as rapidly as possible, but if it became apparent that the Local Government were determined to adhere to the whole terms, then the Dominion of Canada could accede to the terms, and nothing more. They instructed Mr. Edgar to say that the Government would be prepared immediately to undertake the commencement of the work on the Island, traversing northwards towards the point of crossing; prosecuting the surveys on the mainland, getting a passable route along the ridge, and erecting telegraph lines. He was also instructed to state that as soon as the work could be placed under contract, they would spend no less than $1,500,000 within the Province on the railway. He did not know whether this had been accepted or not, but under any circumstances they should have authority to proceed with the work, as they thought would meet the just expectations of the country and the reasonable expectations of the people in British Columbia. The policy he had announced in his election address in November last had been closely criticised by the honourable gentlemen opposite. He had his own impression as to the course to be pursued, and he thought, if he recollected rightly, that the right honourable gentleman opposite had said that if his views were adopted, British Columbia would be justified in seceding from the Union."

No. 61.

The Under Secretary of State for Canada to the Lieutenant-Governor.

DEPARTMENT SECRETARY OF STATE,
10th June, 1874.

SIR,—I have the honour to acknowledge the receipt of your despatch, No. 28, of the 18th ult., purporting to enclose a minute of your Executive Council, and also copy of a telegram founded thereon, and sent by you to the Secretary of State on the 18th ult., on the subject of the mission of Mr J. D. Edgar to the Government of British Columbia.

The minute of Council referred to did not accompany your despatch.

(Signed) EDOUARD J. LANGEVIN,
Under Secretary of State.

No. 62.

The Secretary of State for Canada to the Lieutenant-Governor.

DEPARTMENT SECRETARY OF STATE,
25th June, 1874.

SIR,—I have the honour to acknowledge the receipt of your Despatch, No. 39, of the 9th instant, transmitting a copy of a minute of your Executive Council, together with a copy of a telegram addressed to you by the Honourable the Minister of Public Works, and also of a telegram addressed by you to the Secretary of State, in reply thereto, on the subject of the mission of Mr. J. D. Edgar to British Columbia, in connection with the Pacific Railway.

I have, &c.,
(Signed) EDOUARD J. LANGEVIN,
Under Secretary of State.

63.

The Lieutenant-Governor to the Secretary of State for Canada.

(Copy of No. 46.)   BRITISH COLUMBIA.
Government House, 26th June, 1874.

Minute of Executive Council.

Copy of Telegram.

SIR,—I have the honour to acknowledge the receipt of your Despatch of the 10th instant, referring to my Despatch, No. 28, of the 18th May, and informing me that the Minute of Executive Council, which my said Despatch purported to enclose, had not reached you.

I beg to enclose herewith a duplicate copy of the said Minute of Council, and of the telegram to you based thereon.

I have, &c.,
(Signed)   JOSEPH W. TRUTCH.

No. 64.

Mr. Edgar to the Secretary of State for Canada.

TORONTO, June, 17th, 1874.

SIR,—I have the honour to report that in the month of February last I was requested by the Canadian Government to proceed to the Province of British Columbia on their behalf. My mission was for the purpose of ascertaining the true state of feeling in the Province upon the subject of certain changes which were deemed necessary, in the mode and in the limit of time for the construction of the Canadian Pacific Railway, as well as to attend to any other business required, and to act as Canadian agent in bringing about some such feasible arrangement as might meet the general approval of the Local Government and the people of British Columbia, in place of the original conditions respecting the commencement and completion of the railway that are contained in the Eleventh Article of the Terms of Union. In that clause the language referring to railway construction is as follows:—

"The Government of the Dominion undertake to secure the commencement simul-
" taneously, within two years from the date of Union, of the construction of a railway
" from the Pacific towards the Rocky Mountains, and from such point as may be selected
" east of the Rocky Mountains towards the Pacific, to connect the seaboard of British
" Columbia with the railway system of Canada; and further to secure the completion
" of such railway within ten years from the date of the Union."

The views and policy of his Government upon the question of the Canadian Pacific Railway were communicated to me in several interviews by the Hon. Mr. Mackenzie, and I also had the benefit of conversations upon the same subject with many members of the Administration before I left Ottawa. On the eve of my departure I received from Hon. Mr. Mackenzie certain further instructions and directions for my guidance, which were contained in the following letter:—(*See* No. 34, p. 155.)

When I received the above letter I lost no time, and starting upon my journey and leaving Toronto February 23rd, I arrived upon March 9th at Victoria, the capital of British Columbia. On the day that I landed in Victoria, the Hon. Mr. Walkem, leader of the Local Government, called upon me, and I made him aware of the object of my mission. On the same day I handed him Hon. Mr. Mackenzie's letter of February 16, (see No. 35 p. 157), also informing him that I had letters from His Excellency the Governor-General to his Honour the Lieutenant-Governor, which were next day delivered. Very soon afterwards Mr. Walkem introduced me to his colleagues as the representative of the Canadian Government.

Upon my arrival in the Province, I found that an intense interest was manifested by all the population in whatever related to the question of railway construction. It is difficult at a distance to conceive the importance that is attached to the railway by the British Columbians. On account of the vast construction expenditure, and the sparseness of the population who would participate in the immediate benefits derivable from it, an interest of a direct and personal character is felt upon this subject. The entire white population of the Province, according to the census of 1870, was 8,576 souls. Of this number there were upon the Mainland 3,401, and upon Vancouver Island 5,175. The white population of to-day has probably increased to 10,000. With the exception, perhaps, of the gold miners, who are confined to the Mainland, there is no class in the Province that would not derive immediate personal advantages from the railway construction expenditure. Those in business, in trade, and in agriculture would feel the stimulus instantly; while those of means and leisure would be enriched by the increase in the value of their property. The circumstances of the early settlement of the Province gave it a population of peculiar intelligence; and the fact that most of the rougher kind of labour is performed by Chinamen and Indians has afforded in an especial way to the people of Victoria, the Provincial metropolis, leisure and opportunity for the fullest discussion of their great question of the day. Their keen intelligence and zeal in public affairs suggests a parallel in the history of some of the minor States of ancient Greece and Italy. Although a strong feeling of jealousy of the greatness of Victoria undoubtedly exists in parts of the Mainland, yet that town is the chief centre of public opinion. Its population is almost equal to the whole of the rest of the Province, and in its midst are the head-quarters of Government, of the Courts, of the churches, and of trade. Within three miles there is the fine harbour of Esquimalt, with its arsenal and British ships of war.

To Victoria the question of the location of the railway terminus is all important, because there is nothing in the terms of Union which settles that there shall be any portion of the line upon Vancouver Island; a revocable Order in Council, and the intrinsic merits claimed for the Island location, are the grounds upon which they hope to secure the terminus at Esquimalt. When it became well understood that the surveys were not yet so far advanced as to warrant the Canadian Government in fixing the permanent route and Western terminus of the railway, it was strongly urged upon me by many persons in Victoria that the construction of the line of railway should be at once undertaken by the Dominion from the harbour of Esquimalt to the port of Nanaimo, on the east coast of Vancouver Island, a distance of about seventy miles. It was argued that at whatever point upon the Mainland the Pacific Railway might be brought to the coast, a steam ferry thence to Nanaimo might be established, and would render their portion of railway a means of connection with Esquimalt, which is said to be the finest harbour upon the shores of the Northern Pacific. It was also insisted that from its opening there would be a considerable and profitable traffic over this line in the carriage of coal to Esquimalt from the mines at Nanaimo and Departure Bay.

Moreover, it was contended that in view of the admitted impossibility to complete the construction of the trans-continental railway within the time originally limited, some substantial concessions should be made to the people of the Island, as compensation for their disappointment and prospective losses.

A contention similar to the last mentioned one was also pressed upon me warmly by leading men of the Mainland, who considered that they were now entitled to have some definite understanding arrived at, not so much in regard to the ultimate completion as to the early, vigorous, and continuous construction of the railway upon the Mainland. It was represented that those engaged in agriculture and stock raising in the interior parts of the country were almost without a market for their produce, partly because the gold miners were leaving in considerable numbers, and partly for the reason that in anticipation of railway construction they had raised more crops than usual. The great distance to the coast, and the stupendous mountain ranges to be traversed, prevented them from getting the bulky products of their land to the Island markets of Victoria or Nanaimo. Being familiar with the difficulties to be met with by engineers in seeking for a railway route through their country, the Mainland people were not disposed to blame the Dominion for insisting upon further time and surveys before fixing the location. Their immediate necessities also induced them to attach more importance to the securing of an early and steady expenditure amongst themselves than to the maintaining of any arbitrary time limit for completion, while they also expressed their perfect appreciation of the agreement that a vigorous expenditure of itself involves an accomplishment of the work within a reasonable period.

In the Provincial Constitution of British Columbia the working of representative institutions and responsible parliamentary government may be studied in a simple form. The system is elaborated out of perhaps slender materials, but has been courageously fashioned after the model of the British Constitution. The people are represented by a House of twenty-five members, of whom thirteen are elected from the Mainland and twelve from the Island. In this House sit the Ministers of the Crown, four in number, two being Island members and two from the Mainland. The deliberations are presided over by a Speaker, and due respect for the dignity of the Assembly is maintained by a Sergeant-at-Arms.

Although I had not the fortune to be in the country when the House was in session, I was able to discover among the gentlemen who hold seats a considerable number of much experience and somewhat above the average intelligence of Provincial legislators. To those accustomed to older Canadian constituencies, each with populations varying usually from fifteen to thirty thousand souls, it is somewhat novel to see the smallness of electoral districts in British Columbia. Yet it would be quite unfair to fix the number of electors as the standard of the intelligence of the representative, for one of the ablest of the Provincial Ministers, after an exciting contest at the last election, succeeded in polling but sixteen votes in his constituency, whilst his opponent suffered a decisive defeat, having polled exactly half that number.

The Session of the Provincial Legislature had terminated on the 2nd March, a week before my arrival, and the House had unanimously agreed to a resolution upon the subject or railway clause, in the Terms of Union with the Dominion, which was calculated to have an important bearing upon all negotiations with the local Government for a change in that clause. The language of the resolution is as follows:—"That in view "of the importance of the Railway Clause of the Terms of Union between Canada and "British Columbia being faithfully carried out by Canada, this House is of opinion that "no alteration in the said clause should be permitted by the Government of this Province "until the same has been submitted to the people for endorsation." When I ascertained that this resolution had been passed, that the Provincial Parliament had yet more than a year to run and that the Ministry had in it a sufficient working majority, it at once became apparent that any proposals to alter the railway clause could possess few attractions in the eyes of the party in power. While prepared to admit that the Province would be most reasonable, and would not be disposed to insist at all upon the original time limit for completion, yet members of the Administration, looking at it from their own point of view, very naturally urge that this was a peculiarly unfortunate time to seek any alterations. I also discovered that the first Act of the Provincial Statute Book of 1873-4 contained elements of danger to the continued harmony between the General and Local Governments. This Act became necessary to authorize the Provincial to receive from the Dominion Government the large sums of money, both for the Esquimalt Graving Dock, and for other public works, which the Local Government petitioned the Dominion Government to advance, and which requests the latter complied with as concessions to the Province in excess of what could be claimed under Articles two and twelve of the Terms of Union. A saving clause or proviso was inserted in this Act containing very strong language concerning the rights and wrongs of British Columbia as regards the railway, and adding:—"This Act shall not have any force or "effect unless the above proviso be inserted, in the same words, in any Act of Parlia-"ment of Canada which may be passed for the purposes of this Act."

A profound anxiety at once manifested by Mr. Walkem and his colleagues to ascertain through me if the Canadian Ministry would propose to Parliament to adopt the words of this proviso. When I sought to get from them some proposals or suggestions as to their terms of the concessions that should be made to British Columbia, in consideration of a change in the railway terms, I was continually met by an urgent enquiry as to what was to be done about that clause. As early as the 16th of March, I was informed by telegram that the Dominion Government would not adopt the language of the proviso in their bill, but would make the concessions as originally agreed, and without conditions affecting the railway terms. The announcement of this was received by the Local Ministers with alarm and disappointment, and it afterwards became still more difficult to get a satisfactory discussion of an alteration of railway terms with any of them. Orders in Council were passed by the Local Government upon the subject, and I was continually urged to press upon the Dominion Government the anxiety of the Provincial Ministry for the adoption of the saving clause, and I took many opportunities of doing so. This pressure continued without intermission until the 25th April, when at the request of Mr. Walkem, I sent a despatch to Mr. Mackenzie on behalf of the former, and in his own language urging the adoption of the saving clause.

When, according to instructions, I endeavoured to ascertain from Local Ministers if their unwillingness to submit proposals as to railway to the people arose entirely from our refusal to adopt the saving clause. I found that even such a concession would not induce them to bring about an appeal to the people.

According to instructions received, it was my aim from the very first to take every means of ascertaining the popular view of the railway question. Indeed when it was understood that the Canadian Government had delegated me upon this and general matters, the politeness and hospitable attentions of all classes soon rendered it an easy matter to form some estimate of public opinion. All were as willing to communicate as I was anxious to receive their various views and information. I paid two brief visits to the Mainland, meeting with people of New Westminster, Hope, Yale, and some few other places, and I was so fortunate as to meet, at one time or another, nearly all the members of the Local Legislature, and many other persons of local prominence from the Mainland.

The Lieutenant-Governor and the Hon. Captain Hare, Senior Naval Officer at Esquimalt, kindly afforded me an opportunity of visiting the East Coast of the Island, in company with them, on board of H. M. S. *Myrmidon*.

In discussing the question of the time for the completion of the railway, I elicited a very general expression of opinion that there was no great importance attached to any particular period for completion, but that serious disappointment had been felt at the failure to commence the work of actual construction by July of last year. Much anxiety was felt for an announcement of the policy of Canada upon the subject of the railway, and an extreme desire prevailed to have definite understanding arrived at as to what the Province could expect in place of the original railway terms, which were all but universally admitted to be incapable of literal fulfilment.

The public agitation in Victoria, of February last, might have been mistaken for a movement to insist upon "The terms, the whole terms, and nothing but the terms," or to seek some disloyal alternative. Indeed a portion of the community, who did not sympathize with the excitement, so interpreted it. Yet I was assured by the leaders of that agitation that no such motives or intentions influenced them. The people had been aroused, by what were deemed suspicious circumstances, to fear that efforts would be made, or were being made, to secure from the Local Government an agreement to change the railway terms without a submission to the people who had directly sanctioned the original terms. The local contradictions had scarcely been accepted as satisfactory upon this point, but my denial of it on the part of the Ottawa Government, coupled with the announcement that the latter would not seek to secure any alteration without the sanction of the people of the Province, set that difficulty very much at rest.

Notwithstanding the attitude that was assumed by the Provincial Government against the submission of a proposal, or the opening of negotiations to alter the railway terms, it was quite apparent that popular feeling, all over the Province, was strongly in favour of some definite settlement being arrived at upon the question. The notorious and admitted failure of the original scheme of railway construction had unsettled the business of the country, and the whole community, including even those who would have been the most exacting in bargaining with Canada for new terms, were anxious **to have a proposal** made and to have a full opportunity for discussing and accepting **or rejecting it.**

I felt, therefore, that I should take an early opportunity of arriving at the views of the Local Government upon the subject. I was given an appointment by Mr. Walkem in the first week of April, and then confidentially discussed with his Ministry the whole question of alteration in the railway terms. I may mention that upon this occasion no difficulty was raised as to my authority to represent the General Government.

At this time there was considerable irritation displayed by Ministers upon the subject at the saving clause before alluded to; they would not admit any necessity for a present settlement of the railway question, but still persisted that next year, or some future time, should be awaited for the making of any such propositions; and they were particularly careful to avoid saying what concessions in their opinion would be acceptable to the Province in lieu of the original terms. The attitude of the Local Ministry rendered it more important than ever that the popular feeling should be accurately ascertained, and it was my aim to discover it by unreserved discussion with as many men as possible of the different parties and localities.

It was now quite apparent that the Local Ministers were determined to be obstructive, and it became all the more necessary to satisfy the people in so far as their views were found to be reasonable. After receiving from me the best information I could supply, Hon. Mr. Mackenzie directed me to make the Provincial Government certain proposals which were so arranged as to give large and certain advantages to the Mainland equally with the Island; and on the 6th May, I was instructed to put them formally in writing and give them to the Local Premier and a copy to the Lieutenant-Governor. Upon the 8th May I had prepared, and I read over to Mr. Walkem, the letter of that date containing the proposals (*See* No. 45, p. 159), and upon the following day I handed it to him, and furnished a copy to His Honour the Lieutenant-Governor as directed, accompanied with a short note (*See* No. 46, p. 161). I had made arrangements for another visit to the Mainland to ascertain something more of the feeling there, while the Provincial Government were having the proposals under consideration. Before sailing for New Westminster, however, I received the letter from Mr. Walkem (*See* No. 47, p. 161), in which he raised objections to recognizing me as the agent of the General Government. It struck me as so peculiar a communication on Mr. Walkem's part, after he and his colleagues had recognized me as such agent almost every day for two months, that I felt it would be better not to be too hasty in accepting that as a serious and final reply to the proposals, but to await the lapse of a few days to be occupied by me in visiting New Westminster, Burrard Inlet, Yale, and some other places on the Mainland. Upon returning to Victoria on Saturday, 16th May, I was waited upon by a deputation of leading gentlemen, connected with both sides of local politics, who informed me that it had been announced in the House of Commons at Ottawa, by Hon. Mr. Mackenzie, that proposals had been made on behalf of his Ministry, through myself, to the Provincial Government as to the alteration of the railway terms; and yet that it was denied by members of the Local Ministry, and by their newspaper organ, that any proposals whatever had been made. They represented that the popular feeling was very much excited upon the subject, and that the people were anxious to have the earliest opportunity of considering and deciding upon the question, and I was asked to inform them whether such proposals had been made. Upon receiving an affirmative reply they took their leave, and shortly afterwards, as the intelligence spread, considerable excitement was manifested at the treatment the proposals were receiving at the hands of Local Ministers.

In order to afford Mr. Walkem another opportunity to reply to the proposals, or to consider them, if he were at all desirous of doing so, I again addressed him, and in a letter of 18th May (*see* No. 49, p. 162) endeavoured to point out that he could not ignore the communication of 8th May, and reiterated the request on behalf of the Government of Canada that the proposals should receive the consideration to which they were entitled. In reply to this I received the letter (No. 50, p. 162), and upon the 19th May, under directions from Hon. Mr Mackenzie, I left Victoria upon my return journey without any further official communication with the Local Ministry.

I may be permitted to mention that his Honour the Lieutenant-Governor, throughout the whole of my visit, was always most obliging in giving me upon all public questions very full information, which his large experience in the Province rendered of the highest value. He also manifested an earnest wish to see a definite and amicable settlement of the railway question speedily arrived at between the General and Provincial Governments.

In accordance with the direction contained in the last paragraph of Hon. Mr. Mackenzie's letter to me of the 19th February, I took every opportunity during my stay in British Columbia of noting various matters connected with Dominion business and interests. In several despatches to Heads of Departments, as well as in verbal communications with Ministers, I have already called attention to some important subjects of that kind, and I propose to have the honour of communicating in separate reports or despatches upon several other points of interest and importance connected with Dominion affairs in the Pacific Province.

I have, &c.,

(Signed) J. D. EDGAR.

No. 65.

The Lieutenant-Governor to the Secretary of State for Canada.

(No. 40.) GOVERNMENT HOUSE,
11th, June, 1874.

SIR,—I have the honour to enclose for the consideration of His Excellency the Governor-General a Minute of the Executive Council of this Province, representing that British Columbia is suffering great injury from the failure by Canada to carry out the obligations of the 11th Clause of the Terms of Union, and that it is advisable, in the interests of this Province, that the case be laid before the Imperial Government, by means of a Memorial to be presented to the Secretary of State for the Colonies by the Attorney-General of British Columbia, as Special Agent and Delegate of this Government. In accordance with the advice of my Ministers, I have appointed the Honourable George Anthony Walkem, Attorney-General of this Province, to be such Special Agent and Delegate; and at their request I beg you to inform His Excellency the Governor-General that Mr Walkem has been duly appointed as such Special Agent and Delegate, and to move His Excellency to acquaint the Right Honourable Her Majesty's Principal Secretary of State for the Colonies that Mr. Walkem has been authorized and instructed to place in his hands the Memorial of this Government appealing to Her Majesty, and to support the prayer thereof.

Mr. Walkem will proceed to Ottawa by the next mail, and will take with him a duplicate of this Despatch.

I have, &c.,
(Signed) JOSEPH W. TRUTCH.

No. 66.

Report approved by the Lieutenant-Governor on the 11th June, 1874.

The Committee of Council have had under consideration the Memorandum of the Honourable Provincial Secretary, dated 11th June, 1874, representing that the essential clause of the Terms of Union provided that the Government of the Dominion should secure "the commencement simultaneously of the construction of a Railway from the "Pacific towards the Rocky Mountains, and from such point as may be selected East of "the Rocky Mountains towards the Pacific, to connect the seaboard of British Columbia "with the Railway system of Canada; and, further, to secure the completion of such "Railway within ten years from the date of Union."

That the set time for commencement of the work passed nearly a year ago, and that no commencement of construction has yet been made.

That the Secretary of State of the Dominion has informed this Government that no commencement can be made this year, in consequence of the surveys being incomplete.

That, by order of the Privy Council of Canada, it was decided last year that a portion of the line be located between the harbour of Esquimalt and Seymour Narrows; and that, in consequence of that order, and at the request of the Dominion Government, the lands for a width of twenty miles along that line have been reserved by the Provincial Government.

That the Premier of the Dominion Government has, in an informal manner, but nevertheless in a manner acknowledged to be at the instance of the Dominion Government, offered immediately to undertake the commencement of the work, provided that British Columbia would agree to certain terms of relaxation.

That the relaxation proposed was, that British Columbia should agree to cancel the Railway Clause of the Terms, as regards the mainland part of the Province, and accept in lieu thereof a promise to build a waggon road after the line of railway had been permanently located, on the completion of which, at an undefined time, railway construction would be commenced.

That such proposal has, however, been withdrawn.

That, according to the preamble of the "Canadian Pacific Railway Act, 1874," the railway is to be constructed as rapidly as the same can be accomplished without raising the rate of taxation.

That the bearing of the Dominion Government towards British Columbia is equivalent to the repudiation of the liability of the Dominion to fulfil as far as possible the engagement made respecting the construction of the Pacific Railway.

That, by the course of action taken by the Dominion Government, British Columbia has sustained and is suffering great injury and loss.

That with a view to obtain redress, it is advisable that the case of British Columbia be submitted for the consideration of the Imperial Government.

The Committee concur with the recommendation, and advise that your Excellency do charge the Honourable the Attorney-General and the Provincial Secretary with the preparation of a memorial and remonstrance on behalf of the Province regarding the non-fulfilment of the Terms of Union by the Dominion Government, to be submitted to Her Most Excellent Majesty the Queen in Council.

The Committee further advise, should this Report be approved, that the Honourable George Anthony Walkem be appointed a Special Agent and Delegate, instructed to proceed at once to London, for the purpose of placing the Memorial in the hands of the Right Honourable the Secretary of State for the Colonies, and of supporting the prayer thereof; and request Your Excellency to inform the Governor-General of Mr. Walkem's appointment, and ask that he be provided with a suitable introduction to Her Majesty's Principal Secretary of State for the Colonies.

(Certified) W. J. ARMSTRONG,
Clerk, Executive Council.

No. 67.

Report of the Executive Council, approved by the Lieutenant-Governor on the 11th June, 1874.

On a Memorandum dated 11th June, 1874, from the Honourable the Provincial Secretary, reporting with reference to the breach of the Terms of Union by the Dominion Government, and the Appeal to the Imperial Government thereon arising, that it is advisable that a telegram be sent to the Imperial Government, informing them that British Columbia is about to appeal against the breach, by the Dominion Government, of the Terms of Union, and that a Delegate from this Government is about to leave for London, to lay such Appeal before the Imperial Government.

The Committee concur, and advise that Your Excellency do telegraph to that effect to the Right Honourable the Secretary of State for the Colonies, and also through the proper channel to His Excellency the Governor-General, for the information of the Dominion Government.

(Certified) W. J. ARMSTRONG,
Clerk of the Executive Council.

No. 68.

The Under Secretary of State for Canada to the Lieutenant-Governor.

DEPARTMENT SECRETARY OF STATE,
11th July, 1874.

SIR,—I have the honour to acknowledge the receipt of your despatch, No. 40, of the 11th ult., concerning a copy of a Minute of your Executive Council, in reference to the alleged failure of the Dominion Government to carry out the obligations of the 11th clause of the terms of Union, and recommending that the case be laid before the Imperial

Government by means of a memorial, to be presented to Secretary of State for the Colonies, by the Attorney-General of British Columbia as special agent and delegate of the Government of that Province.

I am, &c.,
(Signed)   EDOUARD J. LANGEVIN,
Under Secretary of State.

No. 69.

Lieutenant-Governor Trutch to the Earl of Carnarvon.

GOVERNMENT HOUSE, VICTORIA,
11th June, 1874.

MY LORD,—I have the honour to state that I have, at the instance of my responsible advisers, addressed to your Lordship a telegraphic despatch to the following effect:—

"*Colonial Secretary, London, 11th June,—*

"Ministry desire to notify you that Delegate proceeds immediately London, present appeal British Columbia against breach by Canada Railway Terms Union."

I have, &c.,
(Signed)   JOSEPH W. TRUTCH.

No. 70.

The Lieutenant-Governor to the Secretary of State, Ottawa, Canada.

VICTORIA, B. C.,
June 11th, 1874.

My Ministers desire me to acquaint Dominion Government that they have resolved to appeal to Imperial Government upon Railway question, and that I have to-day, upon their advice, addressed the Secretary of State for Colonies following Telegram:—

"*Colonial Secretary, London,—*

"Ministry desire notify you that Delegate proceeds immediately London, present "Appeal British Columbia against breach by Canada Railway Terms Union."

I have, &c.,
(Signed)   JOSEPH W. TRUTCH.

No. 71.

The Lieutenant-Governor to the Secretary of State for Canada.

GOVERNMENT HOUSE, VICTORIA,
11th June, 1874.

SIR,—I have the honour to enclose with reference to my telegraphic despatch to you of this day's date, the Minute of my Executive Council, in accordance with the advice contained in which my said despatch, and that to the Right Honourable the Secretary of State for the Colonies, a transcript of which was therein reported for the information of His Excellency the Governor-General, were addressed.

I have, &c.,
(Signed)   JOSEPH W. TRUTCH.

No. 72.

The Lieutenant-Governor to the Secretary of State for Canada.

GOVERNMENT HOUSE, VICTORIA,
11th June, 1874.

SIR,—I have the honour to enclose, for the information of His Excellency the Governor-General a copy of a despatch this day addressed by me to the Right Honourable the Secretary of State for the Colonies, with reference to my telegram to His Lordship of this day's date, a transcript of which has already been telegraphed to you.

I have, &c.,
(Signed) JOSEPH W. TRUTCH.

No. 73.

Report of the Executive Council, approved by the Lieutenant-Governor on the 15th June, 1874.

On a memorandum dated 15th day of June, 1874, from the Honourable the Provincial Secretary recommending that the Memorial hereunto appended of the case of British Columbia be adopted, and presented to the Right Honourable the Secretary of State for the Colonies by the Honourable Mr. Walkem on behalf of the Committee of Council of British Columbia.

The Committee advise that the recommendation be approved.

(Certified) W. J. ARMSTRONG,
Clerk, Executive Council.

No. 74.

Copy of Petition, by Provincial Government, to Her Majesty the Queen, complaining of non-fulfilment of Terms of Union by the Dominion.

To the Queen's Most Excellent Majesty.

MOST GRACIOUS SOVEREIGN :

We, Your Majesty's most dutiful and loyal subjects, the Committee of the Executive Council of the Province of British Columbia, in Council assembled, humbly approach Your Majesty, for the purpose of representing :—

1. That, prior to the 20th day of July, 1871, British Columbia was a Crown Colony, having a Legislative Council, partly nominated by the Crown, and partly chosen by the people :

2. That, by Section 146 of the " British North America Act, 1867," provision was made for the Union of British Columbia with the Dominion of Canada :

3. That, during the years 1868 and 1869, the subject of Union was much discussed in British Columbia, both in the Legislature and throughout the Colony ; and a considerable conflict of opinion existed in relation to the question :

4. That, in obedience to Your Majesty's commands, contained in a Despatch (*see* No. 1, page 139) of the 14th August, 1869, from Your Majesty's Principal Secretary of State for the Colonies to the Governor of British Columbia, the Governor in Council framed the " Proposed Terms of Confederation " (*see* No. 2, page 149), and in the month of February 1870, submitted them to the Legislative Council, by whom they were approved :

5. That these Terms had not been directly submitted to the people for their sanction ; and the Council that approved of them was, at the time, composed of Thirteen Members appointed by the Crown, and Nine chosen by the people :

6. That the " Proposed Terms" were presented for consideration, through Delegates, to the Honourable the Privy Council of Canada, as the basis of an agreement for Union :

7. That, after full discussion between the Delegates of British Columbia and the Committee of the Privy Council, it was mutually agreed that the said Terms should be materially modified; and other Terms, hereinafter called the "Accepted Terms" (see No. 3, p. 140), were substituted for those proposed; and such "Accepted Terms," commonly known as the "Terms of Union," now form the basis of Union between British Columbia and the Dominion.

8. That the main difference between the "Proposed Terms" and the "Accepted Terms," consists in the substitution and insertion of Article 11 in the "Accepted Terms" for Article 8 of the "Proposed Terms," which Articles are herewith submitted:—

ARTICLE 8
OF
"PROPOSED TERMS."

"8. Inasmuch as no real Union can subsist between this Colony and Canada without the speedy establishment of communication across the Rocky Mountains by Coach Road and Railway, the Dominion shall, within three years from the date of Union, construct and open for traffic such Coach Road from some point on the line of the Main Trunk Road of this Colony to Fort Garry, of similar character to the said Main Trunk Road; and shall further engage to use all means in her power to complete such Railway communication at the earliest practicable date; and that surveys to determine the proper line of such Railway shall be at once commenced; and that a sum of not less than One Million Dollars shall be expended in every year, from and after three years from the date of Union, in actually constructing the initial sections of such Railway from the seaboard of British Columbia to connect with the Railway system of Canada."

ARTICLE 11
OF
"ACCEPTED TERMS."

"11. The Government of the Dominion undertake to secure the commencement simultaneously, within two years from the date of Union, of the construction of a railway from the Pacific towards the Rocky Mountains, and from such point as may be selected, east of the Rocky Mountains towards the Pacific, to connect the seaboard of British Columbia with the railway system of Canada; and further, to secure the completion of such railway within ten years from the date of the Union.

"And the Government of British Columbia agree to convey to the Dominion Government, in trust, to be appropriated in such manner as the Dominion Government may deem advisable in furtherance of the construction of the said Railway, a similar extent of public lands along the line of railway throughout its entire length in British Columbia, not to exceed, however, twenty (20) miles on each side of said line, as may be appropriated for the same purpose by the Dominion Government from the public lands in the Northwest Territories and the Province of Manitoba. Provided, that the quantity of land which may be held under pre-emption right or by Crown grant within the limits of the tracts of land in British Columbia to be so conveyed to the Dominion Government shall be made good to the Dominion from contiguous public lands; and provided further, that until the commencement, within two years, as aforesaid, from the date of the Union, of the construction of the said railway, the Government of British Columbia shall not sell or alienate any further portions of the public lands of British Columbia in any other way than under right of pre-emption, requiring actual residence of the pre-emptor on the land claimed by him. In consideration of the land to be so conveyed in aid of the construction of the said Railway, the Dominion Government agree to pay to British Columbia, from the date of the Union, the sum of 100,000 dollars per annum, in half-yearly payments in advance."

9. That this substitution, affording assurance of *speedy Railway communication* with the Eastern Provinces, was made to secure the acceptance of Confederation by the people of British Columbia:

10. That it having been decided that the people of British Columbia should be directly consulted before the "Accepted Terms" became law, Your Majesty, in pursuance of the provisions of the "British Columbia Government Act, 1870," was graciously pleased, by an Order in Council of the 6th day of August, 1870," to so reconstitute the Legislative Council as to allow the Electoral Districts throughout the country to return a majority of Members thereto:

11. That, under the new Constitution of the Council, Writs were issued for the Election of Members to serve therein, and the said "Accepted Terms" were duly submitted to the people for their consideration; and at the subsequent Elections held to

decide the question of Union, the provisions of Article 11 of the Terms of Union formed the main inducement to British Columbia to agree to enter into Confederation; and Members were returned to support the adoption thereof:

12. That such "Accepted Terms" were, on the 23rd day of January, 1871, unanimously agreed to by the Legislative Council; and an humble Address to Your Majesty was at the same time passed, praying that Your Majesty in Council would be graciously pleased " to admit British Columbia into the Union or Dominion of Canada, on the basis " of the Terms and conditions offered to this Colony by the Government of the Dominion " of Canada," which Terms and conditions are those herein referred to as the "Accepted Terms:"

13. That similar Addresses to Your Majesty on the same subject were passed by the Parliament of Canada under the provisions of the 146th Section of the "British North America Act, 1867:"

14. That on the 16th day of May, 1871, Your Majesty, in answer to the said Addresses, was graciously pleased to order and declare (*see* No. 4, page 143) that the Union between British Columbia and the Dominion should take effect on the 20th day of July, 1871—and British Columbia accordingly, became on that day, one of the Provinces of the Dominion of Canada, upon the basis of the "Accepted Terms," or Treaty of Union:

15. That by Article 11 the Dominion undertook "to secure the commencement simul-" taneously, within two years from the date of Union, of the construction of a Railway " from the Pacific towards the Rocky Mountains, and from such point as may be selected " east of the Rocky Mountains towards the Pacific, to connect the Seaboard of British " Columbia with the Railway system of Canada; and further to secure the completion of " such Railway within ten years from the date of the Union." And the Province *in consideration thereof, and " in furtherance of the construction of said Railway," agreed first,—to convey to the Dominion a belt of Public land not exceeding Twenty Miles in width on each side of the Railway in British Columbia; and secondly—to withdraw all its public lands from sale or alienation, except under stringent pre-emption laws, for a period of two years ending on the 20th day of July, 1873* :

16. That accordingly, immediately upon Union, all lands of the Province were withdrawn from sale or alienation.

17. That, the Dominion Government informed the Provincial Government, by Despatch dated the 10th June, 1873, and by an enclosed Order of the Privy Council, (see Nos. 5 and 6, p. 144) based " on a memorandum of the 29th May, 1873, from the Chief " Engineer of the Canadian Pacific Railway," that " Esquimalt, in Vancouver Island," had been "fixed as the Terminus of the Canadian Pacific Railway," and that it had been decided that "a line of Railway be located between the Harbour of Esquimalt and " Seymour Narrows, on the said Island;" and they requested the Provincial Government to convey to the Dominion Government " in trust, according to the 11th paragraph of " the Terms of Agreement of Union, a strip of Land Twenty Miles in width, along the " Eastern Coast of Vancouver Island, between Seymour Narrows and the Harbour of " Esquimalt."

18. That, on the 25th of July, 1873, the Minute of the Executive Council of British Columbia (*see* No. 12. p. 146) relating to the conveyance of the land referred to, was passed and forwarded to Ottawa (*see* No. 7, p. 145) on the following day; and the receipt thereof was acknowledged on the 26th August, 1873, (*see* No. 14, page 148).

19. That, by that Minute, the Provincial Government declined to convey the land referred to, until Railway construction should be commenced as provided by Article 11 of the Terms of Union; but agreed to reserve the said belt (which is coloured red on the accompanying chart of Vancouver Island); being a tract of most valuable land—about 3,200 square miles in extent, abounding in vast mineral wealth and easy of access from the sea,—and this land was accordingly reserved by Order in Council (*see* Nos. 8 and 9, p. 145) on the 30th June, 1873, and by Public Notice on the day following; and has been ever since reserved :

20. That, on the 11th of September, 1873, the Dominion Government intimated their concurrence in the course thus pursued by the Provincial Government, and "submitted (*see* Nos. 15 and 16, p. 149) " that so long as the land which is referred to, is not " alienated from the Crown, but held under Reservation, * * * the object of " the Government of the Dominion will be attained, that object being, simply, that when " the Railway shall come to be constructed, the land in question shall be at the dispo-

"sition of the Government of the Dominion, for the purpose laid down in the 11th "Section of the Terms of Union with British Columbia:"

21. That, on the 22nd September, 1873, the Provincial Government respectfully urged (see Nos. 17 and 18, pp. 149, 150) the Dominion Government to define, by survey, the belt of land referred to, as its reservation was seriously retarding the settlement of Vancouver Island; but to this request no other reply than a mere acknowledgment (see No. 19, p. 150) was sent:

22. That, on the 25th of July, 1873, the Provincial Government, by Order in Council, (see No. 11, p. 146) strongly protested against the breach of the 11th Article, no attempt at construction having been made up to that date; and such protest was forwarded, in Despatch, to the Honourable the Secretary of State, at Ottawa, on the following day (see No. 10, p. 146):

23. That, in the month of August, 1873, the Dominion Government simply acknowledged (see No. 13, p. 148) the receipt of the protest of the 25th July, 1873:—

24. That, on the 24th November following, the Government of the Province again drew the attention of the Dominion, by Despatch and Minute of the Executive Council, (see Nos. 20 and 21, pp. 150, 151) to the protests which had been forwarded and not replied to; and the Dominion Government was requested to state its railway policy for the information of the Provincial Legislature. To this the indefinite reply (see No. 23, p. 151) and no other, was received:

25. That, on the 9th of February, 1874, the Legislative Assembly of British Columbia unanimously protested against the breach of Article 11 of the Terms of Union, and respectfully urged upon Canada "the absolute necessity of commencing the actual con-"struction of the Railway from the Seaboard of British Columbia early in the present "year," (see No. 29, p. 153) and this protest was, on the recommendation of the Executive Council, forwarded to Ottawa in a Despatch of 25th February, 1874, (see No. 30, p. 154) and the receipt thereof was duly acknowledged, but no response thereto has been received (see No. 33, p. 155):

26. That, in the month of February, 1874, the Honourable Mr. Mackenzie, the Premier of Canada, addressed the letter (see No. 35, p. 157) to the Honourable Mr. Walkem, the Attorney-General of British Columbia, introducing Mr. J. D. Edgar, as a gentleman who would "confer" with and ascertain the views of the Members of the Government of British Columbia respecting Railway policy; and this letter was followed by the Correspondence, Official Telegrams, Despatches, and Orders in Council set forth in (see Nos. 35, 40, 41, 42, 45, 47, 48, 49, 50, 51, 53, 54, 55, 56, 57, 59, pp. 157 to 165):

27. That the character, and the substance of the Correspondence, Telegrams, and Despatches may be briefly stated as follows:—

On the 8th day of May, 1874, Mr. Edgar addressed a letter to Mr. Walkem, (see No. 45, p. 159) setting forth the views of Mr. Mackenzie's Administration upon the Railway Clause (Article 11) of the Terms of Union, and making certain suggestions for a change thereof, with a request that they should be considered by the Provincial Government.

As these suggestions gravely affected the interests, both of the Dominion and the Province, and as Mr. Edgar was not accredited by the Dominion Government to make such proposals, it was necessary to ascertain how far they would be binding upon that Government. Accordingly, Telegrams were sent, one (see No. 51, p. 163) by the Provincial Government to the Secretary of State, and the other (see No. 54, p. 163) by Mr. Walkem to Mr. Mackenzie. The only reply was a telegram from Mr. Mackenzie (see No. 53, p. 163), which stated that his letter to Mr. Walkem sufficiently indicated Mr. Edgar's mission; and that he had recalled Mr. Edgar, and was awaiting his return and reports. The inquiry, as to whether Mr. Edgar had power to bind the Dominion Government, remained wholly unanswered.

28. That, Mr. Edgar's letter to Mr. Walkem is made important, by a telegram of the 8th June, 1874, from the Premier of Canada (see No. 56, p. 164) which states that the proposals in Mr. Edgar's letter had been made "on behalf of the Dominion Government," and that they were now withdrawn. To this Telegram, the Provincial Government in substance replied—that it was the first direct communication they had received that those proposals were authoritative, and that it seemed remarkable that by the same communication they should be withdrawn (see No. 59, p. 165):

29. That, in that letter, the Dominion Government proposed "to commence the "construction from Esquimalt to Nanaimo immediately, and push that portion of the

" Railway on to completion with the utmost vigour, and in the shortest practicable time," in consideration of British Columbia consenting to relinquish the definite term fixed in the Treaty of Union for the completion of the Railway; and when " the Surveys and a " proposed Waggon Road on the Mainland can be completed," to make "an annual " minimum expenditure, upon works of construction within the Province, of at least One " million five hundred thousand dollars;" and it further states, that, " to a country like " British Columbia, it is conceded, however, to be an important point, that not only the " prompt and vigorous commencement, but also the vigorous prosecution of the work of " construction, within the limits of the Province should be guaranteed ":

30. That the Dominion Government have no powers to expend public money in railway construction in British Columbia, except under authority of the " Canadian Pacific Railroad Act, 1874," which provides, *inter alia*, for the construction of a section, viz.: the fourth section of the said Railway, to extend from the Western Terminus of the third section, to some point in British Columbia, on the Pacific Ocean:

31. That unless Esquimalt, on Vancouver Island, be the Western Terminal point in British Columbia, on the Pacific Ocean, of the fourth section of the Canadian Pacific Railroad, the Dominion Government cannot expend any public money in the construction of a railway from such point, nor can they claim the reservation of the public lands of the East Coast of Vancouver Island, " for the purposes laid down in the 11th Section of the Terms of Union ":

32. That the following is, as far as can be ascertained, an approximate statement of the exploratory surveys made:—

In 1871 and 1872, there were seven or eight parties engaged, and work was prosecuted with some vigour on the Mainland of British Columbia.

In 1873 two parties left Victoria, as late as the 1st of July, for the interior, and returned in November, that is to say, having, exclusive of travelling time, been engaged in actual work for about three months only. To these parties may be added a third, which had wintered on the Eastern boundaries of the Province.

In 1874 three parties only, exclusive of an explorer sent up the West Coast, started from Victoria for the interior about the 19th May, when the Spring was advanced.

33. That no surveys have been made between Esquimalt and Seymour Narrows, or in any other part of Vancouver Island:

34. That, on the 4th of May, 1874, the Premier of the Dominion Government declared, in his place in the Dominion House of Commons, that " there was no reason to " believe " that it was possible to commence the construction of the Railway in the Province this year (*see* No. 42, p. 159):

35. That, on the 8th May, 1874, the Dominion Government made the offer of *immediate construction on the Island*, as contained in (No. 43, p. 159) before referred to:

36. That, on the 23rd of May, 1874, the Premier of Canada admitted, in his place in the Dominion House of Commons, that " they were quite aware that the Terms of the " Agreement with British Columbia had been violated." (*See* No. 60, p. 165):

37. That the preamble of the " Canadian Pacific Railway Act, 1874," shows that provision for the construction of this work is intended to be made by that Act only as far as can be effected without " further raising the rate of taxation," thus purporting to modify the obligation of Canada, under the Terms of Union, without the consent of British Columbia:

Your Petitioners, therefore, humbly submit—

That British Columbia has fulfilled all the conditions of her agreement under the Terms of Union:

That the Dominion has not completed the necessary Railway Explorations and Surveys; nor, since 1872, has any effort, at all adequate to the undertaking, been made up to the present time:

That notwithstanding the fact that on the 7th day of June, 1873, by Order of the Privy Council, " Esquimalt " was " fixed" *as the point of commencement* on the Pacific, and it was decided that a line should " be located between that harbour and Seymour Narrows;" and notwithstanding, further, that a valuable belt of land, along the line in heated, has ever since been reserved by British Columbia, at the instance of the Dominion, and for the purposes, ostensibly, of immediate construction, the Dominion Government have failed and neglected to commence construction up to the present time:

That although the Government of the Dominion admit that the agreement with

British Columbia has been violated, and acknowledge that immediate construction might be commenced at Esquimalt, and active work vigorously prosecuted upon "that portion of Railway" between Esquimalt and Nanaimo, yet they virtually refuse to commence such construction unless British Columbia consents to materially change the Railway Clause of the Treaty:

That, in consequence of the course pursued by the Dominion, British Columbia is suffering great loss; her trade has been damaged and unsettled; her general prosperity has been seriously affected; her people have become discontented; a feeling of depression has taken the place of the confident anticipations of commercial and political advantages to be derived from the speedy construction of a great Railway, uniting the Atlantic and Pacific shores of your Majesty's Dominion on the Continent of North America.

Your Petitioners, therefore, humbly approach your Majesty, and pray that your Majesty may be graciously pleased to take this, our Petition, into your Majesty's favourable consideration, in order that justice may be done to British Columbia.

And your Petitioners, as in duty bound, will ever pray, &c., &c.

No. 75.

SAN FRANCISCO,
18th June, 1874.

Lieutenant-Governor Trutch, Province of British Columbia, Victoria.

DEAR SIR,—We have just received the following cable message from London:

"LONDON, 18th June.

"Private and confidential. Advise Governor Trutch, Vancouver, by letter, Sproat "says Carnarvon offers to arbitrate between Dominion and Province, both parties con-"curring. Sproat strongly recommends this;" which message you will no doubt understand.

We are, &c.,
(Signed) FAULKNER, BELL, & Co.

No. 76.

BRITISH COLUMBIA,
LIEUTENANT-GOVERNOR'S OFFICE,
June 26th, 1874.

GENTLEMEN,—I am directed by the Lieutenant-Governor to acknowledge the receipt of your letter to him, of the 18th instant, and to thank you for the information it conveys, which is fully understood by His Honour.

I have, &c.,
(Signed) ARTHUR G. J. PINDER,
Private Secretary.

Messrs. Faulkner, Bell & Co., San Francisco, California.

77.

Mr. Walkem to Mr. Mackenzie.

OTTAWA, 4th July, 1874.

SIR,—I have been informed that you intend to leave for Quebec to-day. If this be the case, may I be excused for pressing upon your attention my present very unsatisfactory position in having received no definite information respecting my credentials to the Right Honourable the Principal Secretary of State.

It is considered of great importance by the Government of British Columbia that I should use all possible dispatch in executing my mission to England.

May I therefore request you to inform me when I shall be put in possession of the necessary authority to enable me to accomplish my task?

I have, &c.,
(Signed) GEO. A. WALKEM.

No. 78.

Mr. Buckingham to Mr. Walkem.

OTTAWA, July 4th, 1874.

SIR,—In reply to your letter to Mr. Mackenzie, of this morning's date, enquiring when you can procure your credentials as Delegate of British Columbia to the Imperial Government, I have the honour, by request of Mr. Mackenzie, to say that the necessary Minute of Council has already been forwarded to His Excellency the Governor-General for His Excellency's signature, and that it will be delivered to you immediately the special messenger returns with it to the City.

I have, &c.,
(Signed)   WM. BUCKINGHAM.

No. 79.

Mr. Walkem to the Secretary of State for Canada.

OTTAWA, July 11th 1874.

SIR,—As Mr. Himsworth has arrived from Tadousac, I have the honour to request you to furnish me to-day, if possible, with the documentary authority necessary to accredit me as Delegate from the Government of British Columbia to Her Majesty's Government. The object of my mission has already been stated in a despatch of last June, from the Government of British Columbia to the Dominion Government.

It is of importance that I should leave for England, and bring my work to a close with all convenient speed, hence my request that you will provide me with my letter to-day.

I have, &c.,
(Signed)   GEO. A. WALKEM.

No. 80.

The Secretary of State to Mr. Walkem.

DEPARTMENT SECRETARY OF STATE,
OTTAWA, 11th July, 1874.

SIR,—I have the honour to transmit to you [a certified copy of an Order of His Excellency the Governor-General in Council, on a despatch of His Excellency the Lieutenant-Governor of British Columbia, under date the 11th ultimo, relative to the alleged failure by the Government of the Dominion to carry out the obligations of the 11th Clause of the Terms of Union. In reference to the request of the Lieutenant-Governor, that the Right Honourable the Secretary of State be informed that you have been authorized by the Government of British Columbia, as their Special Agent and Delegate, to submit their memorial appealing to Her Majesty, and to support the prayer thereof, I have to state that a despatch to that effect will be addressed by the Governor-General to the Earl of Carnarvon.

I have, &c.,
(Signed)   R. W. SCOTT.

No. 81.

Report of the Privy Council, approved by the Governor-General in Council on the 8th July, 1874.

On a Despatch, dated 11th June, 1874, from the Lieutenant-Governor of British Columbia, enclosing a Minute of the Executive Council of that Province, representing that British Columbia is suffering great injury from the failure by Canada to carry out the obligations of the Eleventh Clause of the Terms of Union; and that it is advisable, in the interests of that Province, that the case be laid before the Imperial Government, by means of a Memorial to be presented to the Secretary of State for the Colonies by the Attorney-General of British Columbia, as Special Agent and Delegate of that Government.

The Lieutenant-Governor states that, in accordance with the advice of his Ministers, he has appointed the Honourable George Anthony Walkem, Attorney-General of that Province, to be such Special Agent and Delegate, and at their request he begs that Your Excellency be informed that Mr. Walkem has been duly appointed as such Special Agent and Delegate, and that Your Excellency be moved to acquaint the Right Honourable Her Majesty's Principal Secretary of State for the Colonies, that Mr. Walkem has been authorized and instructed to place in his hands the Memorial of that Government appealing to Her Majesty, and to support the prayer thereof.

On the recommendation of the Honourable the Secretary of State, the Committee advise that the above request be acceded to.

       (Certified) W. A. HIMSWORTH,
                Clerk, Privy Council.

No. 82.

The Under Secretary of State for Canada to the Lieutenant-Governor.

            DEPARTMENT OF SECRETARY OF STATE,
               OTTAWA, 13th July, 1874.

SIR,—With reference to my letter of the 11th instant, I have the honour to transmit to you, for the information of your Government, a copy of an Order of His Excellency the Governor-General in Council, and of a letter addressed to Mr. Attorney-General Walkem on the subject of the alleged failure of the Dominion Government to carry out the obligations of the 11th Clause of the Terms of Union.

      I am, &c.,
       (Signed) EDOUARD J. LANGEVIN,
                Under Secretary of State.

No. 83.

The Lieutenant-Governor to the Secretary of State for Canada.

               GOVERNMENT HOUSE,
               Victoria, 28th July, 1874.

SIR,—I have the honour to state that I have received and laid before my Executive Council your despatch of the 13th inst., transmitting a copy of an Order of His Excellency the Governor-General in Council, and of a letter to Mr. Attorney-General Walkem on the subject of Mr Walkem's mission to England in support of the Memorial of this Government to Her Majesty, with reference to the Railway Article of the Terms of Union of this Province with Canada.

      I have, &c.,
       (Signed) JOSEPH W. TRUTCH.

84.

Mr. Walkem to Mr. Mackenzie.

               OTTAWA, July 13th, 1874.

SIR,—I have the honour to forward to you, for your perusal and for the information of your Government, two copies of the Protest of the British Columbia Government (against the breach or infraction of the "Terms of Union" with Canada by the Dominion Government), which I have been authorised to present in person to Her Majesty's Government. Two copies of the Charts referred to in the Protest are also herewith forwarded.

May I request you to be good enough to acknowledge their receipt.

      I have, &c.,
       (Signed) G. A. WALKEM,
                Attorney-General B. C.

No. 85.

The Under Secretary of State to Mr. Walkem.

DEPARTMENT SECRETARY OF STATE,
Ottawa, 13th July, 1874.

SIR,—I am directed to acknowledge the receipt of your letter of this date, addressed to the Honourable Mr. Mackenzie, transmitting two copies of the Protest of the British Columbia Government against the alleged breach or infraction of the Terms of Union with Canada, by the Dominion Government, which you have been authorised to present in person to Her Majesty's Government; and also forwarding two copies of the Charts referred to in the Protest.

I have, &c.,
(Signed) E. J. LANGEVIN.

No. 86.

The Governor-General to the Lieutenant-Governor of British Columbia.

Received 27th July, 1874.

July 3rd, 1874.

SIR,—In obedience to the instructions of the Secretary of State, I have the honour to transmit for your information the enclosed Despatch.

I have, &c.,
(Signed) DUFFERIN.

The Earl of Carnarvon to the Governor-General.

DOWNING STREET, 18th June, 1874.

MY LORD,—The intimation, which I have received by telegraph, of the departure from British Columbia of the President of the Council and Attorney-General of that Province, sent to this country for the purpose of appealing against the course proposed by your Government, and sanctioned by the Dominion Parliament, in regard to the Pacific Railway, together with the Reports of the Proceedings in that Parliament, and other informal communications, have led me to apprehend that the difference of opinion which has unfortunately occurred may not only prove difficult to adjust, but may not impossibly, if it remains long unsettled, give rise to feelings of dissatisfaction and to disagreements, the existence of which within the Dominion would be a matter of serious regret.

2. It is not my wish, nor is it a part of my ordinary duty, to interfere in these questions. They appear to be such as it should be within the province and the competency of the Dominion Government and Legislature to bring to a satisfactory solution; and you will readily understand that Her Majesty's Government would be very reluctant to take any action which might be construed as expressing a doubt of the Dominion Government and Parliament to give the fullest consideration to such representations as may be made on the part of British Columbia, and to deal in the fairest and most liberal spirit with what may be established as being the just claims of that Province.

3. At the same time I am strongly impressed with the importance of neglecting no means that can properly be adopted for effecting the speedy and amicable settlement of a question which cannot, without risk and obvious disadvantages to all parties, remain the subject of prolonged, and it may be acrimonious, discussions; and it has occurred to me that, as in the original terms and conditions of the admission of British Columbia into the union, certain points (as for example the amount of land to be appropriated for the Indians, and the pensions to be assigned to public officers deprived of employment) were reserved for the decision of the Secretary of State; so in the present case it may possibly be acceptable to both parties that I should tender my good offices in determining the new points which have presented themselves for settlement. I accordingly addressed a telegram to you yesterday to the effect that I greatly regretted that a difference should exist between the Dominion and the Province in regard to the railway, and that if both Governments should unite in desiring to refer to my arbitration all matters in

controversy, binding themselves to accept such decision as I may think fair and just, I would not decline to undertake this service.

4. The duty, which under a sense of the importance of interests concerned, I have thus offered to discharge, is of course a responsible and difficult one, which I could not assume unless by the desire of both parties, nor unless it should be fully agreed that my decision, whatever it may be, shall be accepted without any question or demur. If it is desired that I should act in this matter, it will be convenient for each party to prepare a statement to be communicated to the other party, and, after a reasonable interval, a counter statement, and that on these written documents I should, reserving of course to myself the power of calling for any other information to guide me in arriving at my conclusion, give my final decision.

5. I request you to transmit a copy of this despatch with the utmost possible speed to the Lieutenant-Governor of British Columbia. I have communicated to Mr. Sproat, the Agent for British Columbia, for transmission by telegraph to the Government of that Province, the purport of the telegram which I addressed to you yesterday, in order that my offer may come before both parties as soon as possible.

I have, &c.,
(Signed) CARNARVON.

No. 87.

Lieutenant-Governor Trutch to Governor-General.

GOVERNMENT HOUSE, VICTORIA,
29th July, 1874.

MY LORD,—I have the honour to acknowledge the receipt, on the day before yesterday, of Your Lordship's Despatch of the 3rd instant, transmitting, by direction of the Right Honourable the Secretary of State for the Colonies, for the information of this Government, a copy of a despatch from that Minister to Your Lordship proposing himself as arbitrator in the matter under discussion, between the Governments of Canada and this Province, in relation to the 11th Article of the Terms of Union of British Columbia with Canada.

I have submitted Your Lordship's despatch and that from Lord Carnarvon to Your Lordship, therein transmitted, for the consideration and advice of my Executive Council.

I have, &c.,
(Signed) JOSEPH W. TRUTCH.

No. 88.

The Lieutenant-Governor to the Secretary of State for Canada.

GOVERNMENT HOUSE, VICTORIA,
3rd August, 1874.

SIR,—I have the honour to transmit to you for the information of His Excellency the Governor-General, a copy of a despatch addressed by me to Her Majesty's Principal Secretary of State for the Colonies, expressing the acceptance by this Government of the offer made by His Lordship in his despatch of 28th June last, to the Governor-General, to arbitrate in the difference existing between the Government of Canada and this Province, in relation to the Railway Article of the Terms of Union, together with a copy of the Minute of the Executive Council of British Columbia therewith enclosed, expressing the opinions and advice of my responsible Ministers upon Lord Carnarvon's proffered arbitration, and in accordance with which my said despatch to His Lordship, and the telegraphic message therein referred to—and of which a copy is appended—as well as this communication and the telegram to you of this day's date—a copy of which is also attached hereto—are at the same time dispatched.

I have, &c.,
(Signed) JOSEPH W. TRUTCH.

No. 89.

Lieutenant-Governor Trutch to Earl Carnarvon.

GOVERNMENT HOUSE, VICTORIA,
3rd August, 1874.

MY LORD,—I have the honour to state that, on the 28th ultimo, I received and laid before my responsible advisers a copy of Your Lordship's despatch of June 18th, to Governor General the Earl of Dufferin, upon the pending difference between this Province and the Government of Canada, in relation to the Railway Article of the Terms of Union, which despatch was transmitted to me by Lord Dufferin, on the 3rd ultimo, in accordance with Your Lordship's instructions.

I now enclose a Minute of the Executive Council of this Province on your said despatch, and upon the advice of my Ministers therein expressed, I beg to signify my cordial acceptance, on behalf of the Government of British Columbia, of Your Lordship's proffered arbitration, in accordance, in all respects, with the conditions laid down in your said despatch, and to state that I have to-day dispatched a telegraphic message to you to this effect, of which a copy is appended.

A copy of this despatch and enclosures therewith, will be sent by this mail to the Secretary of State for Canada, for the information of His Excellency the Governor-General of Canada.

I have, &c.,
(Signed)   JOSEPH W. TRUTCH.

No. 90.

The Lieutenant-Governor to the Secretary of State for the Colonies.

3rd August, 1874.

Upon advice of Responsible Ministers I acccept on behalf of British Columbia arbitration offered in your Despatch to Lord Dufferin, eighteenth June. Please acknowledge.

(Signed)   JOSEPH W. TRUTCH.

No. 91.

The Secretary of State for the Colonies to Lieutenant Governor.

Your Telegram of August 3rd, received.

(Signed)   CARNARVON.

No. 92.

The Lieutenant-Governor to the Secretary of State for Canada.

VICTORIA, B. C.,
August 3rd, 1874.

My Ministers request me to state for the information of the Governor-General that the following message has been this day telegraphed to Lord Carnarvon:—

"Colonial Secretary, London,—

"Upon advice of Responsible Ministers, I accept on behalf of British Columbia arbitration offered in your despatch to Lord Dufferin, 18th June. Please acknowledge."

(Signed)   JOSEPH W. TRUTCH,
Lieutenant-Governor.

No. 93.

Report of the Executive Council approved by the Lieutenant-Governor on the 5th August, 1874.

The Committee of Council have had under consideration the proposal for a reference to arbitration, of the question between the Province and the Dominion Government, respecting the fulfilment of the Terms of Union, contained in the Despatch dated 18th June, 1874, from the Right Honourable the Earl of Carnarvon, Her Majesty's Principal Secretary of State for the Colonies, to His Excellency the Governor-General, a copy of which has been transmitted for the information of Your Excellency and referred to them for report:—

In the Despatch the Secretary of State observes that he is "strongly impressed with " the importance of neglecting no means that can properly be adopted for effecting the " speedy and amicable settlement of a question, which cannot without risk and obvious " disadvantage to all parties, remain the subject of prolonged, and it may be acrimonious, " discussion."

That it has occurred to him, "that as in the original terms and conditions of the " admission of British Columbia into the Union, certain points were reserved for the " decision of the Secretary of State, so in the present case it may possibly be acceptable " to both parties that he should tender his good offices in determining the new points " which had presented themselves for settlement. That, if both Governments should " unite in desiring to refer to his arbitration all matters in controversy, binding them- " selves to accept such decision as he may think fair and just, he would not decline to " undertake this service."

That the duty, which under a sense of the importance of the interests concerned, he has thus offered to discharge, is of course a responsible and difficult one, which he could not assume unless by the desire of both parties, nor unless it should be fully agreed that his decision, whatever it may be, shall be accepted without any question or demur.

The Committee concur with the Secretary of State in regretting that a difference exists between the Dominion and this Province in regard to the Railway, and that it is most desirable for all parties, that all the questions in controversy should receive a speedy and amicable settlement, and they are of opinion that a reference to arbitration is the course of all others most likely to lead to so desirable a result.

They therefore advise the cordial acceptance by your Excellency of the arbitration of the Secretary of State, in accordance with the conditions laid down in His Lordship's Despatch of the 18th June, 1874; and should this report be approved, they recommend that the acceptance by this Government on behalf of British Columbia of the arbitration of the Right Honourable the Secretary of State for the Colonies, be immediately communicated by Your Excellency to that Minister by telegraph and by mail, that copies of such communications be transmitted simultaneously to the Secretary of State for Canada for the information of His Excellency the Governor-General.

(Certified) W. J. ARMSTRONG,
Clerk Executive Council.

No. 94.

The Under Secretary of State for Canada to the Lieutenant-Governor.

DEPARTMENT OF THE SECRETARY OF STATE,
20th September, 1874.

SIR,—I have the honour to acknowledge the receipt of your despatch, No. 53, of the 3rd instant, and its enclosures, transmitting, for the information of His Excellency the Governor-General, a copy of a despatch addressed by you to the Right Honourable the Secretary of State for the Colonies, expressing the acceptance by your Government of his Lordship's offer, as conveyed in his despatch of the 18th of June last, to arbitrate in the difference between the Government of British Columbia and the Dominion in relation to the Railway Article of the Terms of Union.

Your despatch will be submitted for the consideration of the Government.

I have, &c.,
(Signed) EDOUARD J. LANGEVIN,
Under Secretary of State.

No. 95.

The Earl of Carnarvon to the Governor-General.

Received in OTTAWA, 18th January, 1874.

I regret extremely the difficulty between Dominion of Canada and British Columbia as to Terms of Union in connection with Pacific Railway. Her Majesty's Government are willing to give their good offices in adjusting the matter. If both parties unite in referring all matters of difference to my arbitration, binding themselves to abide by such award as I may deem just and fair, I will not refuse to undertake the duty.

No. 96.

The Governor-General to the Earl of Carnarvon.

(No. 182.)   QUEBEC, 9th July, 1874.

MY LORD,—I have the honour to acknowledge the receipt of your Lordship's Despatch, No. 110, of the 18th June, in which you refer to a misunderstanding that has occurred between the Dominion Government and that of British Columbia, and in which you have made so considerately a suggestion in regard to the settlement of the dispute.

In accordance with your instructions, I have forwarded a copy of the despatch to the Lieutenant-Governor of British Columbia, and I have also communicated it to my Government.

There has not yet been time for them to acquaint me with their view in regard to the extremely considerate and friendly suggestions your Lordship is good enough to convey, but in connection with the subject matter to which the despatch under acknowledgment refers, I have the honour to enclose, for your Lordship's information a memorandum of a Committee of Council on the points in dispute between the Dominion Government and the Government of British Columbia, together with a report by Mr. Edgar of his mission to that Province, accompanied by copies of his correspondence with Mr. Walkem, the Attorney-General of British Columbia.

I am, &c.,
(Signed)   DUFFERIN.

No. 97.

Report of the Privy Council, approved by the Governor-General on the 8th July, 1874.

The Committee of Council, after due deliberation, consider that the proposed mission of Mr. Walkem, Attorney-General of British Columbia, to England on behalf of the Government of that Province, to complain to the Imperial Government of the non-fulfilment by the Dominion Government of the Terms of Union, and the telegraphic message of the Right Honourable the Secretary of State for the Colonies with reference to the said mission, in which he offers his good offices in arriving at some understanding between British Columbia and the Dominion, render it desirable that a brief statement should be submitted showing the position of the question, and the action taken by the present Government of Canada in relation thereto.

The Order in Council under which British Columbia was admitted into the Union provided in the 11th Section that—

"The Government of the Dominion undertake to secure the commencement simul"taneously, within two years from the date of the Union, of the construction of a "railway from the Pacific towards the Rocky Mountains, and from such point as may "be selected east of the Rocky Mountains towards the Pacific, to connect the seaboard "of British Columbia with the Railway system of Canada; and further to secure the "completion of such railway within ten years from the date of the Union."

The passage of such a provision was very strongly opposed in Parliament, the Government of the day securing only a majority of ten in support of the measure. In order to induce even this majority to sustain them, the following Resolution was proposed and carried by the Government:—

"That the railway referred to in the Address to Her Majesty concerning the Union of British Columbia with Canada, adopted by this House on Saturday, the 1st of April, instant, should be constructed and worked by private enterprise, and not by the Dominion Government, and that the public aid to be given to secure that undertaking should consist of such liberal grants of land, and such subsidy in money or other aid, *not increasing the present rate of taxation*, as the Parliament of Canada shall hereafter determine."

The late Government were compelled by their followers in the House to adopt this resolution regarding the taxation consequent on the obligation to build the railway as the condition of obtaining their support. Even with this qualifying resolution promised, the section respecting the railway was carried but by a majority of ten, the usual majority being from fifty to seventy.

It is impossible to conceive how such terms could even have been proposed, as it was quite clear to every person that they were incapable of fulfilment, especially as the British Columbia Legislature never asked such extravagant terms. The clause of the terms adopted by that body having reference to the railway was as follows:

"Inasmuch as no real union can subsist between this Colony and Canada without the speedy establishment of communication across the Rocky Mountains by coach road and railway, the Dominion shall within three years from the date of Union construct and open for traffic such coach road from some point on the line of the Main Trunk Road of this Colony to Fort Garry, of similar character to the said Main Trunk Road; and shall further engage to use all means in her power to complete such railway communication at the earliest practicable date, and that surveys to determine the proper line for such railway shall be at once commenced; and that a sum not less than one million dollars shall be expended in every year from and after three years from the date of Union in actually constructing the initial sections of such railway from the seaboard of British Columbia to connect with the railway system of Canada."

Mr. Trutch, the delegate of the British Columbia Government, present in Ottawa during the discussions on the Terms of Union, expressed himself as follows at a public meeting, in order to reassure those who were apprehensive of the conveyances of so rash an assumption of such serious obligations:—

"When he came to Ottawa with his co-delegates last year, they entered into a computation with the Privy Council as to the cost and time it would take to build the line, and they came to the conclusion that it could be built on the terms proposed in ten years. If they had said twelve or eighteen years, that time would have been accepted with equal readiness, as all that was understood was that the line should be built as soon as possible. British Columbia had entered into a partnership with Canada, and they were united to construct certain public works, but he for one would protest against anything by which it should be understood that the Government were to borrow one hundred millions of dollars, or to tax the people of Canada and British Columbia to carry out those works within a certain time (loud cheers). He had been accused of having made a very Jewish bargain; but not even Shylock would have demanded his 'pound of flesh' if it had to be cut from his own body. (Laughter and cheers."

These expressions show very clearly that the terms agreed to were directory rather than mandatory, and were to be interpreted by circumstances, the essence of the engagement being such diligence as was consistent with moderate expenditure, and no increase in the then rate of taxation.

When the present Government assumed office in November, 1873, the condition of affairs regarding the railway was as follows:—A sum of over a million of dollars had been expended in prosecuting the surveys, over one-half of which was spent in British Columbia, but the engineers had not been able to locate any portion of the line.

A Company under the Presidency of Sir Hugh Allen, had been formed by the late Government to construct the line. That Company had undertaken to complete the railway for a grant of thirty millions of money and a grant of twenty thousand acres of land per mile, retaining possession of the railway when built as their own property. The President of the delegation of the Directors of this Company visited England to make financial arrangements to enable them to commence the work of construction. Their mission proved a total failure. Their failure was so complete that soon after the return of Sir Hugh Allan and his co-delegates from England, they relinquished their charter, and the Government paid them the sum of one million dollars, which had been deposited with the Receiver-General under the terms of the agreement.

The British Columbia Government had also complained that the commencement of the works of construction had not been made within the time provided. Sir John A. Macdonald, however giving an informal opinion that the terms as to commencement were sufficiently and substantially kept by the active prosecution of the surveys.

This Government had therefore to provide some other method for the prosecution of the work, to endeavour to keep substantially good faith with British Columbia, to avoid further taxation and, if possible, secure the consent and co-operation of the Government and people of British Columbia.

The new bill, which has since become law, was prepared, which enables the Government (with the approval of Parliament) to get the work executed in one or several contracts, by a company or companies, which may or may not become proprietors of the line after it is constructed.

Mr. James D. Edgar was dispatched on a special mission to the Province of British Columbia, charged to confer with the Government, and also to visit all classes or parties, and ascertain their views, and to submit any proposal he might be directed to make to the local authorities or to receive any proposition from them and forward the same to Ottawa for consideration. A copy of the instructions sent to Mr. Edgar, and copies of certain telegrams already forwarded, and Mr. Edgar's report accompanying this minute, explain sufficiently the nature and result of Mr. Edgar's mission. It was at first expected that a good understanding would be arrived at, and judging from circumstances, local political complications alone prevented some arrangement being come to.

The reason alleged for refusing to consider the proposition Mr. Edgar was finally directed to make, that Mr. Edgar was not accredited by this Government, was evidently a mere technical pretence. All that Mr. Edgar had to do was simply to present the proposals and ascertain on the spot whether they would be entertained by the Government.

If satisfactory to them, the Dominion Government would, as a matter of course, have them sanctioned in due form; or if any counter proposition had been made, instructions would be given Mr. Edgar concerning them.

The propositions made by Mr. Edgar involved an immediate heavy expenditure in British Columbia not contemplated in the terms of Union, namely the construction of a railway on Vancouver Island, from the Port of Esquimalt to Nanaimo, as compensation to the most populous part of the Province for the requirement of a longer time for completing the line on the mainland. The proposals also embraced an obligation to construct a road or trail and telegraph line across the continent at once, and an expenditure of not less than a million and a half within the Province annually on the railway works on the mainland, irrespective of the amounts which might be spent east of the Rocky Mountains, being a half more than the entire sum British Columbia demanded in the first instance as the annual expenditure on the whole road.

In order to enable the Government to carry out the proposals, which it was hoped the British Columbia Government would have accepted, the average rate of taxation was raised at the late Session about fifteen per cent. The customs duties being raised from fifteen per cent. to seventeen and a half per cent., and the excise duties on spirits and tobacco a corresponding rate, both involving additional taxation exceeding three millions of dollars on the transactions of the year.

The public feeling of the whole Dominion has been expressed so strongly against the fatal extravagance involved in the terms agreed to by the late Government, that no Government could live that would attempt or rather pretend to attempt their literal fulfilment. Public opinion would not go beyond the proposal made through Mr. Edgar to the Government.

There is also reason to believe that local political exigencies alone induce the Government of British Columbia not to entertain these proposals.

Since these propositions have been before the people, meetings have been had on Vancouver's Island and on the mainland, when the action of the local Government was condemned, and a call made to accept the proposals offered. A very influential portion of the local press has also declared in favour of the course pursued by the Dominion Government.

It may not be out of place to mention that the action of the Dominion Government regarding the Graving Dock, shows a desire to do everything that can fairly be asked, whether there be an obligation or not under the Terms of the Union. The Dominion was only bound to guarantee the interest on one hundred thousand pounds at five per cent., for ten years after the Dock should be constructed. The local Government found it impossible to obtain any contractor to undertake the work on the terms they were able to offer, based on the Dominion guarantee, and they solicited this Government to assist otherwise. This was agreed to, and Parliamentary authority was obtained at the late Session to enable the Governor-General in Council to advance $250,000 as the work progressed.

The Report of Mr. Edgar will fully explain the object and effect of his mission as the agent of the Government. The Committee advise, therefore, that a copy of the said Report and appendices be transmitted to the Right Honourable Lord Carnarvon, Secretary of State for the Colonies, with this Minute.

Certified,
(Signed) W. A. HIMSWORTH,
Clerk Privy Council.

No. 98.

The Governor-General to the Earl of Carnarvon.

QUEBEC, 9th July, 1874.

MY LORD,—I have the honour to forward, for Your Lordship's information, a printed circular from the Department of Public Works, inviting proposals for the erection of a line of telegraph along the general route of the Canadian Pacific Railway.

I have, &c.,
(Signed) DUFFERIN.

No. 99.

Canada Pacific Railway—Telegraph Line.

Proposals are invited for the erection of a line of telegraph along the general route of the Canadian Pacific Railway, as may be defined by the Government. The proposals to embrace the following points, viz:—

The furnishing of all materials, labour, instruments, and everything necessary to put the line in operation.

The maintenance of the line for a period of five years after its completion.

In the wooded sections, the land to be cleared to a width of 132 feet, or such greater width as may be necessary to prevent injury to the telegraph from fires or falling trees. Distinct proposals to be made for each of the following sections, such proposals to state the time when the party tendering will undertake to have the telegraph ready for use in each case:

1. Fort Garry to a point opposite Fort Pelly, about 250 miles.
2. Fort Garry to the bend of the North Saskatchewan, about 500 miles.
3. Fort Garry to a point in the longitude of Edmonton, about 800 miles.
4. Lac La Hache, or other convenient point on the existing telegraph system in British Columbia, to Fort Edmonton, about 550 miles.
5. Fort Garry to Nepigon, Lake Superior, about 420 miles.
6. Ottawa to Nepigon, Lake Superior, about 760 miles.

The above distances are approximate. They are given for the general guidance of parties desiring information. Any increase or diminution in the ascertained mileage after construction will be paid for or deducted, as the case may be, at a rate corresponding with the sum total of the tender.

Parties tendering must satisfy the Government as to their ability to carry out the work and maintain it for the specified time.

Proposals addressed to the Minister of Public Works, will be received up to 22nd day of July next.

By Order.

Department of Public Works,   F. BRAUN,
June, 1874.   *Secretary.*

No. 100.

The Governor-General to the Earl of Carnarvon.

OTTAWA, 18th July, 1874.

MY LORD,—I have the honour to enclose a copy of an approved Report of a Committee of the Privy Council, (see No. 81, p. 180) requesting me to inform Your Lordship that Mr. Walkem, the Attorney-General of the Province of Columbia, has been deputed by that Government as a Special Agent to lay before Your Lordship the claims of British Columbia, under the 11th Clause of the Terms of Union with the Dominion of Canada.

I have, &c.,
(Signed)   DUFFERIN.

No. 101.

The Governor-General to the Earl of Carnarvon.

OTTAWA, 22nd July, 1874.

MY LORD,—I have the honour to forward herewith three copies of the Act of last Session, "An Act to provide for the construction of the Canadian Pacific Railway." One copy is attested by the Deputy-Clerk of the Senate.

I have, &c.,
(Signed)   DUFFERIN.

No. 102.

The Governor-General to the Earl of Carnarvon.

OTTAWA, 31st July, 1874.

MY LORD,—I have the honour to transmit a copy of a despatch and enclosure from the Lieutenant-Governor of British Columbia, together with the petition to Her Majesty therein referred to from the inhabitants of Victoria, respecting the non-fulfilment by Canada of the Terms of Union

I have, &c.,
(Signed)   DUFFERIN.

No. 103.

The Governor-General to the Earl of Carnarvon.

SAULT STE. MARIE,
July 31st, 1874.

MY LORD,—In further reference to your public despatch, No. 110, of 18th June, which I communicated to my Ministers, I have the honour to enclose an approved Order in Council, in which my Government sets forth more at large its views with respect to its pending dispute with British Columbia, and expresses a desire that Your Lordship would use your good offices in promoting a settlement of the misunderstanding, in accordance with the suggestion you have been good enough to make.

I have, &c.,
(Signed)   DUFFERIN.

No. 104.

Report of the Privy Council, approved by the Governor-General on the 23rd July, 1874.

The Committee of Council have had under consideration the despatch from the Right Honourable the Secretary of State for the Colonies No. 110, relative to the proposed mission of a member of the British Columbia Government to England, for the purpose of complaining of the alleged non-fulfilment of the Terms of Union between that Province and the Dominion, as to the construction of the Pacific Railway, and containing an offer on the part of Lord Carnarvon in the following terms: "If both Governments "should unite in desiring to refer to my arbitration all matters in controversy, binding "themselves to accept such decision as I may think fair and just, I would not decline to "undertake this service;" and further stating that he could not assume such duty "unless by the desire of both parties, and unless it should be fully agreed that my decision, " whatever it may be, shall be accepted without any question or demur;" concluding with a request that, in the event of this offer being accepted, a statement of the case should be prepared by each Government, to be submitted for consideration.

The Committee advise that Lord Carnarvon be informed that the papers already transmitted to the Colonial Office, with the Minute of Council of July 8th, having special reference to Mr. Walkem's communication in Ottawa of the 15th July, convey substantially all that this Government have to say upon the subject; and that the Government would gladly accept his Lordship's offer, if it were possible to define, with any degree of exactitude, the matter in dispute.

When the present Government assumed office, they found that the British Columbia Government had protested against the non-commencement of works of construction on the railway on or before the 20th day of July, 1873, as agreed to in the eleventh section of the Order in Council relating to the Union. They also found that the means taken by the late Dominion Government for proceeding with the works of construction had totally failed, although the works preliminary to an actual commencement had been prosecuted with all possible dispatch.

There can be no question of the extreme difficulty involved in the survey of a line of railway across an uninhabited continent, a distance of twenty-five hundred miles. To properly complete this survey and ascertain the best route for the railway, would require not two years simply, but at least five or six years, as all experience of works of this magnitude and character both in the Dominion and elsewhere has sufficiently demonstrated.

The expenditure which had taken place up to that time was very large, exceeding one million of dollars, and yet the engineers had been quite unable to locate any portion of the line in the more difficult parts of the country to be traversed.

Under these circumstances the Government conceive that there was no reasonable or just cause of complaint on the part of the British Columbia Government.

No other steps could have been taken further than prosecuting the surveys until the assembling of Parliament towards the close of the month of March of this year.

The Government were then prepared with a new bill, taking ample powers for proceeding with the works as expeditiously as the circumstances of the country would permit. No complaint, official or otherwise, has been made as to the sufficiency of this measure to accomplish the object in view. It was distinctly understood by the British Columbia delegation at the time the Terms of Union were agreed upon, that the taxation of the country was not to be increased on account of this work beyond the rate then existing.

So anxious, however, were the present Government to remove any possible cause of complaint, that they did take means to increase the taxation very materially in order to place themselves in a position to make arrangements for the prosecution of the initial and difficult portions of the line as soon as it was possible to do so,—and, at the same time, a special confidential agent was deputed to British Columbia for the express purpose of conferring with the Government of that Province, and to endeavour to arrive at some understanding as to a course to be pursued which could be satisfactory to British Columbia and meet the circumstances of the Dominion.

It should be mentioned that before the late Government left office it had been distinctly understood, as one of the results of the visit to England by the Directors of the

Allan Company, that an extension of time of at least four years would be absolutely necessary.

Mr. Walkem, of British Columbia, quite understood this, and there is reason to believe that it would have been assented to by all parties.

The proposal made through Mr. Edgar to the British Columbia Government is one which the Dominion Government think should have been accepted as reasonable and just, and as one quite in accordance with the moral obligations imposed on this Government, if not with the actual letter of the agreement.

It must be remembered that British Columbia earnestly petitioned the Dominion Government to modify the Terms of Union in its own favour, in relation to the construction of the Graving Dock. The Dominion Government cordially assented to provide the money for the construction of the work, instead of abiding by the agreement to guarantee merely the Provincial bonds for ten years, as provided by the Terms of Union. This at once shows the liberality of the Dominion Government, and their willingness to consider and meet exceptional circumstances wherever they existed. And this manifestation of liberality on the part of this Government they conceive should have been reciprocated in other matters by the Provincial Government.

The Dominion Government were also willing to exceed the Terms of Union, by constructing a railway on the Island of Vancouver, although they were bound only to reach the *seaboard* of the Pacific.

At the present time, the only violation of the terms of the compact which can be alleged, is that the works of construction were not actually commenced on the 20th July, 1873. But it is doubtful if even that allegation can be upheld.

It was all but impossible to proceed more rapidly with the work of survey, and a very extravagant expenditure was the result of the haste already shown in endeavoring to locate the line.

This may be understood from the fact that the surveys of the Intercolonial Railway, 500 miles long, occupied not less than four years, though the route was through a settled country, and they were then very incomplete, causing subsequent serious embarrassments to the contractors, and the presentation by them of endless claims for compensation.

Mr. Walkem, in his conversations, admits frankly that the literal fulfilment of the terms for the completion of the line on a certain day in 1881 cannot be expected. The only questions, therefore, that can now arise are (1) whether due diligence and expedition have been exerted by the Dominion Government in the prosecution of the works; and (2,) whether the offers of compensation for the alleged non-fulfilment of the terms were just and fair.

While expressing a very strong conviction that everything has been done that could possibly be done under the circumstances, and that the Dominion Government have shown a disposition to go far beyond the spirit of the engagement entered into with British Columbia, considering the expressions of opinion by Mr. Trutch, as the delegate of British Columbia at the time of the union, and the facts set forth in the several documents already forwarded to the Colonial Office, the Committee advise that Lord Carnarvon be informed they would gladly submit the question to him for his decision as to whether the exertions of the Government, the diligence shown, and the offers made, have or have not been fair and just, and in accordance with the spirit of the agreement.

The Committee advise that a copy of this Minute be forwarded to the Right Hon. the Secretary of State for the Colonies. Certified,

(Signed) W. A. HIMSWORTH,
Clerk Privy Council.

No. 105.

Mr. Walkem to the Secretary of State for the Colonies.

LONDON, July 28th, 1874.

MY LORD,—I have the honour to inform Your Lordship of my arrival last evening in London.

The object of my mission, as a Delegate from the Government of the Province of British Columbia to Her Majesty's Government, has, so I have been informed, already been fully explained to Your Lordship. It therefore only remains for me to request Your Lordship to honour me with a personal interview at the earliest hour which may prove convenient. I have the honour, &c.,

(Signed) GEO. A. WALKEM.

No. 106.

Mr. Meade to Mr. Walkem.

DOWNING STREET, 29th July, 1874.

SIR,—In reply to your letter of the 28th instant, I am directed by the Earl of Carnarvon to inform you that he will be happy to see you at this office at 3.30 P. M., on Friday next, the 31st instant. I am, &c.,

(Signed) R. H. MEADE.

No. 107.

Mr. Herbert to Mr. Walkem.

DOWNING STREET, 15th August, 1874.

SIR,—I am directed by the Earl of Carnarvon to acknowledge the receipt of the Petition to the Queen, signed by yourself on behalf of the Executive Council of British Columbia, which you left with his Lordship, on the occasion of your recent interview with him at this office.

After careful perusal of this clearly drawn and temperately expressed statement, and after hearing the further representations which you have since made orally, his Lordship feels that he has before him a full exposition of the views of the Provincial Government; and he desires me to thank you for the judicious manner in which you have discharged the duty entrusted to you.

Lord Carnarvon will be much pleased if he can be the means of adjusting the differences which have arisen; but the subject abounds in details which require close examination; and his Lordship thinks it may be convenient to you to know that he does not anticipate that he will be able, until after two or three weeks, to come to a decision as to the course which he should take.

I am, &c.,

(Signed) ROBERT G. W. HERBERT.

No. 108.

The Earl of Carnarvon to the Governor-General.

(Canada.)

DOWNING STREET, 16th August, 1874.

MY LORD,—With reference to my despatch, No. 110, of the 18th of June, I have now to acquaint you that I have seen Mr. Walkem, the Premier of British Columbia, deputed by his Government to represent to me the claims of the Province relative to the delays which have occurred in the construction of the Pacific Railway; the completion of which works, within a certain understood time, was one of the principal considerations that influenced the Union of British Columbia with the Dominion of Canada in 1871. I will only add on this head, that Mr. Walkem laid his case before me in temperate and reasonable terms.

2. I have also received a telegram from the Lieutenant-Governor of British Columbia, stating that upon the advice of his responsible Ministers he accepts, on behalf of British Columbia, the arbitration which I thought it my duty to offer, and the conditions of which I explained to your Lordship in my despatch of the 18th of June.

3. I have further received your despatch of the 31st July, enclosing copy of the Report of the Canadian Privy Council of the 23rd of July, in which your Ministers express their readiness to submit for my decision the question whether the exertions of the Dominion Government in the prosecution of the work, the diligence shown, and the

offers made by them to British Columbia, have or have not been fair and just, and in accordance with the spirit of the agreement entered into between Canada and British Columbia at the date of the Union.

4. I appreciate the confidence which has been thus placed in me by both parties to this controversy, and so far as lies in my power, I am most desirous of contributing to the settlement of a difference, which although hitherto conducted with great moderation, and in a conciliatory spirit on both sides, might easily assume more serious dimensions.

5. I feel sure that the Dominion Government will agree with me that the sooner this controversy can be closed the better, and that to arrange matters amicably, and with as little resort as possible to formal procedure, will best promote that object, and will be most congenial to the feelings of all parties.

6. With this view, I will proceed to state the case as I understand it, and the impressions which I have formed as to the course that ought to be taken.

The proposals made by Mr. Edgar, on behalf of the Canadian Government, to the Provincial Government of British Columbia, may be stated as follows:—

(1.) To commence at once, and finish as soon as possible, a railway from Esquimalt to Nanaimo.

(2.) To spare no expense in settling, as speedily as possible, the line to be taken by the railway on the mainland.

(3.) To make at once, a waggon road and line of telegraph along the whole length of the railway in British Columbia, and to continue the telegraph across the continent.

(4.) The moment the surveys and road on the mainland are completed, to spend a minimum amount of $1,500,000 annually upon the construction of the railway within the Province.

7. I am under the impression, after conversing with Mr. Walkem, that he is not fully empowered on the part of British Columbia to make specific proposals to the Government of Canada, or to me, as to what terms British Columbia would be willing to accept, but he has stated very clearly, in conversation at this office, the objections entertained by his Government, and in the Province, to the proposals of your Government; and they, or a considerable part of them, are fully set forth in the petition to the Queen, of which, as it has been published in the Colonial press, you no doubt have a copy.

8. Taking each point *seriatim*, as numbered in the last preceding paragraph but one, I understand it to be urged:—

(1.) That nothing is being done by the Dominion Government towards commencing and pushing on a railway from Esquimalt to Nanaimo.

(2.) That the surveying parties on the mainland are numerically very weak; and that there is no expectation in British Columbia or guarantee given on the part of the Dominion, that the surveys will be proceeded with as speedily as possible.

(3.) That the people of British Columbia do not desire the waggon road offered by the Dominion Government, as it would be useless to them; and that even the telegraph proposed to be made along the line of the railway cannot, of course, be made until the route to be taken by the railway is settled.

(4.) That "The moment the surveys are completed," is not only an altogether uncertain, but, at the present rate of proceeding, a very remote period of time, and that an expenditure of $1,500,000 a year on the railway within the Province will not carry the line to the boundary of British Columbia before a very distant date.

8. Mr. Walkem further urges that by section 11 of the Canadian Pacific Railway Act of 1874, it is competent to the Dominion House of Commons to reject at any time the contract for a section of the railway, and thus to prevent the continuous construction of the work.

9. Referring first to this latter point, I do not understand that it is alleged by Mr. Walkem, nor do I for a moment apprehend that the proviso was introduced with any belief that it would delay the construction of the railway. I conceive that all that was intended by it was to retain the power of exercising an adequate supervision over the financial details of the scheme; nevertheless, the objection stated by Mr. Walkem appears to me one which the Dominion Government should seriously consider, as their policy in so important a matter ought not to be left open to criticism, and British Columbia may fairly ask, according to the letter and the spirit of past engagements, for every reasonable security that the railway will be completed as speedily as possible.

10. Strong as are, doubtless, the objections urged by Mr. Walkem to the proposals which I understand Mr. Edgar to have made on behalf of your Ministers, and important as is the subject-matter of controversy, I, as at present advised, can see no reason why the views of both parties should not be reconciled to their satisfaction and with justice to all interests concerned.

11. On the one hand I cannot entertain the least doubt of the sincere intention of the Canadian Government and Parliament to adhere as closely as possible to the pledges given to British Columbia at the time of the Union; to do that which is just and liberal towards the Province, and in fact to maintain the good faith of the Dominion in the spirit if not in the letter of the original agreement under circumstances which I admit to be of no ordinary difficulty.

12. On the other hand, however, it would be unfair to deny that the objections stated by Mr. Walkem have a certain foundation and force, and I have every confidence in order to obtain the settlement of a question of such vital importance to the interests of the whole Dominion, the Canadian Government will be willing to make some reasonable concessions such as may satisfy the local requirements of British Columbia, and yet in no way detract from the high position which the Dominion Parliament and Government ought in my judgment to occupy.

13. I am of opinion, therefore, on a general review of all the considerations of the case, and as an impartial but most friendly adviser, who, if I may be allowed to say so, has the interests of both parties and the prosperity of the whole Dominion deeply at heart, that the following proposals would not be other than a fair basis of adjustment.

14. (1.) That the section of the railway from Esquimalt to Nanaimo should be begun at once.

(2.) That the Dominion Government should greatly increase the strength of the surveying parties on the mainland, and that they should undertake to expend on the surveys, if necessary, for the speedy completion of the work, if not an equal share to that which they would expend on the railway itself if it were in actual course of construction, at all events some considerable definite minimum amount.

(3.) Inasmuch as the proposed waggon road does not seem to be desired by British Columbia, the Canadian Government and Parliament may be fairly relieved of the expense and labour involved in their offer; and desirable as, in my opinion, the construction of the telegraph across the continent will be, it perhaps is a question whether it may not be postponed till the line to be taken by the railway is definitely settled.

(4.) The offer made by the Dominion Government to spend a minimum amount of $1,500,000 annually on the railway within British Columbia, as soon as the surveys and waggon road are completed, appears to me to be hardly as definite as the large interests involved on both sides seem to require. I think that some short and fixed time should be assigned within which the surveys should be completed; failing which, some compensation should become due to British Columbia for the delay.

15. Looking, further, to all the delays which have taken place, and which may yet perhaps occur; looking also to the public expectations that have been held out of the completion of the railway, if not within the original period of ten years fixed by the Terms of Union, at all events within fourteen years from 1871, I cannot but think that the annual minimum expenditure of $1,500,000 offered by the Dominion Government for the construction of the railway in the Province, is hardly adequate. In order to make the proposal not only fair but, as I know is the wish of your Ministers, liberal, I would suggest for their consideration whether the amount should not be fixed at a higher rate, say, for instance, at $2,000,000 a year.

16. The really important point, however, not only in the interests of the Province, but for the credit of the Dominion and the advantage of the Empire at large, is to assume the completion of the railway at some definite period, which, from causes over which your Ministers have had no control, must now, I admit, be much more distant than had been originally contemplated, and I am disposed to suggest as a reasonable arrangement, and one neither unfair to the Dominion nor to British Columbia, that the year 1890 should be agreed upon for this purpose. In making this suggestion, I, of course, conclude that the Dominion Government will readily use all reasonable efforts to complete the line before any extreme limit of time that may be fixed. A postponement to the very distant period which I have mentioned could not fail to be a serious disappointment to the people of the Province, and to all interested in its welfare, and I should not

have suggested it were it not for the full confidence which I felt in the determination of your Ministers to do not merely the least that they may be obliged, but the utmost that they may be able, in redemption of the obligations which they have inherited.

17. I have now only to repeat the strong desire which I feel to be of service in a matter, the settlement of which may be either simple or difficult according to the spirit in which it is approached, a question directly bearing upon the Terms of Union may, if both parties to it will waive some portion of their own views and opinions, be well entrusted to the Imperial authority which presided over that Union, and not improperly, perhaps to the individual Minister whose fortune it was to consider and in some degree to shape the details of the original settlement under which the Provinces of British North America were confederated, and British Columbia ultimately brought into connection with them. If indeed the expression of a personal feeling may, in such a case as this, be indulged, I may perhaps be allowed to say how sincerely I prize the recollection of the share which I was then permitted to have in that great work, how deeply I should grieve to see any disagreement or difference impair the harmony which has been so conspicuously maintained by the wisdom and good feeling of all parties, and how entirely your Lordship and your Ministers may count upon my best efforts in furtherance of every measure that can contribute to the strength and honour of the Dominion of Canada.

18. It will be very convenient if your Government should feel able to reply by telegraph, stating generally whether the modifications which I have proposed, and which seem to me consistent, with the present conditions of the question and with the true construction of the policy adopted by them, are in the main acceptable to them, in order that no unnecessary delay may take place in bringing this matter to a conclusion.

I have, &c.,
(Signed) CARNARVON.

No. 109.

The Governor-General to the Earl of Carnarvon.

OTTAWA, 21st August, 1874.

MY LORD,—In continuation of my despatches, noted in the margin, on the subject
No. 132, 9th July, 207, of the suggestions made by your Lordship for the settlement of the
31st July. differences between the Government of British Columbia and that of
No. 3,677, 29th July, the Dominion, I have the honour to enclose a copy of a despatch from
1874. Lieutenant-Governor Trutch, acknowledging the receipt of the copy I sent him of your Despatch No. 110, of the 18th June. (*See* No. 87, p. 193.).

I have, &c.,
(Signed) DUFFERIN.

No. 110.

The Governor-General to the Earl of Carnarvon.

(CANADA) September 18th, 1874.

MY LORD,—In acknowledging the receipt of your Lordship's despatch, secret, of the 16th of August, in which you have been good enough to convey to me your opinion as to the modifications which might be introduced with advantage into the terms already proffered by my Ministers for the settlement of the dispute now pending between this Government and that of British Columbia, I have the satisfaction of informing you that after a good deal of anxious deliberation Mr. Mackenzie and his colleagues have consented to adopt several suggestions recommended to them by your Lordship, should it be found absolutely impossible to terminate the controversy in any other manner.

2. The general view of my Ministers on the various points referred to are set forth at large in the enclosed Order in Council from which your Lordship will gather that it is with very considerable reluctance they have been induced to make these further concessions, feeling so strongly as they do that their original proposals fairly satisfied the requirements of the case.

3. I have no doubt, however, it will be felt throughout the country that the only mode by which the Dominion could be satisfactorily extricated from the false position in which she was placed by her treaty obligations to fulfil engagements which were physically impossible of execution, was by a large and generous interpretation of the consequent claims against her

4. I have further the honour to transmit a sketch map of the area now under exploration in British Columbia, accompanied by a memorandum by Mr. Fleming, the engineer-in-chief, by which it will be perceived that every effort is being made to hurry forward the surveys with all possible dispatch, and that the employment of any additional staff would uselessly increase the expense without forwarding the work.

I have, &c.,
(Signed) · DUFFERIN.

No. 111.

Report of the Privy Council approved by the Governor-General on the 17th September, 1874.

The Committee of Council have had under consideration the despatch of the Right Honourable Lord Carnarvon relating to the complaints of the British Columbia Government with respect to the Pacific Railway, and suggesting certain modifications of the proposals made by the Dominion Government through Mr. Edgar, on the 8th May last.

These proposals were prompted by a desire to provide against future difficulty, in view of the then well ascertained fact that the terms of Union had become impossible of literal fulfilment, on the one hand, and on the other hand giving due weight to the very strong feeling entertained against the fatal extravagance which these terms involved to the country. The proposals may thus be summarized:—

1. To build a railway from Esquimalt to Nanaimo, on Vancouver Island, in excess of the terms of Union, and to begin the work immediately.

2. To commence the construction of the railway on the mainland as soon as the surveys could be completed, and to expend on the work not less than one and a half millions annually.

3. To take the necessary steps, meanwhile, to secure the construction of a telegraph line across the continent on the located line for the railway, at the same time cutting out the railway track and building thereon a trail or road, which would become available as part of the permanent works.

The arrangement proposed by Lord Carnarvon embodies some amendments. His Lordship suggests:—

· 1st. The immediate construction, as proposed, of the short line on Vancouver Island.

2nd. After the location of the line the expenditure of two millions on the mainland, instead of one and a half millions.

3rd. The increase of the engineering force to double the number now employed; the expenditure on the survey, if not of an amount equal to the proposed annual expenditure on construction, of some other specific sum; the prescribing of a limited time for the completion of the survey; and the payment of a sum of money as compensation in the event of its not being so completed.

4th. The guarantee of the completion of the entire railway in 1890.

It is also suggested that the construction of the telegraph line and road need not be proceeded with, as Mr. Walkem does not consider either as of any use to the Province.

The Committee recommend that the first consideration, which is precisely what was previously offered, be again concurred in.

In regard to the second proposal, the Committee recommend that Lord Carnarvon be informed (if it be found impossible to obtain a settlement of the question by the acceptance of the former offer) that the Government will consent that after the completion of the survey, the average annual minimum expenditure on the mainland shall be two millions. There is every reason to believe now that a majority of the people of Columbia would accept the propositions previously made. Judging from a petition sent from the mainland, signed by 644 names (a copy of which petition is enclosed), there is almost an entire unanimity there in favour of these proposals, and assurances were given very lately by a gentleman of the highest position on the Island that the course of the Local Government would not meet general approval there. An application was made by one prominent gentleman, an ex-member of Parliament, to the Government here, to know if the proposals made would still be adhered to, he pledging himself to secure their acceptance by the bulk of the people here.

It is, therefore, earnestly hoped that no change will be considered necessary, as it will be difficult to induce the country to accept any further concessions.

The third condition requires an increase of the engineer force employed on the surveying service; the completion of the survey within a specific time; and, in case that time should be exceeded, the payment to the Province of a money compensation.

The Committee respectfully submit that the result arrived at by the foregoing suggestion is already being accomplished with the utmost dispatch admitted by the circumstances of the case.

The Chief Engineer was instructed to provide all the assistance he required in order to complete the surveys within the shortest possible period, and he engaged a large force,—a larger force, indeed, than can with profit be employed until the route is definitely determined.

Whatever may be the route finally chosen, the line will of necessity traverse a country with exceedingly rough topographical features for a distance of over five or six hundred miles from the eastern slope of the Rocky Mountains to the extreme limit of the Province on the Pacific.

The country is an immense plateau, which maintains its general elevation to within a few miles of the sea, but often rises into unshapely mountain ranges. Some of these ranges tower to a height of over 9,000 feet.

The boundary of the plateau on the west is the Cascade Range. This forms a huge sea-wall along the coast, and has interposed a much more formidable obstacle to the surveyors than the Rocky Mountains. Attempts have been made at five or six points to pierce the barrier, but, except at the Fraser River and at Bute Inlet, without success.

From the results of last year's explorations, the Bute Inlet route seemed on the whole to be the best, but it is not unassociated with serious difficulties. For a distance of twenty miles the ascent or grade is about 150 feet to the mile.

The straits which form the approach to the harbour from seaward are encumbered by islands, and, when reached, the harbour is found to be destitute of anchorage. The dangers of navigation are increased not alone by the precipitous and rocky shores, but by the rapidity of the tide, which rushes through the narrow channels with a velocity of from seven to nine miles an hour.

It was supposed when work was resumed last Spring that a practicable route would be found from the point where Fleming's line touches the north branch of the Thompson River westward towards what is known as Big Bend, on the Fraser River, from which no serious impediment exists until the commencement of the rapid descent to the sea at Bute Inlet is reached. Had this supposition proved correct, it is probable the Government might have been prepared at the end of this year to proceed with the exact location of the line. But the explorations carried on to the close of July last, resulted in the discovery of a high range of mountains, which fill the country from near the junction of the Clearwater with the Thompson northward to the great Bend of the Fraser; and, without a very long detour south or north, they bar the way to the west. The Chief Engineer, therefore, advised a re-examination of the Fraser Valley, or, more correctly speaking, ravine, inasmuch as no broad valley anywhere exists, the rivers in their courses having cleft ways for themselves through the rocks, which in some cases they have pierced to a depth of 1500 feet by a width of not more than a single mile, thus giving as the normal condition exceedingly precipitous banks. This new examination of the Fraser River route will occupy at least the whole season.

A memorandum from the Chief Engineer will give the strength of the force and show its distribution. Nearly two seasons were passed in examining the Rocky Mountain Range and the Valley of the Columbia, in the endeavour to obtain a favourable pass. The result was that the explorers were driven north to what is known as Jasper House Pass.

These facts are mentioned to give some idea of the enormous labour involved, and the impossibility of placing a large force in the field to do engineering work, when it is not yet known where the engineering work is to be done. The exploratory survey must be tolerably complete before the exact location of any portion of the line can be contemplated or possible, and before plans can be made of bridges and other works of construction required; and nothing but the urgency of the contract so imprudently entered into with British Columbia would otherwise have induced the Government to employ more than half the force now engaged.

As pointed out in previous memorandum, the expenditure to the end of last year in British Columbia alone was considerably over half a million of money more than the whole expenditure upon the two thousand miles eastward of that Province.

The Chief Engineer was informed last winter that it was the desire of the Government to have the utmost expedition used in prosecuting and completing the surveys; and in the engagements which he has entered into these directions have been fully considered.

The fourth engagement involves another precise engagement to have the whole of the railway communication finished in 1890. There are the strongest possible objections to again adopting a precise time for the completion of the lines. The eastern portion of the line, except so far as the mere letter of the conditions is concerned, affects only the Provinces east of Manitoba; and the Government have not been persuaded either of the wisdom or the necessity of immediately constructing that portion of the railway which traverses the country from the west end of Lake Superior to the proposed eastern terminus on Lake Nipissing, near Georgian Bay, nor is it conceived that the people of British Columbia could, with any show of reason whatever, insist that this portion of the work should be completed within any definite time, inasmuch as if the people who are chiefly if not wholly affected by this branch of the undertaking are satisfied, it is maintained that the people of British Columbia would practically have no right of speech in the matter.

It is intended by the Government that the utmost diligence shall be manifested in obtaining a speedy line of communication by rail and water from Lake Superior westward, completing the various links of railway as fast as possible, consistent with that prudent course which a comparatively poor and sparsely settled country should adopt.

There can be no doubt that it would be an extremely difficult task to obtain the sanction of the Canadian Parliament to any specific bargain as to time, considering the consequences which have already resulted from the unwise adoption of a limited period in the Terms of Union for the completion of so vast an undertaking, the extent of which must necessarily be very imperfectly understood by people at a distance. The Committee advise that Lord Carnarvon be informed that, while in no case could the Government undertake the completion of the whole line in the time mentioned, an extreme unwillingness exists to another limitation of time; but if it is found absolutely necessary to secure a present settlement of the controversy by further concessions, a pledge may be given that the portion west of Lake Superior will be completed so as to afford connection by rail with existing lines of railway through a portion of the United States, and by Canadian waters during the season of navigation, by the year 1890, as suggested.

With regard to the ameliorating proposal to dispense with the formation of a road or trail across the country, and the construction of a telegraphic line, on the representation of the British Columbia delegate that neither is considered necessary, it is proper to remark that it is impossible to dispense with the clearing out of a track and the formation of a road of some sort in order to get in the supplies for the railway, and the proposal was, that as soon as the general route of the railway could be determined and the location ascertained, a width of two chains should be cleared out in the wooded districts, a telegraph line erected, and that a sort of road, passable for horses and rough vehicles, should be formed and brought into existence, not as a road independent of the railway, but as an auxiliary to and a necessary preliminary to railway construction, the cost incurred forming part indeed of the construction of the railway itself.

In so vast a country where there are no postal facilities and where there can be no rapid postal communications for many years hence, it is absolutely essential that a telegraph line should be erected along the proposed route, as the only means by which the Government and contractors could maintain any communication. The offer therefore to dispense with a telegraph line is one which cannot be considered as in any way whatever affording relief to the Dominion, the undertaking to construct the telegraph line must rather be looked upon as an earnest of the desire of the Government to do everything in reason, in order to keep within the spirit of its engagements.

The intention of the Government will be seen from the following quotations from the Act of last Session:—

"A line of electric telegraph shall be constructed in advance of the said railway "and branches along their whole extent respectively as soon as practicable after the "location of the line shall have been determined upon."

Having dealt with the modifications suggested by Lord Carnarvon, it is proper to notice *seriatim* the several grounds of complaint as stated in the despatch:

1st. "That nothing is being done by the Dominion Government towards com-"mencing and pushing on a railway from Esquimalt to Nanaimo."

The Dominion has no engagement to build such a railway, and therefore there can be no just complaint that it is not commenced. The construction of such a railway was offered only as compensation for delay in fulfilling the engagement to build a railway to the " Pacific seaboard."

2nd. "That the surveying parties on the mainland are numerically weak, and that "there is no expectation in British Columbia, or guarantee given, that the surveys will "be proceeded with as speedily as possible."

On this point it is sufficient to state that. as remarked elsewhere, the utmost expedition possible has been used, and that the allegations in the petition are incorrect.

3rd. "That the people of British Columbia do not desire the waggon road offered "by the Dominion Government, as it would be useless to them; and that even the tele-"graph proposed to be made along the line of railway cannot of course be made until "the route to be taken by the railway is settled."

It may be noticed in connection with this extraordinary statement that the construction of such a road was one of the conditions imposed by the Local Legislature in their resolutions adopted as the basis whereon to negotiate the Terms of Union. It would therefore seem that such a declaration now is intended more to lessen the value of the proposals made to British Columbia than to indicate public sentiment in the Province. As pointed out elsewhere, the work is practically a part of railway construction, and it is also confidently believed will be of very great advantage to the people generally.

4th. Mr. Walkem further urges "That by Sec. 11 of the Canadian Pacific Railway "Act of 1874, it is competent to the Dominion House of Commons to reject at any time "the contract for a section of the railway, and thus to prevent the continuous construc-"tion of the work."

This is simply a complaint that the present Government provided for Parliamentary supervision over the letting of such vast contracts. It was contended by the opposition in 1872, that in the matter of a contract for so large a work, for which the Dominion was to pay thirty millions of dollars, and allot nearly sixty million acres of land, the formal sanction of Parliament should be obtained. Accordingly, when it became their duty under altered political circumstances to submit a new measure to Parliament, in lieu of the one which had failed of success, they were bound to secure by statutory enactments full control to Parliament over the letting of the contract or contracts.

In all extraordinary contracts entered into by the Government of England or Canada, this course has been followed; as, for instance, in contracts for the conveyance of mails by ocean steamers.

It will also be apparent that no Government decision could prevent future Parliamentary action.

The insertion of this section therefore, is in pursuance of a well settled public policy, not to permit the executive too extensive powers without specific Parliamentary sanction; and even the present opposition demanded that the restriction should apply to minor works on the branches provided for in the Act.

Neither the Canadian Government nor Parliament can be suspected of having inserted such a clause for the improper purpose of using it to retard progress otherwise possible. Nothing has occurred which could justify such a suspicion.

Since the passage of the Act, the Government have placed the grading of the Pembina Branch under contract. and hope soon to place the Nipissing Branch under contract. The contracts for the telegraph lines from Fort William to the existing telegraphic stations in British Columbia will be closed in a few days.

It only remains to say that the Government, in making the new proposals to British Columbia, were actuated by an anxious desire to put an end to all controversy, and to do what is fair and just under very extraordinary circumstances, and that these proposals embraced the most liberal terms that public opinion would justify them in offering.

It is proper, further, to remark that there has been no just cause of complaint at all, inasmuch as the Report of the Chief Engineer shows that nothing more could have been done to forward the work.

The Act passed last Session is a very complete one, and amply provides for the construction of the railway, subject to the Parliamentary supervision referred to.

The lot of British Columbia is cast in with the other North American Provinces, and it becomes the duty of all the Confederated Provinces to consider to some extent the general welfare. It is especially the duty of the smaller Provinces to defer somewhat to the opinions of the old and populous Provinces from which the revenue for the building of all such works is derived.

      Certified.
    (Signed) W. A. HIMSWORTH,
            Clerk, Privy Council.

No. 112.

Copy of Petition.

"That in view of the action taken by an association calling itself 'The Terms of Union Preservation League,' meeting in the City of Victoria, on Vancouver Island, in petitioning Her Most Gracious Majesty the Queen relative to the non-fulfilment of one of the conditions of the Terms of Union, and affirming in said petition that Esquimalt, on Vancouver Island, had been decided to be the terminus of the Canadian Pacific Railway, and that a portion of the line had been located between the harbour of Esquimalt and Seymour Narrows, and praying that Her Majesty act as Arbitrator, and see that justice be done to British Columbia, we, the undersigned, respectfully submit as follows:—

"That in our opinion, the Order of the Privy Council of Canada, of 7th June, 1873, is in no way binding upon Your Excellency's present Government, and that a line of railway along the seaboard on Vancouver Island to Esquimalt is no part of the Terms of Union.

"That in any arrangement which may be entered into for an extension of time for the commencement or completion of the railway, any consideration granted by the Dominion of Canada to the Province of British Columbia, should be such as would be generally advantageous to the whole Province, and not of a merely local nature, benefiting only a section thereof.

"That the league referred to, acting under the impression that further surveys may detract from the favourable opinion now entertained by the Engineers of the Bute Inlet route, are desirous of forcing Your Excellency's Government into an immediate selection.

"That we consider it would be unwise, impolitic, and unjust to select any line for the railway until time be given for a thorough survey of the different routes on the Mainland, believing as we do, that such survey must result in the selection of Fraser Valley route, which is the only one that connects the fertile districts of the interior with the seaboard.

"That as it is evident that the surveys are not yet sufficiently advanced to allow of an intelligent decision on the question of route being arrived at, we consider that a vigorous and immediate prosecution of the surveys by Your Excellency's Government, to be followed in 1875 by the commencement of construction on the Mainland, will be a faithful carrying out of the spirit of the Terms of Union.

"Your petitioners therefore humbly pray that Your Excellency take the views expressed in this our petition into your most favourable consideration."

No. 113.

Mr. Walkem to the Secretary of State for the Colonies.

          LONDON, 10th September, 1874.

MY LORD,—In a letter of the 15th of August last, acknowledging the receipt of the Petition to Her Majesty of the Committee of the Executive Council of British Columbia, Your Lordship was pleased to inform me that you did "not anticipate that you would

" be able, until after two or three weeks, to come to a decision as to the course which
" you should take" upon the subject matter of the Petition.

As the time mentioned has now expired, may I request your Lordship to be good
enough to inform me of the conclusion (if any) which you may have arrived at.

I have, &c.,
(Signed)   GEO. A. WALKEM.

No. 114.

Mr. Malcolm to Mr. Walkem.

DOWNING STREET, 14th September, 1874.

SIR,—I am directed by the Earl of Carnarvon to acknowledge the receipt of your
letter of the 10th instant, and to express to you his regret that he is not at present in a
position to communicate to you any decision, in regard to the Petition of the Executive
Council of British Columbia.
I have, &c.,
(Signed)   W. R. MALCOLM.

No. 115.

Mr. Walkem to the Earl of Carnarvon.

LONDON, October 31st, 1874.

MY LORD,—I now beg leave respectfully to offer, for your Lordship's consideration,
a recapitulation and review of the main points of the question at issue between Canada
and British Columbia, respecting the breach, by the former, of the Railway Agreement
in the Terms of Union.

Although I have been favoured by your Lordship with many and lengthened interviews on this subject, I hope that the grave nature of the interests committed to my
care, as well as the important influence which your Lordship's action at the present
time is sure to exercise upon the political and industrial growth of the Province, will
be a sufficient excuse for again troubling you.

A written communication of the kind proposed may also usefully serve to define
more clearly some of the views, which I have advocated on behalf of the Province.

Before proceeding further, I trust that I may be permitted to tender the expression
of my grateful sense of the attention with which your Lordship has been pleased to
receive, not only the statement of the case of British Columbia as set forth in the
Petition of its Government, but also the comments upon it which I have from time to
time made.

The Provincial Government will be glad to learn—what your Lordship has been
good enough to state—that you have been gratified with the temperate spirit in which
their case has been presented for the consideration of Her Majesty's Government.

It was, as I had the honour to mention at my first interview, with a strong feeling
of regret, that the Government of the Province felt themselves under the necessity of
seeking the advice and intervention of Her Majesty's Government in this matter. The
Provincial Government desired to work in harmony with the Dominion Government,
and I may safely say that such intervention would not have been sought, had a sufficient
effort been made by the Dominion to comply with the spirit of the Railway Agreement.

The key to the general policy of Her Majesty's Government, in relation to British
North America is, so far as I understand, to be found in the preamble of the Act of
Confederation, which briefly declares that " Union would conduce to the welfare of the
" Provinces * * * federally united * * * and promote
" the interests of the British Empire." The Imperial policy thus declared has also been
the policy of Canada. British Columbia likewise has endeavoured on her part loyally
to follow it. It is from a due regard for the principles laid down in the Confederation
Act, and from a natural and, I hope, proper desire to protect her own special interests
as a Province, that British Columbia has protested against the non-fulfilment by Canada
of the Railway Agreement of the Terms of Union.

This Railway Agreement, while purposely and in part framed, as I shall hereafter show, to promote the interests of British Columbia, is not an agreement for the construction of a railway within merely provincial limits, for simply provincial purposes. It is an agreement of a much more comprehensive character, designed, in fact, mainly to advance, and indeed to effect, a real union and consolidation of the British Possessions on the Continent of North America. In the attainment of this great end, British Columbia is, owing to her present isolation, especially interested.

A short reference to a few facts which led to the Union of the Province with Canada will best explain her true position.

In pursuance of the general Confederation policy declared in 1867, Her Majesty's Government in 1869 addressed a despatch to the Governor of British Columbia, expressing a desire that British Columbia should be incorporated with Canada. This despatch not only restates the principles set forth in the Confederation Act, but also shows in what respect they are peculiarly applicable to British Columbia. The following is a quotation from the despatch:—

"Her Majesty's Government," writes the Secretary of State, "anticipate that the interests of every Province of British North America will be more advanced by enabling the wealth, credit, and intelligence of the whole to be brought to bear on every part, than by encouraging each in the contracted policy of taking care of itself, possibly at the expense of its neighbour.

"Most especially is this true in the case of internal transit. It is evident that the establishment of a British line of communication between the Atlantic and Pacific oceans is far more feasible by the operations of a single Government responsible for the progress of both shores of the Continent, than by a bargain negotiated between separate, perhaps in some respects rival, Governments and Legislatures. The San Francisco of British North America would, under these circumstances, hold a greater commercial and political position than would be attainable by the capital of the isolated Colony of British Columbia.

"Her Majesty's Government are aware that the distance between Ottawa and Victoria presents a real difficulty in the way of immediate union. But that very difficulty will not be without its advantages, if it renders easy communication indispensable and forces onwards the operations which are to complete it. In any case it is an understood inconvenience, and a diminishing one, and it appears far better to accept it as a temporary drawback on the advantages of union, than to wait for those obstacles, often more intractable, which are sure to spring up after a neglected opportunity."

Here four propositions are laid down:—

1st. That the Canadian Federal system is based upon a union of the "wealth, credit and intelligence" of the several Provinces, which will, when properly applied, promote the welfare of each.

2nd. That to secure this result, "easy * * * internal * * * communication" through British territory "is indispensable."

3rd. That the absence of this "easy * * * internal * * * communication," and "the distance between Ottawa and Victoria" constitute a real difficulty in the way of immediate union."

4th. That this "real difficulty" will operate as a mere "temporary drawback on the advantages of union," as it will be sure to "force onwards" those "operations" necessary to remove it.

It is to hasten the removal of this "temporary drawback," and to "force onwards," in the sense of the above despatch, these necessary operations, which have been long deferred, that the Government of British Columbia have sought the intervention of Her Majesty's Government.

The strength of the above propositions, viewed in connection with the general confederation policy, was fully recognized by the then Government of the Dominion. They agreed with Her Majesty's Government, that without "easy communication" and "internal transit" between Ottawa and Victoria, the union of British Columbia and Canada could not be effective. Afterwards, when the whole matter was practically studied by the Government of the Dominion, it seems to have been their decided opinion that "easy communication" across the Continent could mean nothing less than a railway; and that, with respect to British Columbia, the "temporary drawback on the advantages" of Confederation, mentioned by Her Majesty's Government, should not be allowed to last for more than ten years from the date of Union.

Hence the Dominion undertook "to secure the commencement simultaneously," on the 20th July, 1873, "of the construction of a railway from the Pacific towards the "Rocky Mountains, and from such point as may be selected, east of the Rocky Moun-"tains, towards the Pacific, to connect the seaboard of British Columbia with the "railway system of Canada; and, further, to secure the completion of such railway "within ten years from" July, 1871. And British Columbia, on her part, entered into certain obligations in favour of the Dominion, with regard to the public lands of the Province. The word "simultaneously," which appears in this agreement, was designedly inserted with two objects:—

1st. That Canada should commence construction works at the two most available points, and thus ensure the early and rapid progress of the railway; and

2ndly. That the admitted disadvantages under which British Columbia would labour until the completion of the main line should to some extent be counterbalanced by the benefits of early expenditure upon railway works in the Province.

The agreement thus entered into was inserted in, and formed the most essential part of, the Terms of Union mutually accepted, in 1871, by British Columbia and Canada. These terms were placed before the people of the Province at a general election. They were shortly afterwards considered and formally approved by the Provincial Legislature. They were subsequently fully debated and accepted by both Houses of the Parliament of Canada; and they were finally sanctioned and ratified by Her Majesty in Council. No question, therefore, could have been more thoroughly ventilated—no conclusion more deliberately arrived at. As a strong practical proof of the continued interest felt by Her Majesty's Government in the success of the Confederation thus established, the Imperial Parliament, in July, 1873, guaranteed a loan of £3,600,000, to be raised by Canada mainly for the construction, among other public works, of the Canadian Pacific Railway.

It may now be useful to present to your Lordship a brief statement of the manner in which the conditions of the Railway Agreement have been observed.

The Petition of the Government of British Columbia shows the following facts:—

That the Province has fulfilled her part of the agreement, and has endeavoured to aid the Dominion Government to carry out their part;

That the Dominion Government have not, during the three years succeeding union, made due effort to complete the railway surveys in British Columbia;

That the Dominion Government did not, on the 20th July, 1873, commence the "simultaneous" railway construction provided for in the agreement;

That they also have hitherto failed to commence any railway construction whatsoever in the Province, though they might have commenced such construction, as they admitted in May last that they were then in a position to begin the railway.

Some further circumstances connected with these matters are detailed in the Petition. It is therein shown that in June, 1873, the Dominion Government selected the harbour of Esquimalt, on the Pacific, as the western terminus of the Canadian Pacific Railway; that they at the same time decided that a portion of the main line should be "located" between this terminus and Seymour Narrows; that some weeks prior to the day named in the Agreement for the commencement of the construction of the main line, they secured from the Provincial Government "in furtherance of such construction" a reserve of a valuable tract of land lying along this projected line, and some 3000 square miles in area; that, as already stated, no construction whatsoever was or has been commenced within the Province; that the land so reserved has been thus rendered comparatively valueless to the Province, as it has ever since been closed to settlement and to the investment of capital.

Against the continuance of the above state of things, the Province, through its Legislature and its Government, from time to time entered protest after protest, but without effect, and without even eliciting any reply from the Dominion Government beyond a formal acknowledgment of the receipt of the despatch enclosing each protest. The last protest was forwarded in February of the present year; subsequently the correspondence took place which is appended to the Petition. From the questions raised by this correspondence, all those which are unimportant may be usefully eliminated. I propose, therefore (subject, perhaps, to a slight digression, where necessary), to confine my observations to the principal points in a letter from Mr. Edgar to myself, which contains certain proposals as regards railway matters.

The Provincial Government did not at the time understand that these proposals were officially made. They were subsequently withdrawn by the Dominion Government, and only at the moment of such withdrawal declared by them to have been made with their authority and on their behalf. The above letter, which thus became invested, though but for a brief time, with an authoritative character, is valuable as the only official intimation to the Provincial Government of the policy of the present Dominion Government on the subject of the Pacific Railway. In addition to certain proposals or offers to British Columbia, the letter contains important statements and some specific admissions which favour the Provincial case.

I shall discuss these offers *seriatim*, and endeavour to ascertain their value taken in connection with the conditions attached to them, which conditions, as I shall afterwards show, virtually amount to a surrender by British Columbia of her existing railway agreement. I shall then offer some comments upon the above statements and admissions, using generally, as far as may be, the language in which they are expressed in the letter, in order to lessen the danger on my part of any inadvertent misconstruction of their meaning.

The offers made are as follows:—

No. 1. The Dominion will "commence construction from Esquimalt to Nanaimo immediately, and push that portion of railway on to completion within the shortest practicable time."

The offer to commence work immediately at Esquimalt (which, as already stated, was selected as the Western Terminus of the main line by an Order of the Privy Council of Canada as far back as June 1873) is simply an offer to do what the Dominion was bound to have done in July 1873, and what they might have done at any time since, and which they admit in this letter was quite practicable in May last. The offer, your Lordship will notice, is a very limited one. No definite provision is made for the extension of the main line beyond Nanaimo (about 60 miles from Esquimalt); nor, indeed, is any definite period fixed for the completion of even this short portion of the railway, which would take neither much time or money to construct. The promise to complete it "in the shortest practicable time,"—a promise in effect attached to all the offers in the letter,—is one which, slightly qualified, is implied in the present and in every other agreement of a similar character, in which no stipulation is inserted for the performance of work within a given time. The phrase is much too elastic in its meaning to admit of any definite interpretation. It may, for the present, therefore, be fairly omitted from special consideration, except as some evidence of a general intention on the part of the Dominion Government. I must assume, what the language conveys, that that the words "that portion of railway," mean the Esquimalt or Nanaimo portion or part of the main railway, which is the only railway referred to in the letter. This would tend to show that the position of the terminus is not questioned. No other allusion to the terminus is made in the letter.

No. 2. The Dominion will prosecute and complete the surveys, and then determine "the location of the line upon the mainland."

This promise is reasonable on the face of it, but it is very vague. In May last the Government of the Dominion informed the Provincial Government that "there was no reason to believe that it would be possible to complete the surveys before the close of the year" 1874. The reasonable inference deducible from this statement is, obviously, that the surveys would be finished at the end of 1874. If a longer period had been deemed necessary for the purpose, the fact would have been stated. Considering the intimation thus given, and looking to the long interval of time that has elapsed without any decision as to the route having been arrived at, it might have been expected that the letter would have positively guaranteed the completion, in 1874, of these and all other indispensable surveys within the Province at least, and have further placed beyond conjecture the commencement of construction works early in 1875. I have been informed by a railway engineer here that, as a matter of practice, the exploratory surveys settle the general bearing or course of a line of railway, and that the subsequent location surveys may be proceeded with at several points along such line simultaneously, and the work of construction be commenced at those points without waiting for the actual location of the whole line. Such being the case, there is no valid reason, in view of all the facts above stated, why this practice should not be followed with respect to the Pacific Railway. The general course of the railway, within the Province at least, should be determined this year, and location surveys, immediately followed by actual construction, should be commenced early in 1875 at various points on the mainland and on the island. This is what British Columbia, above all things, desires, and any definite arrangement which will secure her wants in this respect will give the Province much satisfaction.

> No. 3. The Dominion will "open up a road and build a telegraph line along the whole length of the railway in the Province, and carry the telegraph wire across the Continent."

The performance of this offer, both as to the road and the telegraph line, would depend, in point of time, upon the performance of the preceding offer (No. 2), as the above works would, according to the letter, only be commenced after the completion of the surveys and the location (within the Province) of the whole line along which they are proposed to be constructed. The fact is known to Your Lordship, that the road here meant is a waggon road intended, for a time, at least, to supply the place of the railway. A personal knowledge of the country justifies me in stating that a very large portion of the £50,000 or £60,000 required for its construction would be money simply thrown away. I can also unhesitatingly state that the road would, even as a temporary substitute for the railway, be wholly unacceptable to the Province at large, including the farmers and producers of the "interior," in whose interests, and for whose benefit, it is alleged that the offer is specially made. For the transport of supplies, and to meet engineering necessities along the line, as railway works progress, a merely passable road is necessary, and must be constructed; this, in fact, is all that is required. The telegraph line (when finished) would, doubtless, be useful, but its construction is a question which should be treated independently of the Railway Agreement. The railway is what is required, and the people of the Province would prefer seeing the time and money, which are proposed to be expended on the above works, appropriated to the larger and infinitely more beneficial enterprise.

> No. 4. When "the surveys and road on the mainland can be completed, there shall be in each and every year . . . during the construction of the railway, a minimum expenditure upon the works of construction within the Province of at least 1,500,000 dollars;" and the Dominion "will proceed from the very first with all the works of construction," on the mainland, "that their engineers could sanction."

The expenditure above proposed may be considered, first, in relation to its amount; and next, with reference to the date of its commencement. The amount falls far short of what British Columbia has been led to expect. The cost of the line in British Columbia has been roughly estimated at 35,000,000 dollars (£7,000,000). Assuming this estimate to be correct, and that ten years would see the completion of the railway, the Province, in accepting the Terms of Union, had a fair expectation of an average yearly expenditure within her limits of, say, 3,500,000 dollars (£700,000). After a delay of over three years with its consequent loss to the Province, it is now proposed by the letter that this amount shall be reduced to the sum of 1,500,000 dollars (£300,000). Again, dividing the whole cost 35,000,000 dollars (£7,000,000) by this sum, a period of twenty-three and a half years would be obtained as the time required for the completion of the Provincial section of the line alone, and this period would be only computed from the date when expenditure would be commenced, and not from the date of the letter. It is true that the expenditure proposed is to represent a minimum outlay, which, after several years, might for obvious reasons increase with the progress of the work, but I submit that, in estimating the value of this, or of any similar proposal, the actual figures given—and not contingent amounts which might never be spent—must be the basis of calculation.

Moreover, not only is the proposed expenditure inadequate, but the period when it is to be begun is left largely open to doubt. The letter states that the expenditure will follow the completion, "along the whole length of the railway in the Province," of the waggon road mentioned in offer No. 3. The completion of this road, in turn, has to depend upon the completion of all the surveys, and upon the location of the whole line on the mainland (see offer No. 2); and the completion of these surveys and the location of this line are, in point of time, wholly left open to uncertainty. It is stated, that from the "very first" construction work on the mainland will be done at such places as the sanction of the Engineers will warrant; but this sanction will naturally be deferred until the expenditure which has been proposed to cover construction work generally should be commenced. Taken throughout no offer could well be more indefinite than the above.

Adding all the uncertainties mentioned to the fixed period of twenty-three and a-half years (or even to a reduced period), it would appear that the above offer may be described as one for the postponement of the completion of the line within the Province for a lengthened period, possibly until some time in the next century.

Your Lordship will observe—what I must consider an important matter—that all the preceding offers refer and are strictly confined to the British Columbian portion of the railway. The letter is wholly silent as to the extension of the line beyond the eastern frontier of the Province. British Columbia is thus by implication virtually requested to surrender one of the elements most important to her in the contract, namely, the right to insist upon all rail communication with the Eastern Provinces.

I shall now, as proposed, make a few comments upon certain statements and admissions contained in the letter. Probably the most important of the former is the statement, that the Dominion Government "are advised by their engineers that the physical difficulties are so much greater than was expected, that it is an impossibility to construct a railway within the time limited by the Terms of Union, and that any attempt to do so can only result in wasteful expenditure and financial embarrassment." Upon this point the Provincial Government are without any information save what is afforded by the last Report, as published, of the Chief Engineer of the Dominion Government. A reference to this Report would lead the reader to a rather contrary conclusion to that above expressed. On page 34, section 5, the Chief Engineer makes the following statement:—"It may indeed be now accepted as a certainty that a route has been found generally possessing favourable engineering features, with the exception of a short section approaching the Pacific Coast; which route, taking its entire length, including the exceptional section alluded to, will on the average show lighter work, and will require less costly structures than have been necessary on many of the railways now in operation in the Dominion." It is worthy of notice that this Report, so favourable to the enterprise, is dated only some four months prior to the date of the letter now under discussion. During the interval between these dates, all surveys in the Province had been suspended.

I may further remind your Lordship that the Charter for the construction and completion of the railway in ten years from 1871, according to the Terms of Union, was keenly competed for by two separate combinations, including men of great railway experience, large capital, and high position in the Dominion. These Companies, apparently, did not consider the undertaking to make the railway within the stipulated time impracticable. On the contrary, up to February, 1873, so eager was the competition, and so powerful were the organizations in point of wealth, influence, and ability, that the Dominion Government decided to give the charter to neither; and, upon the two Companies failing to amalgamate, as suggested by the Government, the Government, under certain powers conferred by Parliament, formed a new Company, based upon the principle that each Province should be represented in the undertaking. To this new Company a charter was granted on the 5th of February, 1873. With the political or other causes which subsequently led to the surrender of this charter it is not my duty to deal. The strong fact remains that two responsible and rival companies were willing, and a third undertook, to construct a through-line of railway to connect the east and west of the Dominion in eight years from February 1873. Neither in the Prospectus of the successful Company nor in the voluminous correspondence which took place previously between the two unsuccessful Companies on the subject of their respective claims to the charter, and of their proposed amalgamation, was any doubt expressed as to the possibility of fulfilling this time obligation. Had such a doubt existed, it is fair to infer that the Dominion Government would have requested the assistance of the Province to remove it. No such request was, however, made.

With respect to the statement before your Lordship that the chartered Company considered an extension of four years necessary to place the financial success of the enterprise beyond doubt, the Provincial Government are without any information save what is contained in, or may be inferred from, the last paragraph of section 8 of the Charter granted to the Company, which reads as follows:—The Company "shall complete the whole railway within ten years from the said 20th of July, 1871, unless the last mentioned period shall be enlarged by Act of Parliament, in which case the Company shall complete the whole railway within such extended period." Admitting, for the sake of argument, however, that such extension of four years was deemed necessary, the completion of the line would not have been deferred beyond 1885. The extract already quoted from the Engineer's Report, dated, as it is, about twelve months after the date of the Charter, and made after a further knowledge of the country had been acquired, tends strongly to confirm the views of the respective Companies that the completion of the railway was practicable in 1881, or at the furthest in 1885.

The value of the above facts and correspondence is material as showing, in the first place, that it was considered all important that a definite period should be assigned for the execution of a work upon which Confederation hinges; and in the next place, that 1881, or at most 1885, was a reasonable definition of that period.

The Province, after all her disappointments, above all things desires that the "prompt commencement, continuous prosecution," and early completion of the railway shall be definitely assured or, in the language of the letter, be "guaranteed." The Provincial Government, therefore, strongly, but respectfully, resist the contention of the Dominion Government that the commencement, prosecution, and completion of the line shall be left open to a doubtful and indefinite period.

The further opening statement in the letter, that the Dominion Government are willing "to enter into additional obligations of a definite character for the benefit of the Province" may be said to have been disposed of, as the nature and character of these "obligations" have, in the analysis made of the offers, been already examined. I shall, therefore, pass on to what I have termed the admissions in the letter. The most important of these is an admission which may be inferred from the offer made by the Dominion Government to "commence railway construction immediately from Esquimalt to Nanaimo." Here it is admitted that the Dominion Government were in a position, at least in May last (the date of the letter), if not before, to have begun the railway in the Province. There is, and has been, therefore, no excuse for delay in pushing forward the work.

Of scarcely less importance is a second admission, which reads as follows: "to a country like British Columbia it is conceded, however, to be an important point that not only the prompt and vigorous commencement, but also the continuous prosecution of the work of construction within the limits of the Province should be guaranteed."

To these two admissions may be added a third and last: the Dominion Government, while conceding that railway construction should be commenced at the seaboard of the Province, consider it most important that every effort should be made by them to push forward the construction of the railway on the mainland, in order that the legitimate advantages of expenditure should, as far as possible, fall into the hands of the farmers and producers of the interior.

This is an object which the Provincial Government have much at heart, and strongly desire to see realized.

With the clear and just sense which the Dominion Government thus appear to have of what is due to the Province; with their full appreciation, on the one hand, of the wants of the interior, and, on the other, of the requirements of the Island, it might have been expected that they would, as "a Government responsible for the progress of both shores of the Continent," at least have given some more definite as well as some practical meaning to their expressions of solicitude for the welfare of the people of the Province.

I have thus dwelt upon the letter at considerable length, as your Lordship's attention has been specially directed to it in connection with the present case. I conceive the following to be a synopsis of its offers and conditions: Canada will commence, on the Island, immediate construction of the railway at Esquimalt, and finish about 60 miles of it (time of completion indefinite). On the mainland, she will prosecute the surveys for the remainder of the line, and finish these surveys (time also indefinite). She will thereafter "locate" the line falling within the Province (time also indefinite). When this can be achieved, she will make, along this "located" line, a waggon road (which the Province does not want), and a telegraph line (which the Province has not asked for), and will carry the latter across the Continent (time of completion of both road and telegraph line indefinite). Ultimately, after the completion of the surveys and of the road, but not before, Canada will begin, and will continue railway work in the Province, and spend thereon, year by year, not less than £300,000. (Whether this sum will include the Esquimalt line or not is doubtful. It is the only expenditure offered. As I have shown your Lordship, Canada thus proposes to ensure to the Province the completion of the line within her limits in twenty-three and a half years, or less, dating from the unknown period at which the offered expenditure can be commenced). Canada will do all this work "in the shortest time practicable," a phrase a shade stronger than the words "with due diligence," three words, the construction of which has given rise to much doubt, and to much painful litigation. In consideration of these offers (if accepted), British Columbia shall—1st, abandon all claim to the completion of the Canadian Pacific Railway within a definite time; and, 2ndly, shall (virtually, though not quite so expressed) surrender her right to, and interest in, the completion of about 2,000 miles of the line necessary to connect the eastern frontier with eastern Canada. Apart from the very objectionable features of the last two conditions, the indefinite character of the above proposals made to the Province is in marked contrast to the statement of the Dominion Government that, "to a country like British Columbia," it is important that the early completion of the railway within her limits should be insured; and, therefore, that a guarantee should be given by the Dominion Government for its "prompt commencement" (which depends on the prompt completion of the surveys), and also for "its continuous construction" (which depends on yearly specific expenditure). This concludes my remarks upon the letter.

I have endeavoured to place before your Lordship a full history of the position of British Columbia with respect to Confederation. A very unsatisfactory state of affairs has been disclosed, if the question be regarded simply as a question between the Dominion and one of her Provinces. On the part of the Dominion there have been delays, default, and avowal of default, followed by offers and conditions such as I have described.

The peculiar situation of British Columbia—her remoteness—her weak political position—her dependence on the good faith of the Dominion—the hopes that have been held out and deferred—the grievous loss that has ensued—the consequent utter prostration of her interests, all these give her claims upon Canada, which the present Dominion Government have, as already shown, to a certain extent acknowledged—in words. These claims the Provincial Government hope, will not be overlooked by your Lordship in considering the reasonable measure of justice to which the Province is entitled under the Terms of Union. The Province has not expected anything that is unreasonable, and does not do so now. It is her urgent desire that matters should be forthwith placed on a fair business-like footing, and above all, on a footing of certainty, with proper safeguards to ensure that certainty, so that a good and cordial understanding may be restored and not again be disturbed.

I have, &c.,
(Signed) GEO. A. WALKEM,
President of the Executive Council of British Columbia.

It will be a source of deep satisfaction to Lord Carnarvon if the good feeling between Canada and British Columbia, to the maintenance of which you have contributed by the temperate and reasonable manner in which you have urged the claims of your Province, is permanently confirmed by the aid of his intervention.

I have, &c.,
(Signed) ROBERT G. W. HERBERT.

No. 117.

The Earl of Carnarvon to the Earl of Dufferin.

DOWNING STREET,
November 17th, 1874.

MY LORD,—I duly received your despatch of the 18th September, enclosing an Order in Council, setting forth the views of your Ministers as to the proposals contained in my despatch of the 16th August for the settlement of the controversy between Canada and British Columbia, respecting the Pacific Railway. I subsequently again saw Mr. Walkem, and at his request I have delayed the announcement of the terms which, in my opinion, may properly be laid down as fair and reasonable, until the receipt of a further written communication from him, which has now reached me, and a copy of which I enclose.

The statements thus placed before me are so clear and complete as to assist me materially in appreciating the position in which the question now stands, and in judging without hesitation what modification of the original terms should be adopted. And I would here express my satisfaction at the temperate and forbearing manner in which points involving most important consequences have been argued on both sides, and the pleasure which I feel in being able to think that asperity of feeling or language may have been, in some degree, avoided through the opportunity of submitting the whole case to the independent judgment of one who may at least claim to have the interests of both parties equally at heart.

I explained very fully in my despatch of the 16th August the opinion which I entertained on each of the principal questions at issue, and I need now add but little to the simple statement of my decision. That decision is necessarily, as both parties are aware, in the nature of a compromise, and as such it may perhaps fall short of giving complete satisfaction to either. If, on the one hand, your Ministers, as you inform me, consent with reluctance to the further concessions which, at an earlier stage, I suggested, they will not, on the other hand, fail to bear in mind that even after those concessions are made, British Columbia will receive considerably less than was promised to her as the condition of entering the Dominion. I prefer rather to reflect that, under the amended terms now to be established, British Columbia will, after all, receive very great and substantial advantages from its union with Canada, while the Dominion will be relieved of a considerable part of those obligations which were assumed in the first instance without a sufficient knowledge of the local conditions under which so enormous and difficult an undertaking was to be carried into effect, and to fulfil which would seriously embarrass the resources of even so prosperous a country as Canada.

Adhering, then, to the same order in which, on the 16th August, I stated the principal points on which it appeared to me that a better understanding should be defined, I now proceed to announce the conclusions at which I have arrived. They are:—

1. That the railway from Esquimalt to Nanaimo shall be commenced as soon as possible, and completed with all practicable dispatch.

2. That the surveys on the mainland shall be pushed on with the utmost vigour. On this point, after considering the representations of your Ministers, I feel that I have no alternative but to rely, as I do most fully and readily, upon their assurances that no legitimate effort or expense will be spared, first, to determine the best route for the line, and, secondly, to proceed with the details of the engineering work. It would be distasteful to me, if, indeed, it were not impossible, to prescribe strictly any minimum of time or expenditure with regard to work of so uncertain a nature; but, happily, it is equally impossible for me to doubt that your Government will loyally do its best in every way to accelerate the completion of a duty left freely to its sense of honour and justice.

3. That the waggon road and telegraph line shall be immediately constructed. There seems here to be some difference of opinion as to the special value to the Province of the undertaking to complete these two works; but after considering what has been said, I am of opinion that they should both be proceeded with at once, as indeed is suggested by your Ministers.

4. That $2,000,000 a-year and not $1,500,000, shall be the minimum expenditure on railway works within the Province from the date at which the surveys are sufficiently completed to enable that amount to be expended on construction. In naming this amount I understand that, it being alike the interest and the wish of the Dominion Government to urge on with all speed the completion of the works now to be undertaken, the annual expenditure will be as much in excess of the minimum of $2,000,000 as in any year may be found practicable.

5. Lastly, that on or before the 31st December, 1890, the railway shall be completed and open for traffic from the Pacific seaboard to a point at the western end of Lake Superior, at which it will fall into connection with the existing lines of railway through a portion of the United States, and also with the navigation on Canadian waters. To proceed at present with the remainder of the railway extending, by the country northward of Lake Superior, to the existing Canadian lines, ought not, in my opinion, to be required, and the time for undertaking that work must be determined by the development of settlement and the changing circumstances of the country. The day is, however, I hope, not very distant when a continuous line of railway through Canadian territory will be practicable, and I therefore look upon this portion of the scheme as postponed rather than abandoned.

In order to inform Mr. Walkem of the conclusions at which I have arrived, I have thought it convenient to give him a copy of this despatch, although I have not communicated to him any other part of the correspondence which has passed between your Lordship and me.

It will, of course, be obvious that the conclusion which I have now conveyed to you upholds, in the main, and subject only to some modifications of detail, the policy adopted by your Government with respect to this most embarrassing question. On acceding to office your Ministers found it in a condition which precluded a compliance with the stipulations of Union. It became, therefore, their duty to consider what other arrangements might equitably and in the interests of all concerned be substituted for those which had failed. And in determining to supplement the construction of some part of the new railway by that vast chain of water communications which Nature might seem to have designed for the traffic of a great country, I cannot say that they acted otherwise than wisely. I sincerely trust that the more detailed terms which I have now laid down as those on which this policy should be carried out will be found substantially in accordance with the reasonable requirements of the Province, and with that spirit of generous and honourable adherence to past engagements which ought in an especial degree to govern the dealings of a strong and populous community with a feebler neighbour, and which I well know to be the characteristic of all parties and statesmen alike within the Dominion of Canada.

I have, &c.,

(Signed) CARNARVON.

No. 118.

The Governor-General to the Earl of Carnarvon.

(No. 313.) OTTAWA, 18th December, 1874.

MY LORD,—I have the honour to transmit to your Lordship a copy of an Order of the Privy Council, in which my Ministers convey to your Lordship their best acknowledgment for the pains and trouble you have been good enough to take in promoting the settlement of the difference which has arisen between British Columbia and the Government of the Dominion.

I have, &c.,

(Signed) DUFFERIN.

No. 119.

Report of the Privy Council, approved by the Governor-General in Council on the 18th December, 1874.

The Committee of Council have had under consideration the despatch of the Right Honourable Lord Carnarvon, Secretary of State for the Colonies, of November 17th, conveying a statement of the new terms with British Columbia, which, in his Lordship's opinion, may properly be laid down as fair and reasonable concerning the construction of the Pacific Railway.

In the minute of July 23rd, the Government of the Dominion advised that his Lordship should be informed of their willingness to leave it to him to say whether the exertions of the Government, the diligence shown, and the offers made, were, or were not, fair and just, and in accordance with the spirit of the original agreement, seeing it was impossible to comply with the letter of the Terms of Union in this particular.

The conclusion at which his Lordship has arrived " upholds," as he remarks, in the main, and subject only to some modifications of detail, the policy adopted by this Government on this most embarrassing question.

The minute of Council of September 17th contained a statement of reasons showing why some of these modifications should not be pressed; but the Government, actuated by an anxious desire to remove all difficulties, expressed a willingness to make these further concessions rather than forego an immediate settlement of so irritating a question, as the concessions suggested might be made without involving a violation of the spirit of any Parliamentary resolution, or the letter of any enactment.

The Committee of Council respectfully request that your Excellency will be pleased to convey to Lord Carnarvon their warm appreciation of the kindness which led his Lordship to tender his good offices to effect a settlement of the matter in dispute; and also to assure his Lordship that every effort will be made to secure the realization of what is expected.

Certified.
(Signed) W. A. HIMSWORTH,
Clerk, Privy Council.

No. 120.

The Earl of Carnarvon to the Governor-General.

(Canada.—No. 4.) DOWNING STREET,
4th January, 1875.

MY LORD,—I have the honour to acknowledge the receipt of your despatch of the 18th of December, forwarding to me a copy of an Order of the Dominion Privy Council expressing the acknowledgments of the Government of Canada for the services which I have been fortunate enough to render in promoting the settlement of the differences which had arisen between British Columbia and the Government of the Dominion with respect to the construction of the Pacific Railway.

It has been with great pleasure that I have received this expression of their opinion. I sincerely rejoice to have been the means of bringing to a satisfactory conclusion a question of so much difficulty; of removing, as I trust, all ground of future misunderstanding between the Province of British Columbia and the Dominion, and of thus contributing towards the ultimate completion of a public work in which they, and indeed the whole Empire, are interested.

I have, &c.,
(Signed) CARNARVON.

No. 121.

Telegram.

Mr. Walkem to the Provincial Secretary.

OTTAWA,
January 13th, 1875.

Premier agrees to commence Island location in March, prosecute work vigorously, and prosecute Mainland surveys vigorously. In the interim last Summer's work will be plotted. Railway iron has been ordered for Columbia. Carnarvon's decision adopted.

Legislation upon decision deemed unnecessary by Premier. He manifested very sincere good-will towards Columbia, and received me with generous spirit. Alaska already attended to. Have not settled other business with him. Will telegraph my departure.

(Signed)   GEO. A. WALKEM.

No. 122.

Mr. Walkem to the Secretary of State for Canada.

OTTAWA,
January 23rd, 1875.

SIR,—The Provincial Secretary of British Columbia has requested me, by telegram, to ask you to be good enough to officially communicate, at your earliest convenience, the decision upon Railway matters given by Lord Carnarvon on the 17th November last.

The Government of the Province would appear to have had no official intimation upon the subject; I shall therefore feel obliged to you if you will cause the necessary despatches to be forwarded on Monday next, the 25th instant.

I have, &c.,

(Signed)   GEO. A. WALKEM.

No. 123.

Telegram.

Lieutenant-Governor Trutch to the Earl of Carnarvon.

This Government having received no reply to Railway Memorial, and Legislature being in Session, urgently request to be informed, by telegraph, whether official reply has yet been sent, or may be expected; and whether Canada accepts decision in your despatch handed Mr. Walkem. No communication from Ottawa on subject.

(Signed)   JOSEPH W. TRUTCH.

No. 124.

Telegram.

Mr. Walkem to the Under Secretary of State for the Colonies.

3rd March, 1875.

Authorize Government to use copy Railway despatch you gave me. You stated, and your private letter says, communication through Governor-General, and copy handed me for own convenience.

(Signed)   GEO. A. WALKEM.

No. 125.

Telegram.

The Earl of Carnarvon to the Lieutenant-Governor of British Columbia.

March 4th, 1875.

My despatch to Governor-General, of November 17th, was officially communicated to Mr. Walkem as answer to Railway Memorial, and all other representations. It may of course be published. Dominion Government accepts arrangement.

(Signed)   CARNARVON.

No. 126.

Telegram.

The Provincial Secretary to Hon. A. DeCosmos.

March 2nd, 1875.

Ask Mackenzie to forward Railway despatches. Walkem told they would be sent through Dominion Government, and was only informed of the result as matter of courtesy. Please send some answer immediately.

          (Signed) JOHN ASH.

No. 127.

Telegram.

Hon. Mr. DeCosmos to the Provincial Secretary.

OTTAWA,
March 4th, 1875.

Despatches will be sent; printed copies forwarded.

          (Signed) A. DECOSMOS.

No. 128.

Report on the subject of the Mission of Mr. Walkem, Special Agent and Delegate of the Province of British Columbia to England, with regard to the non-fulfilment by Canada of the Railway Agreement of the Terms of Union.

To the Honourable JOSEPH WILLIAM TRUTCH, *Lieutenant-Governor of British Columbia, &c., &c., &c.*

MAY IT PLEASE YOUR HONOUR:—

  I have the honour to report that, in pursuance of your instructions to me to proceed to England as the Delegate of your Government, there to present to Her Majesty's Government a Petition from your Executive Council complaining of the breach by the Dominion of the Railway Clause of the Terms of Union, and to advocate the cause of the Province, as set forth in such Petition, I left Victoria for Ottawa on the 16th day of June, 1874, and arrived at the latter City on the 29th of the same month. Upon the following day, I made a personal application to the Secretary of State for the Order in Council necessary to place me in official communication with Her Majesty's Principal Secretary of State for the Colonies. I learned that owing to the absence from town of His Excellency the Governor-General, some delay in providing me with it would unavoidably occur. On the 4th July, I addressed Mr. Mackenzie upon the same subject, and, in reply, received his assurance that a special messenger had been dispatched to procure His Excellency's signature to the Order, and that upon his return, it would be handed to me (see Nos. 77, 78, pp. 178, 179.) In answer to my further letter of the 11th, the Order was sent to me, and after its receipt, I proceeded to England by the first Steamer which left Quebec.

  On the evening of the 27th of July, I arrived in London, and on the 28th reported the fact to the Colonial Office, and requested the favour of an interview with Lord Carnarvon (see No. 105, p. 192.) In reply I was informed that His Lordship would grant me an audience on Friday, the 31st July (see No. 106, p. 193), and on that day I accordingly waited upon His Lordship and presented the Petition (see No. 74, p. 174) which accompanies this Report. At a long interview which immediately followed, a full statement of the case of the Province was made by me, and His Lordship was good enough to state that if any further information was required by him, I should be notified to that effect.

My next interview took place with the Under Secretary of State, on the 6th of August, in deference to his wishes, and several matters connected with the Petition were then fully discussed. I may here state that the remarks and arguments offered by me on both these occasions, as well as at all subsequent interviews upon the same subject, are so fully given in substance in a letter which I addressed to Lord Carnarvon on the 31st October (*see* No. 115, p. 202), that I think it unnecessary here to restate them; indeed their repetition would only tend without advantage to burden this report. I may add, however, what has been inadvertently omitted from this letter, that at my first interview I respectfully urged that compensation should, as a matter of equity, be given by the Dominion to the Province, for the very serious loss that the latter had unquestionably sustained by the course which had been pursued by Canada; though, in a strictly legal point of view, damages in such cases were, as I observed, treated as consequential, or, professionally speaking, as too remote to be computed or allowed.

It may here be convenient to allude to the very friendly offer of Lord Carnarvon to act, under certain conditions, as arbitrator between the Dominion and Provincial Governments (*see* No. 86, p 182). Mr. Sproat first informed me in August of the offer, and of its acceptance by the Provincial Government. I heard nothing more of the matter officially, and arbitration was not resorted to.

On the 16th August I received, from the Colonial Office, a written acknowledgment (*see* No. 107, p. 193) of the receipt of the Petition, and also an intimation to the effect that Lord Carnarvon considered that he had the Provincial case fully before him, but that he did not anticipate that he would be able before the lapse of two or three weeks, to decide upon the course he should pursue. At the end of that time I called at the Colonial Office and was told that his Lordship and the Under Secretary of State were absent from town. By the advice of the Acting Under Secretary, I wrote the annexed letter of the 10th of September (*see* No. 113, p. 201), to which I received a reply on the 14th, stating in effect that no conclusion had been arrived at in the matter (*see* No. 114, p. 202).

During September and October some further interviews took place, at the last of which I stated that before the case was closed, I desired, as a matter of record, to put in a letter expressive of the views and opinions which I had held, and of the arguments which, from time to time, I had advanced at the several hearings which had been granted to me. This letter is that of 31st October (*see* No. 115, p. 202), to which I have already invited your Excellency's attention.

On the 13th of November a final interview was at my instance afforded me. I referred to the various points set forth in my last letter. Lord Carnarvon thereupon informed me that in a few days he would state his views upon the whole question in writing, and forward the despatch on the subject to Lord Dufferin for the information of both Governments. At my special request he was good enough to say that a copy would be sent to me. This copy with its covering letter from Mr Herbert, was received by me on the 18th November. On the following day I saw him at the Colonial Office, and understood from him that the official despatches would reach your Excellency through the usual channel.

I delayed my departure from England in the hope of securing further aid from the Imperial Government for the construction of the Esquimalt Graving Dock. My negotiations in this direction were, I am happy to say, successful and will form the subject of a separate report.

On the 17th day of December I sailed from England, and reached Ottawa in the beginning of January. I had conversations at different times with Mr. Mackenzie upon the Railway and other Provincial business; and with a view of affording your Government immediate information upon some of these matters, I asked for and obtained Mr. Mackenzie's authority to state the substance of one of these conversations respecting the Railway and the Alaska Boundary. This I have done in my telegram of the 13th of January last, addressed to the Provincial Secretary (*see* No. 121, p. 212). A copy of this message was, on the same day, handed by me to Mr Mackenzie for his private information. About a week afterwards I learned that your Government had not received the official despatches embodying Lord Carnarvon's conclusions upon the Railway question, and upon enquiry at the Secretary of State's Office, I found that they had not been sent. I therefore requested Mr. Scott, the Secretary of State, by letter of Saturday the 23rd January, to forward them by Monday's mail to Victoria (*see* No. 122, p. 213.) On Monday I failed to see him when I called at his office. The next day I was more fortunate, and he was good enough to assure me that no further delay would occur in their transmission. I shortly afterwards left Ottawa, and reached Victoria on the 18th of last month.

Within the last week the several telegrams (see Nos. 123, 124, 125, 126, 127, pp. 213, 214,) which are appended hereto, have been sent and received upon the subject of the non-arrival of these despatches. The telegram from Lord Carnarvon is especially valuable as containing the only official intimation yet received that the Dominion Government has consented to adopt and follow the recommendations offered by his Lordship in his despatch of the 27th of last November.

Before closing this Report it will, no doubt, be as gratifying to Your Excellency to learn, as it is pleasing to me to state, that I received from Lord Carnarvon and from the Under Secretary of State for the Colonies a full and patient hearing; and every opportunity of placing the case of British Columbia in its true light and in all its bearings before his Lordship was cordially afforded me.

I must also acknowledge, which I do with much pleasure, the able services rendered by Mr. Sproat, the Agent-General of the Province; who upon the railway and all other questions evinced untiring zeal in advancing the interests of British Columbia.

It is worthy of record, that apart from the immediate result of the appeal to England, the Province attracted much attention from the prominence given to the object of my mission. Applications, greatly outnumbering those of any former year, or even number of years, were made at the office of the Agent-General during my stay in London, for full information respecting British Columbia, and its suitability as a home for intending settlers. The interest thus awakened in England has also been extended, in a considerable degree, to the Eastern Provinces; and I can state, from a reference to Mr. Sproat's books, that a number of immigrants, many of whom are in easy circumstances, will arrive here within the next few months.

I may be pardoned for adding that my mission differed but little—if at all—from missions of a similar character. It was not unattended with difficulties, as your Excellency can imagine; nor was my position one of freedom from labour and anxiety in the effort to discharge my duty towards the Province. Questions of a complex and intricate nature were, upon the reference to England of the issues between the two Governments, directly involved in the appeal itself. Further complications on my part would not only have been dangerous but mischievous.

I therefore, during my several interviews in England and at Ottawa, not only refrained from causing irritation between the Dominion and its Province, but endeavored on all occasions to allay it wherever circumstances pointed to its existence. As your Excellency will observe from my last letter to Lord Carnarvon, I laboured—I hope not in vain—to convince Eastern Canada that British Columbia, in the advocacy of her rights, only sought to obtain a reasonable measure of justice without unduly pressing upon the resources of the Dominion, of which she forms a part.

Happily, the grave differences which at one time threatened to create a serious breach between the Dominion and her Western Province are now matters of the past.

For my own part, I trust that I may hereafter have cause to look back with satisfaction upon the settlement which has just been effected, and to reflect with sincere pleasure that under your Excellency's directions it fell to my lot in 1874 to be instrumental in promoting the welfare and advancement of the people of British Columbia.

I have the honour to be,
Your Excellency's most obedient servant,
GEO. A. WALKEM.

Attorney-General's Office,
  8th March, 1875.

No. 129.
The Under Secretary of State to the Lieutenant-Governor.

OTTAWA, 25th March, 1875.

SIR,—I am directed to transmit to you herewith, for the information of your Government, a copy of, an Order of His Excellency the Governor-General in Council respecting the conveyance by the Government of British Columbia to the Government of the Dominion of certain land in connection with the construction of the proposed railway from Esquimalt to Nanaimo in that Province.

I have, &c., (Signed) EDOUARD J. LANGEVIN, *Under Secretary of State.*

No. 130.

Report of the Privy Council, approved by the Governor-General on the 25th March, 1875.

On a memorandum, dated 25th March, 1875, from the Honourable the Minister of Public Works, reporting for the consideration of Council, that prior to the commencement of any works of construction on the proposed Railway from Esquimalt to Nanaimo, which the Dominion Government have agreed to build under the arrangement made through Lord Carnarvon, at the instance of British Columbia, it is essential that the Province of British Columbia should convey by legislation to the Dominion Government in trust, to be appropriated in such manner as the Dominion Government may deem advisable, a similar extent of public lands along the line of railway before mentioned (not to exceed twenty miles on each side of the said line) as may be appropriated for the same purpose by the Dominion from the public lands of the Northwest Territories and the Province of Manitoba, as provided in the Order in Council, Section 11, admitting the Province of British Columbia into Confederation; and that it is desirable that the British Columbia Government should be at once notified that it will be necessary during the present Session of the Legislature of that Province to pass an Act so to appropriate and set apart lands to this extent and for this purpose, the grant to be subject otherwise to all the conditions contained in the said 11th Section of the Terms of Union.

The Committee concur in the above Report of the Minister of Public Works, and recommend that the British Columbia Government be notified accordingly.

Certified,
(Signed)   W. A. HIMSWORTH, *Clerk Privy Council.*

No. 131.

No. 13, Statutes of British Columbia, 1875.

A.D. 1875.

An Act to authorize the grant of certain Public Lands to the Government of the Dominion of Canada, for Railway purposes.

[*Assented to 22nd April, 1875.*]

WHEREAS it is expedient to provide for the grant of public lands to the Dominion Government, required for a Railway between the Town of Nanaimo and Esquimalt Harbour: *Preamble.*

Therefore Her Majesty, by and with the advice and consent of the Legislative Assembly of the Province of British Columbia, enacts as follows:—

1. From and after the passing of this Act there shall be and there is hereby granted to the Dominion Government, for the purpose of constructing, and to aid in the construction of a Railway between the Town of Nanaimo and Esquimalt Harbour, in trust to be appropriated in such manner as the Dominion Government may deem advisable, a similar extent of public lands along the line of Railway before mentioned (not to exceed 20 miles on each side of the said line) as may be appropriated for the same purpose by the Dominion from the public lands of the Northwest Territories and the Province of Manitoba, as provided in the Order in Council, Section 11, admitting the Province of British Columbia into Confederation; such grant to be subject otherwise to all the conditions contained in the said 11th Section of the Terms of Union. *Grant of public lands to Dominion for Railway between Esquimalt and Nanaimo.*

2. All and every the provisions of the "Railway Act, 1868," passed by the Parliament of Canada, in the 31st year of the Reign of Her Majesty, and Chapter 68, including any Acts amending the same, in so far as the provisions therein contained are applicable to the said Railway or any section thereof, and are not inconsistent with or repugnant to the provisions of this Act, shall, *mutatis mutandis*, be considered as forming part of this Act, and are hereby incorporated herewith. *Dominion "Railway Act, 1868," to form part of this Act.*

3. In applying the said Railway Act to the said Railway or any portion thereof— *Interpretation Clause.*

A.D. 1875.

The expression "the Railway" shall be construed as meaning the said Railway, or any section thereof, the construction of which has been undertaken by any contractors:

The expression "the Company" shall mean the contractors for the same; and such contractors shall have all the rights and powers vested in companies by the said Act:

The words "Superior Court" shall be held to mean the Supreme Court of British Columbia:

"Clerks of the Peace" shall be held to mean Chief Commissioner of Lands and Works, Commissioner, and Government Agent, respectively:

"Registry Offices" shall mean the Land Registry Office, Victoria, or any other office named by the Dominion Government.

"Clerk of the Court" shall be held to mean the Registrar of the Supreme Court.

As to maps, plans, etc.

4. As respects the said Railway, the eighth section of the "Railway Act, 1868," relating to Plans and Surveys, shall be subject to the following provisions:—

(*a.*) It shall be sufficient that the map or plan and book of reference for any portion of the line of the Railway, be deposited in the office of the Minister of Public Works of Canada, and at such other places as the said Minister of Public Works may order; and any omission, mis-statement, or erroneous description of any lands therein may be corrected by the contractor with the consent of the Minister, and certified by him; and the Railway may then be made in accordance with such certified correction.

(*b.*) The 11th sub-section of the said 8th section of the Railway Act shall not apply to any portion of the Railway passing over ungranted lands of the Crown, or lands not within any surveyed township in the Province; and in such places, deviations not exceeding five miles from the line shown on the map or plan, approved by the Minister of Public Works, shall be allowed, on the approval of the engineer employed by the said Minister, without any formal correction or certificate; and any further deviation that may be found expedient may be authorized by the Governor in Council, and the Railway made in accordance with such deviation.

(*c.*) The map or plan and book of reference made and deposited in accordance with this section, after approval by the Dominion Government, shall avail as if made and deposited as required by the said "Railway Act, 1868," for all the purposes of the said Act, and of this Act; and any copy of or extract therefrom, certified by the said Minister or his deputy, shall be received as evidence in any court of law in the Province of British Columbia.

(*d.*) It shall be sufficient that a map or profile of any part of the completed Railway be filed in the office of the Minister of Public Works of Canada, and in the office of the Chief Commissioner of Lands and Works, Victoria.

As to incumbrances on lands.

5. The provisions made in sub-sections 30, 31, and 32, of section 9 of the "Railway Act, 1868," as to incumbrances on lands acquired for the said Railway, shall apply to lands so acquired in the Province of British Columbia; the Supreme Court of the Province shall, as to such lands, be held to be the Court intended in the said sub-sections.

Judicial powers.

6. In the Province of British Columbia any Judge of a Superior or County Court shall have all the powers given by the said Act to a County Judge.

Short Title.

7. This Act may be cited as the "Esquimalt and Nanaimo Railway Act, 1875."

No. 132.

The Under Secretary of State to the Lieutenant-Governor.

OTTAWA, 10th November, 1875.

SIR,—I am directed to transmit to you, for the information of your Government, a copy of an Order of His Excellency the Administrator of the Government in Council, on the subject of the difficulties existing between the Government of the Dominion and that of British Columbia, arising out of the agreement, made in 1871, for the construction of the Canadian Pacific Railway.

I beg to express my regret at the delay which has occurred in forwarding this document. It arose from the fact of the officer, whose duty it was to furnish a copy of the Order in Council to this Department, for transmission to your Government, having inadvertently omitted to do so.

I have, &c.,
(Signed)   EDOUARD J. LANGEVIN,
Under Secretary of State.

No. 133.

Report of the Privy Council, approved by the Administrator of the Government, on the 20th September, 1875.

The Committee of Council have had under consideration the difficulties arising out of the agreement made in 1871, for the construction of the Canadian Pacific Railway. Mr. Edgar's mission to British Columbia last year was based upon the view that the conditions of that agreement were quite impracticable of fulfilment. The proposals submitted by him to the British Columbia Government were briefly that, the limitation of time being given up, Canada should undertake that one million and a half of dollars should be expended upon construction within that Province in each year after location, and that the building of a waggon road along the line of the proposed railway construction should precede actual railway construction.

It was further proposed to build a Railway on Vancouver Island, from Esquimalt to Nanaimo.

The propositions were either not considered by the Government of British Columbia, or, if considered, they were rejected by them, and they subsequently appealed to the Imperial Government, invoking their intervention. The result of this appeal was an offer from the Right Honourable Lord Carnarvon, Secretary of State for the Colonies, of his good offices to promote a settlement.

The Privy Council in their Minute of the 23rd July, 1874, advised " that Lord Car-
" narvon be informed they would gladly submit the question to him for his decision as
" to whether the exertions of the Government, the diligence shown, and the offers made,
" have or have not been fair and just, and in accordance with the spirit of the agree-
" ment." Lord Carnarvon in his Despatch of August 16th, acting upon this Minute, and upon agreement on the part of British Columbia to abide by his decision, made certain suggestions, of which the most important were—that the amount of yearly expenditure within the Province, after location, should be not less than two millions of dollars; that the period of completion should be the year 1890, and that the Railway from Esquimalt to Nanaimo should be at once commenced.

The Canadian Government in their Minute of Council of September 17th, stated
" that while in no case could the Government undertake the completion of the whole
" line in the time mentioned, and extreme unwillingness exists to another limitation of
" time, yet, if it be found absolutely necessary to secure a present settlement of the con-
" troversy by further concessions, a pledge may be given that the portion West of Lake
" Superior will be completed so as to afford connection by rail with existing lines of
" railway through a portion of the United States, and by Canadian waters during the
" season of navigation, by the year 1890, as suggested."

It was further agreed that after location, two millions should be expended yearly upon construction in British Columbia, and that a Railway from Esquimalt to Nanaimo should be built.

It must be borne in mind that every step in the negotiations was necessarily predicated upon and subject to the conditions of the Resolution of the House of Commons, passed in 1871, contemporaneously with the adoption of the Terms of Union with British Columbia, subsequently enacted in the Canadian Pacific Railway Act of 1872, and subsequently re-enacted (after a large addition had been made to the rate of taxation) in the Canadian Pacific Railway Act of 1874; that the public aid to be given to secure the accomplishment of the undertaking "should consist of such liberal grants of land and "such subsidy in money or other aid, *not increasing the then existing rate of taxation*, as "the Parliament of Canada should thereafter determine."

This determination not to involve the country in a hopeless burden of debt is sustained by public opinion everywhere throughout the Dominion, and must of necessity control the action of the Government, and it cannot be too clearly understood that any agreements as to yearly expenditure, and as to completion by a fixed time, must be subject to the condition thrice recorded in the Journals of Parliament, that no further increase of the rate of taxation shall be required in order to their fulfilment.

The sanction of Parliament to the construction of the proposed Railway from Esquimalt to Nanaimo was necessarily a condition precedent to the commencement of the work.

The other important features of the arrangement, namely the limitation of time for the completion of a certain portion, and the specification of a yearly expenditure, were deemed to be within the meaning of the Pacific Railway Act, 1874, subject, of course, to the condition already mentioned, and which was referred to in the Minute of Council of December 18th, 1874, when the Government "expressed a willingness to make those 'further concessions rather than forego an immediate settlement of so irritating a ques-'tion, as the concessions suggested might be made without involving the violation of "the spirit of any parliamentary resolution or the letter of any enactment."

The proposed Railway from Esquimalt to Nanaimo does not form a portion of the Canadian Pacific Railway as defined by the Act; it was intended to benefit local interests, and was proposed as compensation for the disappointment experienced by the unavoidable delay in constructing the Railway across the Continent. The work is essentially a local one, and there are obvious reasons against the Canadian Government, under ordinary circumstances, undertaking the construction of such works, and in favour of their being built, if at all, by virtue of Provincial action.

The Bill which the Government introduced into the House of Commons to provide for building this Railway, evoked a considerable degree of opposition in that House and in the country, and, although passed by the House of Commons, it was afterwards rejected in the Senate, and thus there is imposed upon the Government the duty of considering some other method of meeting all just expectations of the people of British Columbia, whose Government has not suggested to this Government any solution of the difficulty.

It would seem reasonable that the people of British Columbia should construct this work themselves, or (if they think other local public works more advantageous) should, in lieu of this, themselves undertake such other local public works, and that the compensation to be given them by Canada for any delays which may take place in the construction of the Pacific Railway should be in the form of a cash bonus to be applied towards the local Railway, or such other local works as the Legislature of British Columbia may undertake, Canada also surrendering any claim to lands which may have been reserved in Vancouver Island for railway purposes.

The sum of $750,000 would appear to the Committee to be *a liberal* compensation, and the Committee advise that the Government of British Columbia be informed that this Government is prepared to propose to Parliament at its next Session, the legislation necessary to carry out the views contained in this Minute as to the construction of the Pacific Railway and the compensation to be given to British Columbia for delays in such construction.

The Committee further advise that a copy of this Minute be transmitted to the Right Honourable the Secretary of State for the Colonies.

       Certified,
        (Signed)   W. A. HIMSWORTH,
               Clerk Privy Council, Canada.

Extract from the speech of the Hon. Mr. Blake, "Debates of the House of Commons of the Dominion of Canada, 1880," vol. II., p. 1429.

" Shortly after the close of the Session (April, 1875) I entered the Administration upon a distinct understanding in reference to the Pacific Railway. That understanding was that the Carnarvon terms having failed by reason of the action of Parliament, *a moderate money compensation should be offered to the Province for past and future delays in the construction of the Pacific Railway.*"

No. 134.

The Lieutenant-Governor to the Secretary of State.

(No. 69.)

GOVERNMENT HOUSE,
29th November, 1875.

SIR,—I have the honour to state that I received on the day before yesterday, and have this day laid before my Executive Council, your Despatch of the 10th instant, and the copy therewith transmitted, of an Order of His Excellency the Administrator of the Government in Council, on the subject of the difficulties existing between the Government of the Dominion and that of this Province, arising out of the agreement made in 1871, for the construction of the Canadian Pacific Railway.

I have, &c.,

(Signed) JOSEPH W. TRUTCH.

No. 135.

The Lieutenant-Governor to the Secretary of State,

(No. 73.)

GOVERNMENT HOUSE,
6th December, 1875.

SIR,—With reference to your Despatch of the 10th ultimo and the Order of His Excellency the Administrator of the Government in Council, a copy of which was therewith transmitted, on the subject of the existing difficulties between the Government of the Dominion and that of this Province, arising out of the agreement for the construction of the Canadian Pacific Railway specified in the Terms of Union of British Columbia with the Dominion, I have the honour to enclose herewith a copy of a Minute of my Executive Council thereon, and to request you to lay the same before His Excellency the Governor-General, and in accordance with the advice of my Ministers, expressed in that Minute. I have to state, for the information of His Excellency, that the proposals contained in the above referred to Order of His Excellency the Administrator of the Government are respectfully declined by this Government, and to strongly urge that the Railway agreement be carried out according to the Terms thereof.

I beg also to enclose a copy of a Despatch, which, upon the advice of my Ministers, I have this day addressed to the Right Honourable Her Majesty's Principal Secretary of State for the Colonies, forwarding to that Minister a copy of the Minute of my Executive Council, herewith transmitted.

I have, &c.,

(Signed) JOSEPH W. TRUTCH.

The Committee dissent from many of the views expressed in the above Minute, and see no reason for consenting to any variation of or departure from the Terms of the Railway Agreement therein referred to. They therefore advise that the proposals contained in the Minute be unhesitatingly but respectfully declined by Your Excellency, and that the Dominion Government be so informed; and further, that that Government be strongly impressed with the absolute necessity of the Railway Agreement being carried out, according to the terms thereof.

The Committee further advise that a copy of this Minute (if approved) be transmitted to the Right Honourable the Secretary of State for the Colonies.

Certified,
(Signed) W. J. ARMSTRONG.
Clerk Executive Council.

No. 137.

The Lieutenant-Governor to the Secretary of State for the Colonies.

GOVERNMENT HOUSE,
6th December, 1875.

MY LORD,—I have the honour to transmit to Your Lordship, in accordance with the advice of my Ministers, a copy of a Minute of my Executive Council, expressing the views of this Government on the proposals conveyed in the Order of His Excellency the Administrator of the Government of the Dominion in Council, on the subject of the difficulties existing between the Government of the Dominion and that of British Columbia, arising out of the agreement made in 1871 for the construction of the Canadian Pacific Railway, a copy of which Order in Council has already been transmitted to Your Lordship, as this Government understands from the concluding paragraph thereof.

I have, &c.,
(Signed) JOSEPH W. TRUTCH.

No. 138.

The Lieutenant-Governor to the Secretary of State.

(No. 2.) GOVERNMENT HOUSE,
8th January, 1876.

SIR,—With reference to my despatch to you, of the 6th ultimo, covering a copy of a Minute of my Executive Council, expressing the views of this Government upon the proposals conveyed in the Order of His Excellency the Administrator of the Government in Council, transmitted in your despatch of the 10th November last, respecting the existing difficulties between the Government of the Dominion and that of this Province, arising out of the agreement for the construction of the Canadian Pacific Railway specified in the Terms of Union of British Columbia with Canada, I have the honour to enclose, for submission to His Excellency the Governor-General, a Minute of my Executive Council, conveying certain further comments on this subject, which my Ministers consider advisable to be urged in replication to the said Order in Council.

I have also to state that I have this day, upon the advice of my Ministers, forwarded to Her Majesty's Principal Secretary of State for the Colonies, a copy of the said Minute of Council, herewith transmitted in a covering despatch, of which a copy is appended hereto.

I have, &c.,
(Signed) JOSEPH W. TRUTCH.

No. 139.

Report of the Executive Council, approved by the Lieutenant-Governor on the 4th January, 1876.

The Committee of Council have had before them the Minute of the Honourable the Privy Council of Canada, of the 20th September, 1875, with its covering Despatch of the 10th November last, relative to the construction of the Canadian Pacific Railway.

The general features of the above Minute are such, that this Government found no difficulty in coming to a decision upon it. To avoid possibly prejudicial delays a reply was promptly sent "unhesitatingly but respectfully declining" the proposals, and dissenting generally from the views contained in the Minute, it being considered preferable, in a matter of such importance, to leave for a further communication such comments as the details of the Minute might seem to fairly challenge.

The Committee have now to remark that the Minute, at the outset, refers to Mr. Edgar's letter, and gives a brief, but inaccurate statement of its proposals. It omits to mention the offer of the Dominion Government to immediately construct the Telegraph line in and beyond the Province; and in the next place it incorrectly states that that Government proposed to build "*a Railway*" from Esquimalt to Nanaimo.

Mr. Edgar's letter, it will be found, expresses the inability of the Dominion to construct the Pacific Railway within the period stipulated. It therefore proposes that if this time limit for the completion *of the whole line* be surrendered, the Dominion will, immediately commence "*that portion*" which lies between Esquimalt and Nanaimo. The language of the letter is that "they" (the Dominion Government) "propose to "commence construction from Esquimalt to Nanaimo immediately, and to push *that* "*portion* of Railway on to completion with the utmost vigour, and in the shortest "practicable time."

This extract conveys but one meaning, viz.:—that the line between Esquimalt and Nanaimo was regarded by the present, as it was by the past, Canadian Ministry, as a "*portion of*" the main line.

It now appears from the published correspondence forwarded by the Dominion Government to England, that in their Minute of the 18th August, 1874, they disavowed Mr. Edgar's offer, inasmuch as they alleged (what is repeated in their present Minute) that the Esquimalt line "does not form a portion of the" main line; that "it was in-"tended to benefit local interests, *and was proposed as compensation* for the disappointment "experienced by the unavoidable delay in constructing the Railway across the Continent."

Of these changed views, and certainly unexpected statements, this Government had no intimation until some time after the publication of the correspondence by the Canadian Parliament. During the negotiations this correspondence was not communicated to this Government, otherwise exception would have been taken at the time to several portions of it, which are very objectionable.

The statement that the work in question was proposed as "compensation" is a manifest error, for no such proposal was ever made or hinted at, as will appear by reference to Mr. Edgar's letter. It is also, to a certain extent, inconsistent with the subsequent request made by the Dominion Government to this Province on the 25th March, 1875, for a conveyance (which was granted) of a belt of land along the line between Esquimalt and Nanaimo, similar in extent to that prescribed by the Terms of Union for the Pacific Railway, "and subject otherwise to all the conditions contained "in the 11th Section of the said Terms."

The Dominion Government were not entitled to the land, except under the "Terms of Union." Their agreement with Lord Carnarvon gave them no new claim to it, if the line was not to form part of the Pacific Railway.

It is further alleged in the Minute under consideration, that "the sanction of Parlia-"ment to the construction of the proposed railway between Esquimalt and Nanaimo "*was*" (that is, when Lord Carnarvon's settlement of 1874 was made,) "necessarily a "condition precedent to its commencement;" while, on the other hand, the Premier, in his place in the Commons, said, on the 5th March, 1875, after reading this Settlement to the House:—

"The Terms recommended by Lord Carnarvon, *and which we have accepted,* are "simply these: *That, instead of one and a half millions, we propose to expend two millions* "*a year within the Province* of British Columbia, and we propose to finish *the railway con-*"*nection through the Province* and downward to the point indicated by the year 1890, being "an extension of time of nine years. With respect to the question raised by my Hon-"ourable friend from South Bruce, *I······· I have no··· stock from Parliament.* "*We have no authority* ······· , but merely to continue to act··· to Parliament this decision, "and rely upon the House supporting us in accepting the Terms." (Hansard, p. 511.)

The next point in the Minute is that the agreement for an annual railway expenditure of $2,000,000 in the Province, and for the completion of the line from the Pacific to Lake Superior by 1890, "must" be contingent upon and subject to the conditions of the Resolution passed by the Commons in 1871, contemporaneously with the Terms of Union, and subsequently enacted and re-enacted in the Pacific Railway Acts of 1872-1874 respectively. This Resolution, as quoted in the Minute, reads:—"The aid to be "given to secure the accomplishment of the undertaking should consist of such liberal "grants of land, and such subsidy in money, or other aid, not increasing the then existing "rate of taxation, as the Parliament of Canada should thereafter determine." It is to be remarked that the following important part of the Resolution has not been given in this quotation, viz.:—" *That the Railway should be constructed and worked by private "enterprise and not by the Dominion Government."* That Government seem to have overlooked the fact that the above conditions were so materially changed in 1874 that they were practically abandoned. The rate of taxation was then increased, and, by the Railway Act of 1874 the construction of the railway was placed in the hands of the Government instead of being entrusted to private enterprise. Even had the original Resolution been binding on this Province, no such modifications of it as those above indicated could have been of any effect as regards this Province, until the consent of its Legislature had been obtained thereto. But British Columbia, in fact, was never even consulted as to either the original Resolution or its modification; nor was any intimation given to this—or, as far as known, to the Imperial Government that such a Resolution had been passed by the Canadian Commons, as an intended qualification of the Terms of Union. It could not possibly have had any such effect, as the Address containing the "Terms" was passed by the House of Commons on the 1st of April, 1871, and the Resolution was not submitted to the House until *some days afterwards*, and was *not carried until the 11th April.*

Therefore, the Dominion Government cannot be sustained in their contention that the "Terms of Union" should be controlled by and be subject to the Resolution and the Act above mentioned.

Looking at the question practically, the Resolution and Statute were severally submitted to the House as indications of the schemes at different periods matured by the Government for the *purpose of providing means* for fulfilling the Railway agreement with British Columbia; and should the Act, like the Resolution, fail in its object, some other measure must necessarily be devised for the above purpose.

With respect to the cash bonus of $750,000 to be offered (provided the sanction of Parliament be obtained) " as compensation for the *delays which may take place* in the "construction of the Pacific Railway," it is evident that *future delays of a very grave character are seriously contemplated*, otherwise such an offer never would have been made, before even construction in the Province has been attempted, and before the expiration of the first year of the fifteen given for the completion of the railway hence to Lake Superior. Under these circumstances this offer can only be regarded as a proposed indemnity for a contemplated indefinite postponement of the construction of the work. The agreements for annual railway expenditure and for completion of the line within a fixed time are the only guarantees given that the railway will be constructed this century. An acceptance of this proposed bonus would be equivalent to a surrender of those guarantees, and an abandonment by British Columbia for all time to come of her right to protest against future delays, however protracted. The amount offered represents the average cost of only about 20 miles of railway, and is little more than one-third of one year's promised expenditure in the Province.

The other portions of Lord Carnarvon's Settlement, which declare that the waggon road and telegraph line should be constructed immediately, " as suggested by " the Dominion Government, have not been touched upon in the Minute. The waggon road has not been commenced, though twelve months have elapsed since it was promised, and though its immediate construction as a forerunner of railway work was strenuously insisted upon by the Dominion Government. The *immediate* erection of the telegraph line was, for the same reason, also declared to be indispensable; but work on this line though begun last spring, has been abandoned indefinitely. The proposal to construct it formed a very material element in the consideration of British Columbia's appeal to England, as the heavy cost of the undertaking was weighed, against the claims advanced by the Province.

The facts and incidents which forced the Provincial Government to appeal to the Imperial Government in 1874 need not be repeated. After nearly six months spent in negotiations, proposals were submitted by Lord Carnarvon to the Dominion Government for their approval. To these proposals they gave their deliberate and unreserved assent on the 18th December, 1874. In their Minute of that date, they stated that the proposals could be *accepted " without involving a violation of the spirit of any parliamentary resolution "or the letter of any enactment;"* and that *"the conclusion* at which his Lordship has "arrived *upholds,* as he remarks, *in the main and* subject only *to some modification of detail,* "the policy adopted by this Government on this most embarrassing question."* They therefore "respectfully request that your Excellency will be pleased * * * * *to assure his* "*Lordship that every effort will be made to secure the realization of what is expected.*"

Thus apparently ended a most unpleasant as well as unprofitable and irritating dispute, which had lasted for about eighteen months, and which resulted in a most carefully considered Settlement—a Settlement that, in the opinion of the Dominion Government, upheld their own railway policy and violated neither the spirit nor the letter of any parliamentary provision. Notwithstanding these facts, and the strong assurance given that "every effort" would be made to redeem their pledges, the Dominion Government only, nine months afterwards, (as appears by their Minute of the 20th September last) virtually decided to ignore these engagements. The construction of the Island section of the railway is to be abandoned. The agreements to *immediately* construct the waggon road and telegraph line have already been violated, and no assurance whatever remains that they will ever be constructed. The stipulations—most important of all—for an annual railway expenditure in the Province, and for completion of the railway within a fixed time, are now held by the Dominion Government to be contingent upon conditions which, though incidentally referred to in their first and last despatches to Lord Carnarvon, were never offered for his Lordship's consideration; nor was it contended that they should control any settlement that might be made. In justice to all parties, the Dominion Government should have placed their whole case before Lord Carnarvon, and not have reserved this point for contention and for sudden announcement nearly twelve months after the date of what was supposed and intended to be a final settlement of all differences upon railway matters. If the contention referred to were conceded, the Settlement would virtually be reduced to a nullity, as the Ministry of the day would be free to use the bulk, and indeed all, of their available revenue for general public purposes, and thus leave little or nothing for the railway project.

The delay in the transmission of the Minute of Council now under consideration deserves notice. It was passed on the 20th September last, and was detained at Ottawa until the 19th of November—some seven weeks—"owing," as alleged by the Under Secretary of State, "to the fact of the officer whose duty it was to furnish a copy of the Order in Council to this Department for transmission * * * * * having inadvertently omitted to do so." To the Dominion Government this detention proved most opportune. By a singular coincidence they were during this period engaged in negotiating a heavy loan in England, $7,250,000 of which, it is publicly reported, they succeeded last October in borrowing on the Imperial guarantee, in which the Province is specially interested, as it was mainly given to aid in the construction of the Pacific Railway. Owing to the detention alluded to, the Provincial Government were not afforded an opportunity of protesting in the proper quarter, against the guarantee being used under existing circumstances. With respect to that guarantee, the importance and value of a good understanding with British Columbia upon Railway matters has been and is well understood by the Dominion Government. On the 16th of February, 1875, the Canadian Minister of Finance stated in his speech upon the Budget:—"I think it would have "placed us at a certain disadvantage with the Imperial Government and British Colum- "bia, if we asked for the Imperial guarantee while there was any dispute between our- "selves and that Province as to the construction of the Pacific Railway,"—(Hansard, 1875, page 163.) This statement, it will be observed, was made about two months after the Settlement of 1874 had been effected. Before using the guarantee, it might have been expected that the Dominion Government would have taken every precaution to have informed this Government of their determination to re-open the Settlement, and not fulfil its terms.

It is also worthy of observation that, during the same period and about the 20th of September last, the survey parties on the Island were materially strengthened; and the line of railway between Esquimalt and Nanaimo has, since then, been practically located for its whole length. Steel rails were also landed at these two places, so that the people of the Province had every confidence in the early commencement of the work, and had no reason for suspecting that, at this very time, the Dominion Government had resolved to abandon and ignore the terms of their settlement with Lord Carnarvon.

The history of the railway agreement would be a recital of unnecessary delays by the Dominion, and of consequent disappointments to British Columbia of a most discouraging and damaging character. Direct pecuniary loss to a large proportion of her people and an utter prostration of most important interests have been the result of the non-fulfilment of promises made with every semblance of deliberation and good faith. Distrust has unfortunately been created where trust and confidence should have been inspired. It would be mischievous to conceal this state of affairs.

It has fallen to the lot of British Columbia, though politically weak, to defend and preserve the agreement for the construction of the Pacific Railway upon which Confederation depends.

The Committee of Council urge that the terms of Lord Carnarvon's Settlement be strictly carried out, and they strongly protest against their violation by the Dominion Government.

The Committee respectfully request that Your Excellency will be pleased, if this Minute be approved, to cause copies thereof to be severally forwarded to the Dominion Government and to the Right Honourable the Secretary of State for the Colonies.

Certified,
(Signed)   W. J. ARMSTRONG,
Clerk, Executive Council.

No. 140.

The Lieutenant-Governor to the Secretary of State for the Colonies.

GOVERNMENT HOUSE,
8th January, 1876.

MY LORD,—With reference to my despatch to your Lordship, dated the 6th ultimo, transmitting a copy of a Minute of my Executive Council, expressing the views of this Government on certain proposals conveyed in the Order of His Excellency the Administrator of the Government of the Dominion in Council, in relation to the existing difficulties between the Government of the Dominion and that of this Province, arising out of the agreement for the construction of the Canadian Pacific Railway, I have the honour to enclose for Your Lordship's consideration, at the request of my Ministers, a Minute of my Executive Council, conveying certain further comments on this subject, which my Ministers consider advisable to be urged in replication to the said Order in Council.

I have, &c.,
(Signed)   JOSEPH W. TRUTCH.

No. 141.

Extract from Journals, Legislative Assembly, British Columbia.

Report of the Committee of the Whole, with respect to the Canadian Pacific Railway.

21st January, 1876.

Your Committee appointed by this Honourable House to consider and report upon the correspondence between the Governments of the Dominion and of the Province with regard to the Canadian Pacific Railway, respectfully report as follows:—

1. That it appears that the Dominion Government have almost wholly disregarded the terms of the Settlement effected through the mediation of the Right Honourable the Secretary of State for the Colonies, for the purpose of carrying out the Railway Agreement in our Terms of Union.

2. The Dominion Government have not commenced Railway construction, either on the Island or on the Mainland, or the waggon road or engineering trail intended to

facilitate railway work on the Mainland; though as part of the Settlement the "immediate construction" of a portion of these works was promised by the Dominion Government in December, 1874. The agreement, in the Settlement, for the immediate construction of the Provincial section of the Trans-Continental Telegraph Line has also been violated.

3. That with respect to the promised active prosecution of the surveys, your Committee have no authoritative information upon which a correct opinion can be based.

4. That the Dominion Government have, by Minute of the Privy Council of the 20th of September, 1875, intimated their intention to virtually ignore the Settlement effected by them with Lord Carnarvon, and have stated that they will submit their views, as expressed in the Minute, to Parliament at its ensuing Session, as the policy which should be adopted with respect to their railway engagements with the Province.

5. That the Dominion Government have affirmed, in their Minute of September, that the section of Railway on *Vancouver Island* is not part of the Pacific Railway, but that it was offered to this Province as compensation for local losses caused by delays in the construction of the Pacific Railway; but your Committee do not find that such an offer of compensation was ever made or even suggested to the Province.

6. That the Dominion Government state in their Minute of the 20th of September last, that " it cannot be too clearly understood" that they will not abide by, or observe the agreements in the Settlement for an annual railway expenditure of $2,000,000 in the Province, and for the completion of the railway from the Pacific to Lake Superior, by the year 1890, if the performance of such agreements should interfere with the conditions of a Resolution passed by the House of Commons in 1871, after our Terms of Union had been assented to by that body. The terms of this Resolution were, in effect, that the Railway should be constructed and worked by private enterprise, and not by the Dominion Government; and that subsidies in land and money, to an extent that would not increase the then rate of taxation, should be given in aid of the work by the Government.

7. Your Committee find that the terms of the Resolution were abandoned in 1874, the rate of taxation having been increased, and the construction of the Railway having been undertaken by the Government, instead of being confided to private enterprise.

8. Your Committee would observe that the Resolution was at best merely an indication of the scheme matured by the Government to provide means to fulfil their Railway engagements with the Province; that it never was submitted to the people or Government of British Columbia; nor was it, so far as known, submitted in 1871 to the Imperial Government for consideration, when the Terms of Union were passed; or in 1874, to Lord Carnarvon, during the negotiations which preceded the Settlement. The Resolution therefore cannot, for plain constitutional, as well as legal reasons, control either the Terms of Union, or the Settlement made to carry them out.

9. That no compensation has been offered by the Dominion Government for the proposed abandonment of the section of railway on *Vancouver Island*, or for the broken engagements to build the waggon road and telegraph line, or for any of the past disastrous and ruinous delays in the construction of the Pacific Railway on the Mainland or Island.

10. That an indemnity, however, to the amount of $750,000—the cost of about twenty miles of railway—has been offered to British Columbia, for any *future* delays which may occur in the construction of the Railway, and that this sum will, subject to the assent of Parliament, be paid as a cash bonus to the Province, if the agreements for yearly Railway expenditure, and for completion of the Railway to *Lake Superior* by 1890, be surrendered by the Province.

11. That the Provincial Government have declined to accept the offer of $750,000, and have recorded their dissent from the views expressed by the Dominion Government in their Minute in Council of September last.

12. That your Committee are of opinion that the Provincial Government have, by declining such offer, acted in the interests of this Province.

13. That the Province entered Confederation upon a distinct and specific agreement that, as " no real union could exist without " [eas]y communication" between *British Columbia* and *Eastern Canada* through British territory, the Canadian Pacific Railway should be constructed by the Dominion as a Federal work of political and commercial necessity.

14. That the aim of the Province is to secure practical Confederation and its anticipated advantages, in lieu of theoretical union with its losses and many disappointments.

15. That as the Dominion Government have failed to observe their Railway engagements with the Province, and have intimated, as stated, their intention not to carry them out, your Committee advise that your Honourable House do appoint a Committee to draft and submit to the House an humble Address to Her Majesty, setting forth all the circumstances connected with the subject of this Report, and praying that Her Majesty may be graciously pleased to at once move the Dominion Government to carry out the conditions of the Settlement effected through the mediation of Lord Carnarvon, and agreed to by them.

142.

The Lieutenant-Governor to the Secretary of State for the Colonies.

BRITISH COLUMBIA, GOVERNMENT HOUSE,
2nd February, 1876.

MY LORD,—I have the honour to enclose herewith a Petition to Her Majesty the Queen, from the Legislative Assembly of this Province, praying in regard to the unfulfilled obligations of Canada to British Columbia respecting the construction of the Canadian Pacific Railway, that Her Majesty may be graciously pleased to cause the Dominion Government to be immediately moved to carry out the terms of the settlement effected through your Lordship's intervention in November, 1874.

I also enclose a copy of the Address from the Legislative Assembly with which this Petition was handed to me, together with a copy of a Minute of my Executive Council, expressing their entire and earnest concurrence in the prayer of the said Petition, and, following the advise of my Ministers, expressed in that Minute, and in compliance with the request of the Assembly, I have the honour to forward their said Petition to your Lordship, and to respectfully solicit that it may be laid before Her Majesty, and that Her Majesty will be graciously moved to favourably consider the same and to order the signification of Her Royal pleasure thereon to be communicated to this Government as soon as practicable.

I have, &c.,
(Signed) JOSEPH W. TRUTCH.

No. 143.

Petition of the Legislative Assembly of the Province of British Columbia.

To the Queen's Most Excellent Majesty.

MOST GRACIOUS SOVEREIGN:—

We, Your Majesty's most dutiful and loyal subjects, the Members of the Legislative Assembly of the Province of British Columbia, in Session assembled, humbly approach Your Majesty for the purpose of representing:—

1. That, on the 31st day of July, 1874, the Government of this Province humbly presented a Petition to Your Majesty, alleging (amongst other matters) that the main inducement which led British Columbia to enter the Dominion of Canada, on the 20th day of July, 1871, was the Agreement by the latter to commence in two and complete in ten years from that date the construction of the Canadian Pacific Railway; and that this Agreement had been violated by Canada. The Petitioners, therefore, prayed that Your Majesty would, under the circumstances set forth in the Petition, be graciously pleased to cause justice to be done to British Columbia. To this Petition your present Petitioners (the Legislative Assembly) beg leave to refer Your Majesty.

2. That after protracted negotiations on the subject between Your Majesty's Right Honourable Secretary of State for the Colonies (the Earl of Carnarvon) and the Dominion Government, His Lordship was pleased to signify his conclusions upon the question in dispute, in the following language:—

"(1.) That the railway from Esquimalt to Nanaimo shall be commenced as soon as possible, and completed with all practicable dispatch.

"(2.) That the surveys on the mainland shall be pushed on with the utmost vigour.

* * * * * * * * * *

"It would be distasteful to me, if, indeed, it were not impossible, to prescribe strictly any minimum of time or expenditure with regard to work of so uncertain a nature; but, happily, it is equally impossible for me to doubt that your Government will loyally do its best in every way to accelerate the completion of a duty left freely to its sense of honour and justice.

"(3.) That the waggon road and telegraph line shall be immediately constructed. There seems here to be some difference of opinion as to the special value to the Province of the undertaking to complete these two works; but after considering what has been said, I am of opinion that they should both be proceeded with at once, as, indeed, is suggested by your Ministers.

"(4.) That 2,000.000 dollars a year, and not 1,500,000 dollars shall be the minimum expenditure on railway works within the Province from the date at which the surveys are sufficiently completed to enable that amount to be expended on construction. In naming this amount, I understand that, it being alike the interest and the wish of the Dominion Government to urge on with all speed the completion of the works now to be undertaken, the annual expenditure will be as much in excess of the minimum of 2,000,000 dollars as in any year may be found practicable.

"(5.) Lastly, that on or before the 31st December, 1890, the railway shall be completed and open for traffic from the Pacific seaboard to a point at the western end of Lake Superior, at which it will fall into connection with the existing lines of railway through a portion of the United States, and also with the navigation on Canadian waters. To proceed, at present, with the remainder of the railway extending, by the country northward of Lake Superior, to the existing Canadian lines, ought not, in my opinion, to be required, and the time for undertaking that work must be determined by the development of settlement and the changing circumstances of the country. The day is, however, I hope not very distant when a continuous line of railway through Canadian territory will be practicable, and I therefore look upon this portion of the scheme as postponed rather than abandoned." [*Vide* despatch, Lord Carnarvon to Lord Dufferin, 17th November, 1874, No. 117, p. 210.]

3. That the Dominion Government, one month later, assented to these conclusions or proposals, and stated, in effect, that the proposals would be carried out as they upheld in the main their own policy on the question and violated neither the letter nor the spirit of any parliamentary provision. The Settlement thus effected was intended and supposed to be final and conclusive. [*Vide* despatch, Lord Dufferin to Lord Carnarvon, 18th December, 1874, No. 118, p. 211.]

4. Your Petitioners, the Legislative Assembly, with great regret, feel compelled to state that the Dominion Government have almost wholly disregarded the terms of the above Settlement, as they have not commenced the promised railway construction, either on the Island or on the Mainland, or the waggon road or engineering trail intended to facilitate railway work on the Mainland; nor has the agreement, in the Settlement, for the immediate construction of the Provincial section of the Trans-Continental Telegraph Line been carried out.

5. That with respect to the promised active prosecution of the surveys, your Petitioners have no authoritative information upon which a correct opinion can be based.

6. That the Dominion Government have, by Minute of their Privy Council of the 20th of September, 1875, intimated their intention to virtually ignore the above Settlement, and have stated that they will submit their views, as expressed in the Minute, to Parliament at its ensuing Session, as the policy which should be adopted with respect to their railway engagements with the Province. [*See* No. 133, p. 219.]

7. That the Dominion Government have affirmed, in their Minute of September, that the section of railway on Vancouver Island is not part of the Pacific Railway, but that it was offered to this Province as compensation for local losses caused by delays in the construction of the Pacific Railway; but your Petitioners do not find that such an offer of compensation was ever made or even suggested to the Province.

8. That the Dominion Government state in their Minute of the 20th of September last, that "it cannot be too clearly understood" that they will not abide by or observe the agreements in the Settlement for an annual railway expenditure of $2,000,000 in the Province, and for the completion of the railway from the Pacific to Lake Superior, by the year 1890, if the performance of such agreements should interfere with the conditions of a Resolution passed by the House of Commons in 1871, after our Terms of Union had been assented to by that body. The terms of this Resolution were, in effect, that the Railway should be constructed and worked by private enterprise, and not by the Dominion Government; and that subsidies in land and money, to an extent that would not increase the then rate of Dominion taxation, should be given in aid of the work by the Government.

9. That your Petitioners find that the terms of the Resolution were abandoned in 1874, the rate of taxation having been increased, and the construction of the railway having been undertaken by the Government, instead of being confided to private enterprise.

10. Your Petitioners respectfully submit that the Resolution was at best merely an indication of the scheme matured by the Government to provide means to fulfil their railway engagements with the Province; that it never was submitted to the people or Government of British Columbia; nor was it, so far as known, submitted in 1871 to Your Majesty's Government for consideration, when the Terms of Union were passed; or in 1874, to Lord Carnarvon, during the negotiations which preceded the Settlement. The Resolution, therefore, cannot for plain constitutional as well as legal reasons control either the Terms of Union or the Settlement made to carry them out.

11. That no compensation has been offered by the Dominion Government for the proposed abandonment of the section of railway on Vancouver Island, or for the broken engagements to build the waggon road and telegraph line, or for any of the past disastrous and ruinous delays in the construction of the Pacific Railway on the Mainland or Island.

12. That an indemnity, however, to the amount of $750,000—the cost of about twenty miles of railway—has been offered to British Columbia, for any *future* delays which may occur in the construction of the railway, and that this sum will, subject to the assent of Parliament, be paid as a cash bonus to the Province, if the agreements for yearly railway expenditure, and for completion of the railway to Lake Superior by 1890, be surrendered by the Province.

13. That the Provincial Government have declined to accept the offer of $750,000, and have recorded their dissent from the views expressed by the Dominion Government in their Minute in Council of September last.

14. That your Petitioners are of opinion that the Provincial Government have, by declining such offer, acted in the interests of this Province.

15. That the Province entered Confederation upon a distinct and specific agreement that, as "no real union could exist" without "speedy communication between" British Columbia and Eastern Canada through British territory, the Canadian Pacific Railway should be constructed by the Dominion as a Federal work of political and commercial necessity.

16. That the aim of the Province is to secure practical Confederation and its anticipated advantages, as indicated in the Terms of Union, in lieu of theoretical union with its losses, deprivations, and many disappointments.

17. That your Petitioners humbly solicit Your Majesty's attention to the Minutes of the Executive Council of this Province lately forwarded to the Right Honourable the Secretary of State for the Colonies, and dated respectively the 6th day of December, 1875, and the 4th day of January, 1876, as your Petitioners wholly agree with the views and statements therein set forth.

18. That British Columbia has fulfilled all the conditions of her agreement with Canada.

19. That by reason of the repeated violations by Canada of its railway engagements with this Province, all classes of our population have suffered loss; provident anticipations based on these engagements have resulted in unexpected and undeserved failure, and in disappointment of a grave and damaging character; distrust has been created where trust and confidence should have been inspired; trade and commerce have been mischievously unsettled and disturbed; the progress of the Province has been seriously

checked; and "a feeling of depression has taken the place of the confident anticipations "of commercial and political advantages to be derived from the speedy construction of "a railway which should practically unite the Atlantic and Pacific shores with Your "Majesty's Dominion on the Continent of North America."

20. Your Petitioners, therefore, humbly submit that they are at least entitled to have the conditions of the Settlement effected through the intervention of the Right Honourable the Secretary of State carried out in letter and in spirit.

Your Petitioners, therefore, humbly approach Your Majesty, and pray that Your Majesty may be graciously pleased to cause the Dominion Government to be immediately moved to carry out the terms of the said Settlement.

And your Petitioners, as in duty bound, will ever pray, &c.

(Signed) JAMES TRIMBLE,
Speaker.

No. 144.

The Lieutenant-Governor to the Secretary of State for Canada.

BRITISH COLUMBIA, GOVERNMENT HOUSE,
2nd February, 1876.

SIR,—I have the honour to enclose herewith, for the information of His Excellency the Governor-General, a copy of a Despatch which, upon the advice of my Ministers, I have this day addressed to the Right Honourable Her Majesty's Principal Secretary of State for the Colonies, together with a copy of the documents therewith transmitted, being a Petition to Her Majesty the Queen from the Legislative Assembly of this Province, respecting the existing Railway Question between the Dominion and that of British Columbia, the Address of the Legislative Assembly with which that Petition was handed to me, and a Minute of my Executive Council expressing their views and advice to me in relation to the said Address and accompanying Petition.

I have, &c.,
(Signed) JOSEPH W. TRUTCH.

No. 145.

Telegram.

The Lieutenant-Governor to the Secretary of State for the Colonies.

4th February.

Earl Carnarvon, Colonial Secretary, London.

Ministry desire me inform you Petition unanimously adopted by Legislative Assembly, praying Dominion Government be immediately moved to carry out Railway Agreement, was dispatched to you yesterday.

(Signed) J. W. TRUTCH.

No. 146.

Telegram.

The Lieutenant-Governor to the Secretary of State for Canada.

VICTORIA, B. C., 4th February, 1876.

Hon. R. W. Scott, Secretary of State, Ottawa.

My Ministers desire me to inform you that a Petition to the Queen, praying that Dominion Government may be immediately moved to carry out the Terms of the Settlement of the Canadian Pacific Railway question effected by Lord Carnarvon, has been unanimously adopted by the Legislative Assembly, and dispatched to Lord Carnarvon yesterday. A copy of the Petition was forwarded at the same time to you.

(Signed) J. W. TRUTCH.

No. 147.

The Lieutenant-Governor to the Secretary of State for Canada.

British Columbia, Government House,
4th February, 1876.

Sir,—I have the honour to enclose herewith a copy of a Minute of my Executive Council, in accordance with the purport of which I have this day addressed to you and to the Right Honourable Her Majesty's Principal Secretary of State for the Colonies respectively, the telegraphic despatches transcripts of which are also enclosed.

I have, &c.,
(Signed)   Joseph W. Trutch.

No. 148.

The Secretary of State to the Lieutenant-Governor.

(520 on 912.)

Ottawa, 17th March, 1876.
[Received 11th April, 1876.]

Sir,—Adverting to previous correspondence on the subject, I have the honour to transmit to you, for the information of your Government, six copies of an Order of His Excellency the Governor-General in Council, on the Address to Her Majesty the Queen, enclosed in your Despatch, No. 8, of the 2nd ultimo, on the subject of the Canadian Pacific Railway.

(Signed)   R. W. Scott,
Secretary of State.

No. 149.

Report of the Privy Council, approved by the Governor-General on the 13th March, 1876.

The Committee of Council have had under consideration the Despatch from the Lieutenant-Governor of British Columbia, dated 2nd February, 1876, on the subject of the Pacific Railway, enclosing amongst other papers a copy of an Address to Her Majesty, from the Legislative Assembly of British Columbia.

1. In that Address the Legislative Assembly states, " that the Dominion Government have almost wholly disregarded the terms of the settlement, as they have not commenced the promised Railway construction, either on the Island or on the Mainland, or the waggon road or engineering trail intended to facilitate railway work on the Mainland, nor has the agreement in the settlement for the immediate construction of the Provincial section of the Trans-Continental Telegraph Line been carried out."

2. Upon this allegation the Committee would observe, that although the Government took very step in their power to secure the construction of the proposed Esquimalt and Nanaimo Railway, the Bill for that purpose, which they carried through the House of Commons, was defeated in the Senate.

3. With reference to railway construction on the Mainland, the present Government always insisted, and it was part of the arrangement, that they should not be called upon to locate the line before the surveys were sufficiently complete for that purpose. The Government is not even yet in a position to determine the location, and this must of course precede the commencement of construction.

4. As to the proposed waggon road or engineering trail, this road was alleged by British Columbia to be valueless, but it was explained by the Government of Canada, (as indeed is stated in the Address), that it was intended to facilitate the construction of the railway (of which it would in fact be a part), and that it would be built upon the location line of the railway.

5. The railway not being yet located it is of course impossible to construct the waggon road.

6. The same observations apply to the telegraph line which was to be constructed along the located line of the railway for the purposes thereof. It is to be observed, however, that contracts have been entered into by the Government for the entire telegraph line from Lake Superior to the Pacific, of which five hundred miles have been built; and that the contractor for the part in Columbia, having the bulk of his material on hand, is ready to commence construction as soon as the line is located.

7. The Address proceeds to state "that with reference to the promised active prosecution of the surveys, the Assembly have no authoritative information upon which a correct opinion can be based."

8. Upon this statement the Committee have only to observe that the utmost diligence has been used in prosecuting the surveys, and in fact the extreme haste induced by an earnest desire to fulfil as far as practicable the Terms of Union, has in several instances prevented so thorough an examination of the country as should be made in order to secure the best location. The Committee must add that the members of the Columbia Legislature can hardly be ignorant of the enormous expenditure made in that Province in connection with the surveys.

9. The Address states "that the Dominion Government have, by a Minute of the Privy Council, of 20th September, 1875, intimated their intention to virtually ignore the settlement;" * * * * * * * and further that they "have affirmed that the section of the railway on Vancouver Island is no part of the Pacific Railway, but was offered to the Province as compensation for local losses caused by delays in the construction of the Pacific Railway, but your petitioners do not find that such an offer of compensation was ever made or even suggested to the Province."

10. On these statements the Committee would observe that the Government of Canada, so far from ignoring, have used their best endeavours to carry out the terms of the arrangement.

11. There is no pretence for saying that the Esquimalt and Nanaimo Railway was under the Terms of Union, a work, the construction of which was obligatory on Canada, as part of the Pacific Railway.

12. By these terms the western terminus of the railway is prescribed to be a point on the Pacific seaboard to be fixed by the Governor in Council; and thus the question became not a matter of bargain between Canada and Columbia, but part of the executive policy of Canada.

13. The first action connecting in the remotest degree the Government of Canada with the construction of any railway on Vancouver Island took place on the seventh of June, 1873, two years after the Union, when an Order in Council was passed which (most improvidently in the view of the Committee) declared that Esquimalt should be the terminus of the railway.

14. By this policy, had it remained unreversed, the Government would have been obliged to provide for the construction of over 160 miles of railway on Vancouver Island, at a probable cost of over seven millions five hundred thousand dollars; besides the building of a railway from the head of Bute Inlet and the bridging of the Narrows, a work supposed to be the most gigantic of its kind ever suggested, and estimated to cost more than twenty millions, making a total estimated cost of over twenty-seven millions and a half dollars.

15. The present Government from the beginning declined to adopt or maintain this part of the policy of its predecessors, either by bridging the Narrows, or by constructing any works on Vancouver Island as part of the Pacific Railway; but even had they done otherwise, such a course, however unwise, would not have altered the facts already detailed, which show conclusively that the Island Railway was not stipulated for by the Terms of Union.

16. The attitude which the present Government have always assumed upon this subject appears from the instructions to Mr. Edgar, of 19th September, 1874, which contains the following paragraphs:—

17. "You will remember that the Dominion is bound to reach the *seaboard of the Pacific* only, not Victoria or Esquimalt, and you will convey an intimation to them that any further extension beyond the waters of Bute Inlet, or whatever other portion of the sea-waters may be reached, may depend entirely on the spirit shown by themselves in assenting to a reasonable extension of time, or a modification of the terms originally agreed to." * * * * * * * *

18. "You will take special care not to admit in any way that we are bound to build the Railway to Esquimalt, or to any other place on the Island, and while you do not at all threaten not to build there, to let them understand that this is wholly and purely a concession, and that its construction must be contingent on a reasonable course being pursued regarding the other parts of the scheme."

19. The whole tenor of the subsequent correspondence and action of this Government has been in strict accordance with this view. The Minute of Council of 8th July, 1874, transmitted to Lord Carnarvon, contains the following paragraph:—

20. "The proposition made by Mr. Edgar involved an immediate heavy expenditure in British Columbia not contemplated by the Terms of Union, namely: the construction of a railway on Vancouver Island, from the port of Esquimalt to Nanaimo, as compensation to the most populous part of the Province for the requirement of a longer time for completing the line on the Mainland."

21. The Minute of the 23rd July, 1874, also transmitted to Lord Carnarvon, contains the following paragraph:—

22. "The Dominion Government were also willing to exceed the Terms of Union by constructing a railway on the Island of Vancouver, although they were bound only to reach the seaboard of the Pacific."

23. The Minute of the 17th September, 1874, also transmitted to Lord Carnarvon, contains the following paragraphs:—

24. "The proposals may thus be summarized:—1. To build a railway from Esquimalt to Nanaimo, on Vancouver Island, in excess of the Terms of Union, and to begin the work immediately." * * * * * * *

25. "It is proper to notice *seriatim*, the several grounds of complaint as stated in the despatch. 1st. That nothing is being done by the Dominion Government towards commencing and pushing on a railway from Esquimalt to Nanaimo."

26. "The Dominion has no engagement to build such a Railway, and therefore there can be no just complaint that it is not commenced. The construction of such a railway was offered only as compensation for delay in fulfilling the engagement to build a railway to the Pacific seaboard."

27. The same view was recognized and acted upon last Session by the introduction of a Bill to authorize the construction of a Railway from Esquimalt to Nanaimo, a course which would have been unnecessary had that line formed part of the Pacific Railway; and also by the Minute of Council of 22nd March, 1875, which pointed out to the British Columbia Government that it was essential that legislation should take place in British Columbia for the appropriation of certain lands in respect of that railway, a step which would have been unnecessary had it formed part of the Pacific Railway, but the necessity for which was recognized by the British Columbia Government and Legislature, which passed an Act for the purpose.

28. It is impossible to doubt that the British Columbia Government and Legislature were, when that Act was passed, well aware of the views of the Canadian Government and Parliament, which, however, they never repudiated, the first expression of dissatisfaction therewith being contained in the Minute of Council of British Columbia, dated 4th January, 1876.

29. The Committee have only to repeat that Canada being under no obligation to construct a railway upon Vancouver Island as part of the Pacific Railway, the proposal to construct that line was obviously and necessarily intended as a compensation, or concession, to the Province of British Columbia for delays in the construction of the Pacific Railway.

30. The Address proceeds to refer to the statement in the Minute of Council of this Government of 20th of September last, upon the subject of the Parliamentary provisions that no further increase of the rate of taxation should be required in order to the construction of the railway.

31. The Address affirms that the terms of the resolution referred to "were abandoned in 1874, the rate of taxation having been increased, and the construction of the railway having been undertaken by the Government, instead of being confided to private enterprise," and proceeds to submit that "the resolution was at best merely the indication of a scheme matured by the Government to provide the means to fulfil their railway engagements with the Province; and that it was never submitted to the people or Government of British Columbia; nor was it, so far as known, submitted in

"1871 to Her Majesty's Government for consideration, when the Terms of Union were passed; or in 1874 to Lord Carnarvon, during the negotiation which preceded the settlement. The resolution, therefore, cannot for plain constitutional as well as legal reasons control either the Terms of Union or the settlement made to carry them out."

32. The Committee would observe that the resolution in question was passed within a few days of the time at which the Terms of Union were assented to by the House of Commons; that it was well known, that in order to secure the consent of a majority of the House to these ruinous terms, the Government of that day were obliged to promise to their supporters the introduction of such a resolution; and that the then delegate, now the Lieutenant-Governor of British Columbia, was present and aware of, and doubtless an assenting party to the arrangement.

33. The present Government, however, have never contended that the Resolution was of the same force as if it had been embodied in the Terms of Union. On the contrary, they share the opinion expressed at the time by a large minority of the House of Commons, that it was of the last importance, in order to secure Canada from embarrassing complications and exorbitant and possibly ruinous demands, that the terms of the resolution should be so embodied. In that effort the Opposition were unsuccessful, and the consequences of their failure cannot be ignored. Had the Opposition succeeded, and so enabled the Government to argue that the Terms of Union were absolutely and technically controlled by the terms of the resolution, they would not have considered themselves called on to offer new terms to British Columbia. It was because they felt that they could not fairly take this ground that new terms were proposed. But the Government have always contended that in considering this question in a moral and equitable point of view—trying it as it should be tried, as a question of honour—it is impossible for British Columbia, under the circumstances shortly stated, to hold herself entirely absolved from considering that resolution, which should be treated as an ingredient in estimating the extent of the moral obligation of Canada towards the Province.

34. The Committee cannot assent to the suggestion that the increase of taxation involved an abandonment of the resolution.

35. It is true that, animated by a desire honourably to fulfil to the utmost of their ability the improvident engagements to which the country had been committed, the Parliament of Canada did, at the instance of the Government in the Session of 1874, largely increase the rate of taxation; but no such increase could under any circumstances deprive the Government or Parliament of its right to advert to the resolution in question as still continuing to be an element to be considered—much less could it have that effect when, contemporaneously with the increase of taxation, an Act was passed reiterating that resolution as forming part of the policy of Parliament on the subject.

36. The like observation applies to the suggestion that the resolution was abandoned by the provisions of the Act of 1874, permitting the Government to construct the whole or part of the work.

37. The plan proposed by the late Government had failed. The Company which it chartered had been unsuccessful in raising the necessary funds; had acknowledged its failure, and had asked for the concession of more favourable terms. That concession not having been granted, it had asked for a cancellation of its charter and the repayment of the million of dollars deposited as security for the execution of the work. These requests had been granted, and the Company had been dissolved.

38. In providing under such circumstances for the execution of the work, it was prudent, if not necessary, to take power for the construction of the railway, in whole or part, as a public enterprise, first because it was impossible to assert after the failure of the former scheme, that it possessed the elements of success, and also because, pending the completion of the surveys, the power so taken might enable some progress to be made. But the power of constructing the work by means of a private company, should that be found possible, remains, and can at the proper time be exercised.

39. Again, in the very Act which authorized the construction by the Government, the resolution in question was recited and re-enacted, thus rendering it utterly impossible to contend successfully that Parliament was, by that Act, abandoning the resolution.

40. The resolution having been so re-enacted in the Statute under whose provisions alone the Administration had power to deal with the question, was referred to in more than one of the Minutes transmitted to Lord Carnarvon during the negotiation for settlement.

41. The Address inaccurately states the position taken in the Minute of 20th September upon this subject, which is as follows:—

"It must be borne in mind that every step in the negotiation was necessarily pre-dicated upon, and subject to the conditions of the resolution of the House of Commons passed in 1871, contemporaneously with the adoption of the Terms of Union with British Columbia, subsequently enacted in the Canadian Pacific Railway Act of 1872, and subsequently re-enacted after a large addition had been made to the rate of taxation, in the Canadian Pacific Railway Act of 1874—that the public aid to be given to secure the accomplishment of the undertaking, should consist of such liberal grants of land and such subsidy in money or other aid, *not increasing the then existing rate of taxation*, as the Parliament of Canada should thereafter determine. This determination not to involve the country in a hopeless burden of debt, is sustained by public opinion every-where throughout the Dominion, and must of necessity control the action of the Government; and it cannot be too clearly understood that any agreements as to yearly expenditure, and as to completion by a fixed time, must be subject to the con-dition thrice recorded in the Journals of Parliament, that no further increase of the rate of taxation shall be required in order to their fulfilment. The sanction of Par-liament to the construction of the proposed railway from Esquimalt to Nanaimo, was necessarily a condition precedent to the commencement of the work.

42. "The other important features of the arrangement—namely, the limitation of time for the completion of a certain portion and the specification of a yearly expen-diture, were deemed to be within the meaning of the Pacific Railway Act, 1874, subject of course to the condition already mentioned and which was referred to in the Minute of Council of December 18th, 1874, when the Government expressed a willing-ness to make these further concessions rather than forego an immediate settlement of so irritating a question, as the concessions suggested might be made without involving a violation of the spirit of any Parliamentary resolutions or the letter of any enactment."

43. The British Columbia Government and Legislature were, of course, aware of the passing of the resolution, and of its enactment in the Statutes of 1872 and 1874; but they never made any objection to these provisions.

44. The Committee, for the reasons assigned, wholly dissent from the view that the resolution has been abandoned.

45. The Address proceeds to state that "no compensation has been offered by the Dominion Government for the proposed abandonment of the section of railway on Vancouver Island or for the broken engagements to build the waggon road and telegraph line, or for any of the past disastrous and ruinous delays in the construction of the Pacific Railway on the Mainland or Island.

46. "That an indemnity, however, to the amount of $750,000—the cost of about 20 miles of railway—has been offered to British Columbia for any future delays which may occur in the construction of the railway, and that this sum will, subject to the assent of Parliament, be paid as a cash bonus to the Province, if the agreements for yearly railway expenditure and for completion of the railway to Lake Superior by 1890, be surrendered by the Province."

47. The Committee having already dealt with several of these statements, it is un-necessary to repeat their argument. The proposal of the Government was to construct the Esquimalt and Nanaimo Railway as compensation for delays upon receiving a grant of a large area of land on Vancouver Island.

48. Parliament declining to authorize the construction of that railway, the Govern-ment proposed to invite Parliament to pay in cash (towards the construction of local public works, to be determined on and built by British Columbia herself) seven hundred and fifty thousand dollars as a substituted compensation.

49. This sum seems to be but little regarded by the Legislature of British Columbia; but it appears to the Committee to be a very liberal offer. The population of the Province is estimated at ten thousand; that of the Dominion may be called four millions. A like expenditure at the same rate on public works over the whole Dominion would reach three hundred millions of dollars. An allotment at this rate to British Columbia is far from insignificant

50. Nor was this sum offered on the condition stated in the Address. It was not proposed that the Province should surrender the agreement for a yearly expenditure

and the completion of the Railway to Lake Superior. It was simply stated that the agreement was—as it was by the Government intended to be—as by the law it necessarily must have been—as, unless Parliament should alter the law, it must have remained—subject to the condition so often repeated, with reference to the increase of taxation. Were it found possible to carry out fully those terms of the agreement without such increase, the Government proposed to do it. Were that found impossible, the Government proposed to carry out those terms so far as practicable consistently with the condition, which was itself a fundamental part of any arrangement the Government could lawfully make; but the Committee must repeat their conviction that the people of Canada would not consent to enter unconditionally into arrangements which, though less onerous than the Terms of Union, would yet involve such a burden as might, but for the condition, plunge the country into ruin.

51. The Address states that "the aim of the Province is to secure practical Confederation and its anticipated advantages as indicated in the Terms of Union, in lieu of theoretical Union, with its losses, deprivation and many disappointments;" and "that by reason of the repeated violation by Canada of her railway engagements, all classes of the British Columbia population have suffered loss. Provident anticipations based upon these engagements have resulted in unexpected and undeserved failure and in disappointment of a grave and damaging character; distrust has been created where trust and confidence should have been inspired; trade and commerce have been mischievously unsettled and disturbed; the progress of the Province has been seriously checked, and a feeling of depression has taken the place of the confident anticipations of commercial and political advantages to be derived from the speedy construction of a railway which should practically unite the Atlantic and Pacific shores with Your Majesty's Dominions on the continent of North America."

52. The Committee would observe that they cannot assent to the view that the Union with British Columbia has occasioned loss and deprivation to that Province. On the contrary, the results, financially to the Dominion and to British Columbia respectively, even ignoring all railway expenditure in the Province, show that enormous pecuniary advantages have been derived by Columbia from Canada.

53. Appended hereto is a statement of the financial results of the Union from July, 1871, up to December, 1875, which shows that after crediting British Columbia with all revenue received from it, and apart from all railway expenditure, Canada has expended for British Columbia one million two hundred and three thousand dollars over her receipts from that Province.

54. The Committee must further observe that the tenor of the representations now under consideration would seem to indicate that the object of the Legislature of British Columbia is less to secure the completion of the work as a national undertaking in such a way and on such terms as may best conduce to the welfare of the whole community, than to enforce the immediate and continued expenditure within their own Province at whatever cost to Canada of many millions of money, for which they cannot pretend to have given an equivalent; and that their chief grievance is that their people have not as yet derived, in addition to the other financial benefits of Union, the gains and profits to be expected from the expenditure of these millions in their midst. To these views must be mainly referred the allegations, unfounded as they appear to the Committee, of disastrous and ruinous delays, and as to all classes of the population having suffered loss and deprivations.

55. The Committee cannot but observe that the spirit which (ignoring the general welfare, and the importance to the whole of Canada of avoiding disaster from a premature commencement and a reckless prosecution of the Pacific Railway) presses so urgently for an enormous expenditure with a view to reap vast profits for the small population amongst which it is to be made, is hardly calculated to induce the people of Canada to second the efforts of the Administration to redeem as far as they can the appalling obligations to which, by the Terms of Union, the country was committed.

56. The Committee remark with regret that the Assembly of British Columbia should have expressed their entire agreement with the views and statements set forth in the Minute of the Executive Council of that Province dated 4th January, 1876, which, besides some allegations and arguments substantially repeated in the Address, contains with reference to the transmission of the Minute of Council of 20th September last,

imputations upon the honour and good faith of the Canadian Government so gross that they must decline to discuss it.

57. The policy of the Government of Canada was to do everything in their power to fulfil in other respects the terms of the arrangement recently entered into in the manner set forth in their Minute of 20th September and referred to in this Minute; nor did the Government hesitate to intimate their readiness to propose a liberal compensation for delays in substitution of that provided by the arrangement, but to which Parliament declined to assent.

58. The Committee regret that the Legislature of British Columbia should have refused their proposal.

59. It remains only to endeavour to construct the Pacific Railway as rapidly as the resources of the country will permit.

60. The Committee recommend that copies of this Minute should be transmitted to the Secretary of State for the Colonies, and to the Lieutenant-Governor of British Columbia. Certified.

(Signed)   W. A. HIMSWORTH,
Clerk Privy Council, Canada.

Revenue and Expenditure in British Columbia.

REVENUE.

	1871-72.	1872-73.	1873-74.	1874-75.	1875-½ year.
	$ cts.	$ cts.	$ cts.	$ cts.	$ cts.
Customs	353,844 00	303,865 99	325,787 29	414,331 85	249,039 40
Excise	1,457 11	5,425 53	10,674 84	11,181 01	4,300 06
Post Office	177 54	16,740 90	9,504 20	12,264 11	6,495 02
Ocean Service		24,732 72	12,449 20	2,975 12	5,981 45
Telegraph		14,310 48	10,120 72	9,480 18	2,529 07
Railway &c.		12,513 39	295 40		
Miscellaneous		1,113 42	3,915 97	2,157 29	1,160 01
Share by popul'n of interest on investments &c.	7,809 00	6,310 00	8,435 00	11,674 00	1,829 00
Total Consolidated Fund	363,288 19	385,330 03	391,192 62	464,072 56	275,333 01

EXPENDITURE.

	1871-72.	1872-73.	1873-74.	1874-75.	1875-½ year.
	$ cts.	$ cts.	$ cts.	$ cts.	$ cts.
Charges on debt by population	84,913 00	80,524 00	85,752 00	99,889 00	48,913 00
Local Offices in charges of management	2,851 77	6,969 13	10,135 53	0,850 70	3,294 44
Share of Civil Government by population					
Local Offices in Civil Government	8,473 00	9,730 00	10,832 00	11,185 00	5,032 00
Justice	7,591 31	8,499 12	13,671 31	11,444 60	4,505 16
Penitentiary		42,001 32	42,717 00	30,658 55	10,742 17
Legislation	28,588 05	35,061 32	15,864 45	20,311 00	4,525 77
Immigration and quarantine			10,050 41	500 00	2,085 00
Marine Hospital	16,917 24	19,392 18	1,231 12	3,881 81	1,150 32
Pensions	55 00	5,000 00	3,016 59	4,579 35	2,021 93
Militia	474 27		4,478 17	8,743 80	5,426 18
Public works and buildings	804 67	22,639 04	47,631 65	42,375 48	84,075 22
Ocean and river service	56,155 83	68,984 72	64,555 67	95,236 74	30,762 60
Light-houses and coast service	15,171 83	13,207 01	30,560 90	24,782 70	11,291 08
Subsidy	214,000 00	216,289 75	220,293 05	225,049 65	130,230 00
Indians	556 95	20,000 00	29,000 00	25,000 00	13,660 50
Miscellaneous	1,374 49	321 97	19,631 47	1,350 31	
Customs	17,065 00	24,477 56		119,050 37	10,087 12
Excise		1,085 77	6,137 00	5,318 40	3,765 55
Post Office	37,397 13	60,370 91	68,686 67	70,055 58	25,000 00
Telegraph	15,848 67	51,990 77	23,021 19	32,774 21	9,411 76
Total expenditure	510,221 01	641,381 70	702,441 39	767,043 34	401,571 81
Total revenue	363,298 08	385,330 03	391,192 62	464,072 56	275,333 01
Excess of expenditure	140,923 83	265,051 73	371,248 77	303,975 78	126,238 80
Pacific Railway expenditure	90,400 00	310,823 80	108,431 85	184,247 30	177,241 32
Total excess of expenditure	237,323 83	572,875 59	479,680 62	487,123 14	303,460 12

Total expenditure		$3,083,505 21
Total revenue		1,879,226 36
Excess of expenditure		1,204,338 91
Add Pacific Railway expenditure		870,144 36
Total excess of expenditure		2,080,483 30

JOHN LANGTON,
Auditor.

No. 150.

The Lieutenant-Governor to the Secretary of State for Canada.

British Columbia, Government House,
11th April, 1876.

Sir,—I have the honour to state that I have this day received and laid before my Executive Council, your Despatch of the 17th ultimo, and the six copies therewith enclosed, of an Order of His Excellency the Governor-General in Council on the Address to Her Majesty the Queen, forwarded in my Despatch to you, No. 8, of the 2nd February, in reference to the Canadian Pacific Railway.

I have, &c.,
(Signed)   Joseph W. Trutch.

No. 151.

Report of the Honourable the Executive Council, approved by His Excellency the Lieutenant-Governor on the 11th day of April, 1876.

The Committee of Council request your Excellency to address a message (by telegraph) to the Secretary of State for the Colonies, inquiring whether the Address to Her Majesty the Queen from the Legislative Assembly of British Columbia, in relation to the Canadian Pacific Railroad, has been received by his Lordship; and, if so, when an answer thereto may be expected by your Excellency; and representing that the Legislative Assembly is now in session, and that it is of the most urgent importance to the interests not only of this Province, but of the Empire, that an indication of Her Majesty's decision in this matter should be communicated to your Excellency before the House is prorogued, and if necessary by telegraphic despatch.

Certified.
(Signed)   T. Basil Humphreys,
          Clerk of the Executive Council.

No. 152.

Telegram.

The Lieutenant-Governor to the Secretary of State for the Colonies.

11th April.

Earl Carnarvon, Colonial Secretary, London.

This Government anxious to learn whether Petition of Assembly respecting Railway received—if so, when answer will reach here? Legislature in Session. Government considers most important to Provincial and Imperial interests that decision be communicated before Prorogation. If necessary by telegraph.

(Signed)   J. W. Trutch.

No. 153.

Telegram.

The Secretary of State for the Colonies to the Lieutenant-Governor.

April 13th, 1876.

Lieutenant-Governor, British Columbia.

Petition duly received. Reply impossible until explanations about to arrive from Dominion Government have been received.

(Signed)   Carnarvon.

No. 154.

Report of the Executive Council approved by the Lieutenant-Governor on the 22nd day of April, 1876.

The Committee of Council respectfully request Your Excellency to acknowledge, by telegraphic despatch, the receipt of Lord Carnarvon's telegram of the 13th April, 1876, and to state that the Legislature of this Province will remain in session about twenty days from this 22nd day of April, and that this Government again urge that it is of the utmost importance that the decision upon the Petition from the Legislative Assembly to Her Majesty, respecting the Railway question, be communicated to Your Excellency before the House is prorogued.

Certified,
(Signed)   T. BASIL HUMPHREYS,
Clerk of the Executive Council.

No. 155.

The Lieutenant-Governor to the Secretary of State for Canada.

GOVERNMENT HOUSE,
(No. 25.)   Victoria, 22nd April, 1876.

SIR,—I have the honour to state, for the information of His Excellency the Governor-General, that, upon the advice of my Ministers, expressed in a Minute of Executive Council, a copy of which is herewith enclosed, I have to-day addressed to the Right Honourable H. M. Principal Secretary of State for the Colonies, a telegraphic message and also a despatch by mail, a copy of which is also enclosed, containing a transcript of that message in further relation to the Petition from the Legislative Assembly of British Columbia to Her Majesty the Queen respecting the Canadian Pacific Railway.

I have, &c.,
(Signed)   JOSEPH W. TRUTCH.

No. 156.

Telegram.

The Lieutenant-Governor to the Secretary of State for the Colonies.

22nd April.

Earl Carnarvon, London.

My Ministers request me acknowledge your telegram thirteenth instant, and state Legislature will continue sitting twenty days, and again urge most important that decision on petition be communicated before prorogation.

(Signed)   JOSEPH W. TRUTCH.

No. 157.

Telegram.

The Secretary of State for the Colonies to Lieutenant-Governor.

27th April.

Lieutenant-Governor, British Columbia.

I entertain great hope that difficulties of Railway question can be satisfactorily overcome, but fear it will be impossible for my reply, which must be fully considered, to reach British Columbia within time mentioned in your telegram of twenty-second.

(Signed)   CARNARVON.

No. 158.

The Lieutenant-Governor to the Secretary of State for Canada.

(No. 38.) — British Columbia, Government House,
3rd June, 1876.

Sir,—With reference to your Despatch of 17th March last, the receipt of which was duly acknowledged by me on the 17th April, transmitting six copies of an Order of His Excellency the Governor-General in Council on the Address to Her Majesty the Queen from the Legislative Assembly of this Province, in relation to the questions at issue between the Government of the Dominion and that of this Province respecting the agreement in the Terms of Union for the construction of the Canadian Pacific Railway, I have the honour to enclose, herewith, for the information of His Excellency the Governor-General, in accordance with the advice of my Ministers, a copy of a Minute of my Executive Council submitting certain remarks upon that Order in Council. I also enclose for His Excellency's information a copy of a Despatch which, in further accordance with the advice of my Ministers expressed in this Minute, I have this day addressed to the Right Honourable Her Majesty's Principal Secretary of State for the Colonies, covering a copy of the said Minute of my Council.

I have, &c.,
(Signed) Joseph W. Trutch.

No. 159.

Report of the Executive Council, approved by the Lieutenant-Governor on the 3rd day of June, 1876.

The Committee of Council having had before them the Minute of the Privy Council of Canada, of March 13th last, commenting upon the Address and Petition to Her Majesty by the Legislative Assembly of British Columbia, desire to submit the following remarks in relation thereto:—

That that Minute in no way disproves or even disputes the material facts stated in the said Address, but rather seeks to account for them; nor does it in their opinion weaken the force of the representations based on those facts; and that they would be well satisfied that the argument in this case should be submitted to any impartial tribunal, just as it is left by the reply in the Minute of the Government of Canada upon that Address.

That they desire, however, to deny distinctly that British Columbia has at any time, through any delegate or agent, either directly or indirectly, consented or agreed that the Railway obligations of Canada towards British Columbia, under the Terms of Union, should be subject to the limitation specified in the Resolution adopted by the House of Commons of Canada on the 11th day of April, 1871.

That such a limitation virtually nullifies those obligations altogether, as, indeed, is now in fact claimed by the Government of the Dominion.

That they protest against the unwarranted assumption in that Minute that British Columbia has in any way assented or become bound, either legally or in honour, to such an abrogation of the Railway Article of the Terms of Union.

That they equally repel the charge that this Province, from sordid and selfish craving "for the gains and profits to be expected from the expenditure of millions in their " midst, on the construction of the Pacific Railway," has ever sought to exact the literal fulfilment of the Railway Agreement, regardless of the general welfare of Canada, even to the involvement of the Dominion, of which she is a Province in financial ruin, as is asserted in that Minute. That, on the contrary, British Columbia has always been ready to adopt a reasonable view of that agreement, as is fully shown by the cordial concurrence of her Government and people in the modification of that agreement effected in 1874, through the Right Honourable the Secretary of State for the Colonies.

That the Government of Canada, however, now evade compliance with the requirements of that modified agreement, or seek to qualify or virtually nullify it by a condition certainly not clearly or openly stated (if stated at all) when that modification was decided upon by the Secretary of State for the Colonies and accepted unreservedly by that Government.

That British Columbia never urged, nor desired, nor would she have concurred in any such expenditure of the public funds of Canada, in the construction of the Pacific Railway, as could be shown to be beyond the financial ability of the Dominion, but that she has claimed and does claim a right to form and express an independent opinion as to the extent to which that financial ability should be exerted on this great national enterprise; and she holds that, though in other respects an integral part of Canada as a Province of the Dominion, she is entitled, in respect of this question of the non-fulfilment of the Terms upon which she entered the Dominion, to a position as independent as she occupied in negotiating those Terms, a position of entire equality with that which attached to the Dominion itself, the other party to those negotiations.

That as regards the suggestion by the Government of Canada in the Minute of Privy Council of 20th September last, that British Columbia should receive a bonus of $750,000 "as compensation for any delays which may take place in the construction of "the Pacific Railway," it seems to be intimated in the subsequent Minute of March 13th, although it is yet far from being distinctly stated, that such bonus was offered in lieu of the proposed section of railroad between Esquimalt and Nanaimo only, and that it was never intended that the acceptance of that bonus by British Columbia should relieve Canada from any of the conditions of the settlement of the Railway agreement effected in 1874, other than that providing for the construction of that particular section of railroad. If such was the intention of that offer, it is much to be regretted that it was expressed in the Minute of 20th of September in language which certainly conveys a very different meaning, and fully warrants the conclusion, and none other, which the Government and people of British Columbia derived from it, viz: that the acceptance of the proffered bonus would be held to preclude British Columbia from any further assertion of her rights under the Railway Article of the Terms of Union. It is yet more to be regretted that the Government of Canada, on learning that the true intent of their suggestion had been, as they allege, misapprehended, have not, in plain language, renewed that suggestion in the spirit of the desire expressed in their last Minute, to propose "a liberal compensation for delays, in substitution of that provided by the "arrangement recently entered into in 1874, but to which Parliament declined to "assent."

That as to the contention in the Minute of the Privy Council of Canada of 20th of September last, that the "proposed railway from Esquimalt to Nanaimo does not form a portion of the Canadian Pacific Railway, as defined by the Act; it was proposed as compensation for the disappointment experienced by the unavoidable delay in constructing the Railway across the continent," which contention is renewed in their subsequent Minute, the Committee observe that the Order in Council of 7th June, 1873, by which it is decided that "Esquimalt be fixed as the terminus of the Canadian Pacific Railroad," has never been repealed or reversed, as far as the Committee are aware, by any subsequent Order of Council or other instrument of equal validity. Certainly no such subsequent Order of Council has been communicated to the Government of British Columbia.

That, whatever may have been the intention of the Government of Canada in offering to construct immediately the portion of road between Esquimalt and Nanaimo, that offer was never accepted by the Government of British Columbia.

That the Government of British Columbia, did, however, accept the settlement effected in 1874 through the Secretary of State for the Colonies, and that the Government and people of British Columbia are loyally ready to abide in all respects by that settlement, and to be bound by all its conditions as they may be defined by the Secretary of State for the Colonies.

That the Government and Legislature of British Columbia, desirous then, as they still are, to do all in their power to give effect to that settlement, without hesitation complied last year with the request of the Government of Canada for the conveyance to that Government, by Act of this Legislature, of certain lands along the line of the proposed Railroad between Esquimalt and Nanaimo, in aid of the construction of that portion of road, of the extent and on the conditions stipulated in the 11th Article of the Terms of Union.

That the Government of Canada, in their application for the conveyance of those lands by Act of this Legislature, gave no intimation that such conveyance by legislation was specially requisite on account of the proposed road from Esquimalt to Nanaimo not being part of the Canadian Pacific Railroad; nor was such a consideration presented in any way to the Government or Legislature of British Columbia.

That the Committee hold, on the contrary, that such legislation would have been equally required for the full legal conveyance of the lands applied for, whether the portion of road towards the construction of which they were appropriated were part of the Canadian Pacific Railroad or not, and that similar legislation would be requisite for the conveyance to the Dominion of any lands in respect of the construction of any portion of the Canadian Pacific Railroad, under the 11th Article of the Terms of Union, by which the Government of British Columbia "agree to convey" certains lands on the conditions therein stated, this Government being incompetent to duly carry that agreement into effect without being further specially empowered so to do by the Legislature of the Province.

That the contention that the portion of road between Esquimalt and Nanaimo is not part of the Pacific Railway is wholly immaterial if—as seems to be indicated in the last Minute of Privy Council—that portion of road was undertaken in 1874 as compensation for delay which had then already occurred in the commencement of the Pacific Railroad, and for such further delay only in its construction and completion as is stipulated in the settlement effected by the Secretary of State for the Colonies.

That, with regard to the comparative statement of the Revenue and Expenditure of the Dominion in British Columbia since union, which is appended to and commented upon in the Minute of Privy Council of 13th March, it would not be difficult to show that that statement is not altogether a fair exhibit of the account. That a large part of the expenditure charged against British Columbia is incidental to the extension of the system of Confederation over a new Province. That the revenue derived by the Dominion from British Columbia is shown by that statement to have steadily and largely increased, viz.: as $363,298 08 for the year 1871–2 is to $275,333 01 for the first half of the year 1875–6, the expenditure increasing also in about the same proportion; that whilst it may confidently be anticipated that at least that ratio of increase of revenue will be maintained, the increase of expenditures, on the other hand, may be expected to be proportionately reduced after the completion of those public buildings and other public works, the construction of which was provided for in the Terms of Union, and to which a considerable part of the expenditure of the past three years is chargeable.

That even if it could be shown from a comparison of the expenditure and receipts of the Dominion in British Columbia since Union, that enormous pecuniary advantages have, as is asserted in that Minute, resulted to this Province, such a financial balance against British Columbia would be but insignificant in comparison with the infinitely more important and lasting benefits which she justly anticipates from the construction of the Pacific Railroad in accordance with the Terms of Union, not indeed so much from the expenditure of money in its construction as from the results to the Province and to the Dominion of its completion and the establishment thereby of a great highway for trade and travel within British territory from the Atlantic to the Pacific, and the immigration consequent therefrom into this Province.

That the introduction, by the Government of the Dominion of such a discussion as to the financial results to Canada and British Columbia respectively, from the introduction of that Province into the Dominion, appears to the Committee most unfortunate, and is certainly not pertinent to the question at issue. British Columbia has never complained of having been unfairly dealt with in the apportionment of General Expenditure by the Dominion, nor would the Committee desire to assume that such expenditure, either in British Columbia or elsewhere, has been directed by any other motive than that of promoting the general welfare of the Dominion as a whole, without seeking to purchase, by undue apportionment of the public funds, the consent of this or any other Province to an abandonment of just claims under the Terms of Union.

That the manifestation by the Government of Canada of their sentiments towards British Columbia, expressed in the concluding paragraphs of their last Minute, followed as it has been by the adoption by a large majority of the House of Commons in the recent Session—all the members of the Government in that House being of that majority—of a Resolution to the effect that the Pacific Railroad shall not be built if its construction entail on Canada any increase of taxation, has painfully impressed us, and the community we represent, with the conviction that the Government of Canada do not intend to press the construction of that railroad beyond the convenience of that Government after providing for all other public works of apparently more direct and local interest to the majority in Eastern Canada, nor to have any regard to the contract for its completion entered into by Canada in the Terms of Union, and renewed in modified terms in the Settlement effected in 1874, by the Right Honourable the Secretary of State for the Colonies, except subject to that convenience.

That the Committee, again, humbly submit that British Columbia is, at least, entitled to have the conditions of that settlement carried out in letter and in spirit; and they humbly and earnestly renew the prayer of the Petition to Her Majesty from the Legislative Assembly of the Province; that the Dominion Government be immediately moved to carry out the terms of that settlement.

That they have the fullest confidence that Her Majesty will not require Her loyal subjects in this Province, however numerically weak, to submit to injustice and injury from the majority, however great, to whom they united themselves at Her Majesty's instance, on distinct and carefully considered terms, in claiming the performance of which, even in a modified form, they are met with reproaches and charged with ignominious motives.

That, unless means be speedily taken to remove this sense of slight and injustice, now felt by the people of British Columbia, and to satisfy them that the substantial rights of the Province will be maintained, this growing alienation of sentiment must result prejudicially to the interests of the Empire.

The Committee respectfully request that your Excellency will be pleased, if this Report be approved, to cause copies thereof to be severally forwarded to the Right Honourable the Secretary of State for the Colonies and to the Honourable the Secretary of State for Canada.

Certified,
(Signed) T. BASIL HUMPHREYS,
Clerk of the Executive Council.

No. 160.

The Governor-General's Secretary to Lieutenant-Governor Trutch.

GOVERNOR-GENERAL'S OFFICE, OTTAWA,
12th June, 1876.

SIR,—I am directed by the Governor-General to transmit to you, for the information of your Government, a copy of a despatch which His Excellency has received from the Right Honourable the Secretary of State for the Colonies, having reference to a Memorial addressed to the Queen from the Legislative Assembly of British Columbia, and to a Report of a Committee of the Privy Council of the Dominion, in regard to the construction of the Canadian Pacific Railway.

I have, &c.,
(Signed) E. G. P. LITTLETON.

No. 161.

The Earl of Carnarvon to the Earl of Dufferin.

DOWNING STREET,
May 23rd, 1876.

MY LORD,—I have received your Despatch No. 75, of the 17th March, in which you enclose a Report of a Committee of your Privy Council, drawn up in reference to a Petition to the Queen from the Legislative Assembly of British Columbia, having reference to the course proposed to be taken by the Canadian Government with regard to the construction of the Pacific Railway.

2. The Petition of the Legislative Council of British Columbia was forwarded, as you are aware, by the Lieutenant-Governor of the Province, who had also previously

communicated to me the Minutes of his Executive Council, dated the 6th of December, 1875, and 4th January, 1876, relating to the same subject.

3. I have learnt with sincere pleasure that, with the concurrence of your Ministers, you contemplate a progress through the Western portion of the Dominion, as apart from the advantages likely to arise from your becoming personally acquainted with British Columbia and its inhabitants, your intercourse with the principal persons of the Province, and the information you will be able to gather, will be very valuable in enabling me to appreciate the situation.

4. I should have been anxious to take the papers, to which I have referred, at once into consideration, and to offer my assistance, so far as it might have been effective, in the settlement of the question which has unfortunately been at issue between the two Governments; but it appears to me that the benefits likely to be derived from your visit will be so great, that I prefer to postpone my consideration of the papers till after that event.

5. It seems to me quite unnecessary for Her Majesty's Government to review the arguments advanced by the British Columbian Government in their Minute of Council of the 4th January, as to whether or no the Nanaimo Railway had ever been spoken of, or regarded, as an integral portion of the main line, or the results suggested as flowing from this proposition, inasmuch as the Dominion Government during the course of their recent negotiations volunteered to build it, as an independent undertaking, and on circumstances rendering the execution of the project impossible, proposed, as I understand, to ask Parliament to vote in substitution a money payment, a modification, the principle of which I think reasonable.

6. I am glad to perceive that your Ministers recognise the fact that the resolution of the House of Commons passed a few days after the Terms of Union had been ratified by the Dominion Legislature, could not be regarded as having the same force or significance, as if it had formed an integral part of the treaty agreed to by both parties, though even apart from the weight claimed for the resolution itself, the condition asserted in it, namely that the aid to be granted to the construction of the Pacific Railway should not be such as to increase the existing rate of taxation, involves of course a principle, of which neither British Columbia nor any other part of the Dominion should lose sight.

7. I cannot but suppose that the complaints which have reached me from the Government of British Columbia have been founded upon a misapprehension, both with reference to the expression used in the Canadian Minute in Council of the 20th of September, in regard to the cash bonus of $750,000, which it was proposed to award to the Province, as well as to the intentions of the Dominion Ministers. From the reports of the engineers which you have forwarded to me, I am led to believe that no exertions have been spared in the prosecution of the extremely difficult surveys which must necessarily precede the location of the line, and I cannot help entertaining every confidence that the Dominion authorities will continue to exercise effectual diligence in the prosecution of the work.

8. Whilst I fully sympathize with the anxieties which must be felt by those charged with the responsibility of bringing this very great enterprise to a successful termination, and readily acknowledge the difficulties which attend it, I confidently trust that the inhabitants of British Columbia will not fail to remember that they are not merely inhabitants of a Province, but of a great Dominion, and that they will not be less anxious than any of their fellow subjects in any other part of the country to see the work conducted under such circumstances as will be most conducive to the welfare of the community at large.

9. I heartily approve of your journey to British Columbia, and doubt not that the fact of your Ministers concurring so entirely in the visit will be recognized by the inhabitants of the Province as a proof of their good will and solicitude, and I wish it to be understood that no course could have been suggested which would have been more in accordance with my own views. It is indeed because I attach so much importance to the project and entertain so confident a hope of the results likely to arise from it, that I propose to postpone my reply to the Minutes in Council which have been communicated to me from British Columbia and from Canada respectively, and to defer laying before Her Majesty the Petition from the Provincial Assembly, until after I shall have heard from you from Victoria.

10. It only remains for me to notice the complaint of the British Columbian Gov-

ernment that the Minute of Council of September 20th, 1875, of your Government, was not forwarded to them until after a long delay. After the explanations which have been given of this occurrence I am certain that the Government of British Columbia will feel as convinced as I myself am, that it was merely owing to an unfortunate oversight, and I regret that it should have been thought to warrant an imputation which ought never to have been made.

You will be so good as to communicate this Despatch to the Lieutenant-Governor of British Columbia.

I have, &c.,
(Signed) CARNARVON.

No. 162.

The Missing Despatch from the Dominion Government relating to the Reservation of Railway Lands, received in July, 1876, not published until 4th February, 1879

No. 47. (COPY.)
W. S. BOYLE, P. S.

The Lieutenant-Governor to the Secretary of State for Canada.

GOVERNMENT HOUSE,
VICTORIA, B. C., 4th July, 1876.

SIR,—I have the honour to state that I have this day received and laid before my Executive Council your Despatch of the 13th ultimo, and the copy therewith transmitted, of an Order of His Excellency the Governor-General in Council, and of the Memorandum of the Honourable the Minister of Public Works therein referred to, in relation to a conveyance from this Government to that of the Dominion of a tract of land twenty miles in width on each side of the portion of the Canadian Pacific Railway Line surveyed and located in this Province.

I have, &c.,
(Signed) JOSEPH W. TRUTCH.

No. 163.

The Secretary of State to the Lieutenant-Governor.

[Copy sent to Executive Council, 4th July.—(Signed) J. W. T.]

No. 44. (COPY.)
W. S. BOYLE, P. S.

OTTAWA, 13th June, 1876.
[Received 4th July, 1876.]

SIR,—I have the honour to transmit to you herewith, for the consideration of your Government, a copy of an Order of His Excellency the Governor-General in Council, and of the Memorandum of the Honourable the Minister of Public Works, therein referred to, representing the expediency of obtaining from the Government of British Columbia a conveyance of land twenty miles in width on each side of the portion of the Canadian Pacific Railway Line surveyed and located in that Province.

I am, &c.,
(Signed) R. W. SCOTT,
Secretary of State.

No. 164.

Report of the Privy Council, approved by the Governor-General on the 9th June, 1876.

The Committee of Council have had under consideration the Memorandum from the Honourable Mr. Mackenzie, submitting the expediency of obtaining from the Government of British Columbia a conveyance of land twenty (20) miles in width on each side of the portion of the Canadian Pacific Railway Line surveyed and located in that Province, and they respectfully submit their concurrence therein, and advise that a copy thereof, and of this Minute, be transmitted to the Government of British Columbia.

Certified.
(Signed)   W. A. HIMSWORTH,
Clerk, Privy Council.

OTTAWA, 7th June, 1876.

The undersigned has the honour to report:—

That, under the terms by which British Columbia entered the Dominion of Canada, the Government of that Province agreed to convey to the Dominion Government, in trust, to be appropriated in such manner as the Dominion Government may deem advisable, in furtherance of the construction of what is known as the Canadian Pacific Railway, a similar extent of public lands along the line of Railway throughout its entire length in British Columbia, (not to exceed, however, twenty miles on each side of said line, as may be appropriated for the same purpose by the Dominion Government from the public lands of the North-West Territories and the Province of Manitoba.

That the Government of Canada have, already, by Orders in Council, withdrawn from sale or settlement all lands in the Province of Manitoba within twenty miles on each side of the Railway line surveyed, and also for a district twenty miles to the westward of Fort Pelly, in the North-West Territories, and further extending from a point twenty miles westerly of Fort Pelly to a point twenty miles westerly of the mouth of Battle River, and further for twenty miles on each side of the Railway from a point twenty miles westerly of the Battle River to Jasper House, in the Yellow Head Pass, through the Rocky Mountains.

That the line of Railway has been defined and located through part of the Province of British Columbia, and that it is desirable, with a view of enabling the Government of Canada to proceed with the construction of the Railway, that the lands along such line of Railway, and for twenty miles on each side of the line, may be conveyed to the Dominion Government in accordance with the 11th paragraph of the Terms of Union.

The description of the line so located, to which reference is above made, is as follows:—Commencing at a point on the eastern boundary of British Columbia, in the Yellow Head Pass, through the Rocky Mountains, the line follows down the Valley of the River Fraser to Grand Rapids, a distance of about 185 miles; thence westerly, turning the north end of the Cariboo Range and cutting off the great bend of the Fraser, it crosses the latter near the mouth of Willow River; thence south-westerly to a point near the confluence of the Rivers Stewart and Chilacoh.

The undersigned further recommends that communication be had to this effect with the Lieutenant-Governor of British Columbia, requesting that the lands along the line of Railway, as herein described, and for twenty miles on each side of the said line, be forthwith conveyed to the Dominion Government, and that it be represented that an Order of the Lieutenant-Governor in Council, appropriating this tract of land, will at present suffice as a sufficient conveyance of the same, but that it is further suggested that an Act be passed by the Legislature of British Columbia conveying and vesting such appropriation in Her Majesty, for the purposes of the Government of Canada, and to be appropriated in such manner as the said Dominion Government may deem advisable in furtherance of the construction of the said Railway.

He further recommends that in order to give due information to the public, and to prevent squatters or the pre-emption of any portion of the land so conveyed, the Lieutenant-Governor should be invited to give public notice of the passing of such Order in Council, and of the conveyance of the said lands as herein mentioned and herein comprised.

(Signed)   A. MACKENZIE.

No. 165.

Address of His Excellency the Governor-General of Canada, on the subject of the Relations between the Dominion Government and British Columbia, in respect to the Canadian Pacific Railway, delivered at Government House, Victoria, Sept. 20th, 1876, to a Deputation of the Reception Committee.

GENTLEMEN,—I am indeed very glad to have an opportunity before quitting British Columbia of thanking you, and through you the citizens of Victoria, not only for the general kindness and courtesy I have met with during my residence amongst you; but especially for the invitation to the banquet with which you have honoured me. I regret extremely that my engagements did not permit me to accept this additional proof of your hospitality; but my desire to see as much as possible of the country, and my other engagements, forced me most reluctantly to decline it. I shall, however, have a final opportunity of mingling with your citizens at the entertainment arranged for me at Beacon Hill this afternoon, to which I am looking forward with the greatest pleasure. Perhaps, gentlemen, I may be also permitted to take advantage of this occasion to express to you the satisfaction and enjoyment I have derived from my recent progress through such portions of the Province as I have been able to reach within the short period left at my disposal. I am well aware I have visited but a small proportion of your domains, and that there are important centres of population from which I have been kept aloof. More especially have I to regret my inability to reach Cariboo, the chief theatre of your mining industry and the home of a community with whose feelings, wishes, and sentiments it would have been very advantageous for me to have become personally acquainted. Still by dint of considerable exertion I have traversed the entire coast of British Columbia from its southern extremity to Alaska. I have penetrated to the head of Bute Inlet. I have examined Seymour Narrows, and the other channels which intervene between the head of Bute Inlet and Vancouver Island. I have looked into the mouth of Dean's Canal, and passed along the entrance of Gardner's Channel. I have visited Mr. Duncan's wonderful settlement at Metlakatlah, and the interesting Methodist mission at Fort Simpson; and have thus been able to realize what scenes of primitive peace and innocence, of idylic beauty, and material comfort can be presented by the stalwart men and comely maidens of an Indian community under the wise administration of a judicious and devoted Christian missionary. I have passed across the intervening Sound of Queen Charlotte Island to Skidegate, and studied with wonder the strange characteristics of a Hydah village with its forest of heraldic pillars. I have been presented with the sinister opportunity of a descent upon a tribe of our Pagan savages in the very midst of their drunken orgies and barbarous rites; and after various other explorations I have had the privilege of visiting, under very gratifying circumstances, the Royal City of New Westminster. Taking from that spot a new departure, we proceeded up the valley of the Fraser where the river has cloven its way through the granite ridges and bulwarks of the Cascade range, and along a road of such admirable construction, considering the engineering difficulties of the line and the modest resources of the colony when it was built, as does the greatest credit to the able administrator who directed its execution. Passing thence into the open valleys and rounded eminences beyond, we had an opportunity of appreciating the pastoral resources and agricultural capabilities of what is known as the bunch grass country. It is needless to say that wherever we went we found the same kindness, the same loyalty, the same honest pride in their country and its institutions which characterize the English race throughout the world, while Her Majesty's Indian subjects on their spirited horses, which the ladies of their families seemed to bestride with as much ease and grace as their husbands and brothers, notwithstanding the embarrassment of one baby on the pommel and another on the crupper, met us everywhere in large numbers and testified in their untutored fashion their genuine loyalty and devotion to their White Mother. Having journeyed Eastward as far as Kamloops and admired from a lofty eminence in its neighbourhood what seemed an almost interminable prospect of grazing lands and valleys susceptible of cultivation, we were forced with much reluctance to turn our faces homewards to Victoria. And now that I am back, it may, perhaps, interest you to learn what are the impressions I have derived during my journey. Well, I may frankly tell you that I think British Columbia a glorious Province—a Province which Canada should be proud to possess, and whose association with the Dominion she ought to regard as the crowning triumph of Federation. Such a spectacle as its coast line presents is not to be paralleled by any country in the world. Day after day for a whole week, in a vessel of nearly 2,000 tons, we threaded an interminable labyrinth of watery lanes and reaches that wound endlessly in and out of a network of islands, promontories, and peninsulas for thousands of miles, unruffled by the slightest swell from the adjoining ocean, and presenting at every turn an ever shifting combination of rock, verdure, forest, glacier, and snow-capped mountain of unrivalled grandeur and beauty. When it is remembered that this wonderful system of navigation, equally well adapted to the largest line of battle-ship and the frailest canoe, fringes the entire seaboard of your Province and communicates, at points sometimes more than a hundred miles from the coast, with a multitude of valleys stretching eastward into the interior, while at the same time it is furnished with innumerable harbours on either hand, one is lost in admiration at the facilities for inter communication which are thus provided for the future inhabitants of this wonderful region. It is true at the present moment they lie unused except by the Indian fisherman and villager, but the day will surely come when the rapidly diminishing stores of pine upon this continent will be still further exhausted, and when the nations of Europe as well as of America will undoubtedly be obliged to recur to British Columbia for a material of which you will by that time be the principal depository. Already from an adjoining port a large trade is being done in lumber with Great Britain, Europe, Australia, and South America, and I venture to think that ere long the ports of the United States will perforce be thrown open to your traffic. I had the pleasure of witnessing the overthrow by the axes of your woodmen of one of your forest giants, that towered to the height of 250 feet above our heads, and whose rings bore witness that it dated its birth from the reign of the Fourth Edward; and where it grew, and for thousands of miles along the coast beyond it, millions of its contemporaries are awaiting the same fate. With such facilities of access as I have described to the heart and centre of your various forest lands, where almost every tree can be rolled from the spot upon which it grew to the ship which is to transfer it to its destination, it would be difficult to over-estimate the opportunities of industrial development thus indicated; and to prove that I am not over-sanguine in my conjectures, I will read you a letter recently received from the British Admiralty by Mr. Innes, the Superintendent of the Dockyard at Esquimalt:

" From various causes, spars from Canada, the former main source of supply, have " not of late years been obtainable, and the trade in New Zealand spars for top-masts has " also completely died away. Of late years the sole source of supply has been the casual " cargoes of Oregon spars, imported from time to time, and from these the wants of the " service have been met. But my Lords feel that this is not a mode to be depended " upon, more especially for the larger sized spars."

Their Lordships then proceed to order Mr. Innes to make arrangements for the transhipment for the dockyards of Great Britain of the specified number of Douglas pine which will be required by the service during the ensuing year,—and what England does in this direction other nations will feel themselves compelled to do as well. But I have learnt a further lesson: I have had opportunities of inspecting some of the spots where your mineral wealth is stored, and here again the ocean stands your friend, the mouths of the coal pits I have visited almost opening into the hulls of the vessels which are to convey their contents across the ocean. When it is further remembered that inexhaustible supplies of iron ore are found in juxtaposition with your coal, no one can blame you for regarding the beautiful Island on which you live as having been especially favoured by Providence in the distribution of its natural gifts. But still more precious minerals than either coal or iron enhance the value of your possessions. As we skirted the banks of the Fraser we were met at every turn by the evidences of its extraordinary supplies of fish; but scarcely less frequent were the signs afforded us of the golden treasures it rolls down, nor need any traveller think it strange to see the Indian fisher-man hauling out a salmon on to the sands from whence the miner beside him is sifting the sparkling ore. But the signs of mineral wealth which may happen to have attracted my personal attention are as nothing, I understand, to what is exhibited in Cariboo, Cassiar, and along the valley of the Stickeen, and most grieved am I to think that I have not had time to testify by my presence amongst them the sympathy I feel with the adventurous prospector and the miner in their arduous enterprises. I had also the satisfaction of having pointed out to me where various lodes of silver only await greater facilities of access to be worked with profit and advantage. But perhaps the greatest surprise in store for us was the discovery, on our exit from the pass through the Cascade range, of the noble expanse of pastoral lands and the long vistas of fertile valleys which opened up on every side as we advanced through the country; and which, as I could see with my own eyes from various heights we traversed, extended in rounded upland slopes or in gentle depressions for hundreds of miles to the foot of the Rocky Mountains, proving, after all, that the mountain ranges which frown along your coast no more accurately indicate the nature of the territory they guard than is the wall of breaking surf that roars along a tropic beach identical with the softly undulating sea that glitters in the sun beyond. But you will very likely say to me, of what service to us are these resources which you describe, if they and we are to remain locked up in a distant and at present inaccessible corner of the Dominion, cut off by a trackless waste of intervening territory from all intercourse, whether of a social or of a commercial character, with those with whom we are politically united? Well, gentlemen, I can only answer: Of comparatively little use, or at all events of far less profit than they would immediately become were the railway upon whose construction you naturally counted when you entered into Confederation once completed. But here I feel I am touching upon dangerous ground. You are well aware from the first moment I set foot in the Province I was careful to inform every one who approached me that I came here as the Governor-General of the Dominion, the Representative of Her Majesty, exactly in the same way as I had passed through other Provinces of the Dominion, in order to make acquaintance with the people, their wants, wishes, and aspirations, and to learn as much as I could in regard to the physical features, capabilities, and resources of the Province; that I had not come on a diplomatic mission, or as a messenger, or charged with any announcement, either from the Imperial or from the Dominion Government. This statement I beg now most distinctly to repeat. Nor should it be imagined I have come either to persuade or coax you into any line of action which you may not consider conducive to your own interests, or to make any new promises on behalf of my Government, or renew any old ones; least of all have I a design to force upon you any further modification of those arrangements which were arrived at in 1874 between the Provincial and Dominion Governments under the auspices of Lord Carnarvon. Should any business of this kind ever have to be perfected, it will have to be done in the usual constitutional manner through the Secretary of State. But though I have thought it well thus unmistakably and effectually to guard against my journey to the Province being misinterpreted, there is, I admit, one mission with which I am charged—a mission that is strictly within my functions to fulfil—namely, the mission of testifying by my presence amongst you and by my patient and respectful attention to everything which may be said to me, that the Government and the entire people of Canada, without distinction of party, are most sincerely desirous of cultivating with you those friendly and affectionate relations, upon the existence of which must depend the future harmony and solidity of our common Dominion. Gentlemen, this mission I think you will admit I have done my best to fulfil. I think you will bear me witness that I have been inaccessible to no one, that I have shown neither impatience nor indifference during the conversations I have had with you, and that it would have been impossible for any one to have exhibited more anxiety thoroughly to understand your views. I think it will be further admitted that I have done this, without in the slightest degree seeking to disturb or embarrass the march of your domestic politics. I have treated the existing Ministers as it became me to treat the responsible advisers of the Crown in this locality, and I have shown that deference to their opponents which is always due to Her Majesty's loyal opposition. Nay, further, I think it must have been observed that I have betrayed no disposition either to create or foment in what might be termed, though most incorrectly, the interest of Canada, any discord or contrariety of interest between the Mainland and the Island. Such a mode of procedure would have been most unworthy; for no true friend of the Dominion should be capable of any other object or desire than to give universal satisfaction to the Province as a whole. A settlement of the pending controversy would indeed be most lamely concluded if it left either of the sections into which your community is geographically divided unsatisfied. Let me then assure you on the part of the Canadian Government, and on the part of the Canadian people at large, that there is nothing they desire more earnestly or more fervently than to know and feel that you are one with them in heart, thought, and feeling. Canada would indeed be dead to the most self-evident considerations of self-interest and to the first instincts of national pride if she did not regard with satisfaction her connection with a Province so richly endowed by Nature, inhabited by a community so replete with British loyalty and pluck, while it afforded her the means of extending her confines and the outlets of her commerce to the wide Pacific and the countries beyond. It is true circumstances have arisen to create an unfriendly and hostile feeling in your minds against Canada. You consider yourselves injured, and you certainly have been disappointed. Far be it from me to belittle your grievances, or to speak slightingly of your complaints. Happily my independent position relieves me from the necessity of engaging with you in any irritating discussion upon the various points which are in controversy between this Colony and the Dominion Government. On the contrary, I am ready to make several admissions. I don't suppose that in any part of Canada will it be denied that you have been subjected both to anxiety and uncertainty on points which were of vital importance to you. From first to last since the idea of a Pacific Railway was originated, things, to use a homely phrase, have gone "contrairy" with it, and with everybody connected with it, and you in common with many other persons have suffered in many ways. But though happily it is no part of my duty to pronounce judgment in these matters, or to approve, or blame, or criticise the conduct of any one concerned, I think that I can render both Canada and British Columbia some service by speaking to certain matters of fact which have taken place within my own immediate cognizance, and by thus removing from your minds certain wrong impressions in regard to the matters of fact, which have undoubtedly taken deep root there. Now, gentlemen, in discharging this task—I may almost call it this duty—I am sure my observations will be received by those I see around me in a candid and loyal spirit, and that the heats and passions which have been engendered by these unhappy differences will not prove an impediment to a calm consideration of what I am about to say, more especially as it will be my endeavour to avoid wounding any susceptibilities, or forcing upon your attention views or opinions which may be ungrateful to you. Of course I well understand that the gravamen of the charge against the Canadian Government is that it has failed to fulfil its treaty engagements. Those engagements were embodied in a solemn agreement which was ratified by the respective Legislatures of the contracting parties, who were at the time perfectly independent of each other, and I admit they thus acquired all the characteristics of an international treaty. The terms of that treaty were (to omit the minor items) that Canada undertook to secure, within two years from the date of the union, the simultaneous commencement at either end of a railway which was to connect the seaboard of British Columbia with the railway system of the Dominion, and that such railway should be completed within ten years from the date of union in 1871. We are now in 1876. Five years have elapsed, and the work of construction even at one end can be said to have only just begun. Undoubtedly under these circumstances everyone must allow that Canada has failed to fulfil her treaty obligations towards this Province, but unfortunately Canada has been accused not only of failing to accomplish her undertakings, but of what is a very different thing,—a wilful breach of faith in having neglected to do so. Well, let us consider for a moment whether this very serious assertion is true. What was the state of things when the bargain was made? At that time everything in Canada was prosperous: her finances were flourishing, the discovery of the Great North West, so to speak, had inflamed her imagination; above all things railway enterprise in the United States and generally on this continent was being developed to an astounding extent. One trans-continental railway had been successfully executed, and several others on the same gigantic scale were being projected; in fact it had come to be considered that a railway could be flung across the Rocky Mountains as readily as across a hay field, and the observations of those who passed from New York to San Francisco did not suggest any extraordinary obstacles to undertakings of this description. Unfortunately one element in the calculation was left entirely out of account, and that was the comparative ignorance which prevailed in regard to the mountain ranges and the mountain passes which intervened between the Hudson Bay Company's possessions and our Western Coast. In the United States, for years and years, troops of emigrants had passed Westward to Salt Lake City, to Sacramento, and to the Golden Gate; every track and trail through the mountains was wayworn and well known; the location of a line in that neighbourhood was pre-determined by the experience of persons already well acquainted with the locality. But in our case the trans-continental passes were sparse and unfrequented, and from an engineering point of view may be said to have been absolutely unknown. It was under these circumstances that Canada undertook to commence her Pacific Railway in two years, and to finish it in ten. In doing this she undoubtedly pledged herself to that which was a physical impossibility, for the moment the engineers peered over the Rocky Mountains into your Province they saw at once that before any one passage through the devious range before them could be pronounced the best, an amount of preliminary surveying would have to be undertaken which it would require several years to complete. Now there is a legal motto which says *nemo teneatur ad impossibile*, and I would submit to you that under the circumstances I have mentioned, however great the default of Canada, she need not necessarily have been guilty of any wilful breach of faith. I myself am quite convinced that when Canada ratified this bargain with you she acted in perfect good faith and fully believed that she would accomplish her promise, if not within ten years, at all events within such a sufficiently reasonable period as would satisfy your requirements. The mistake she made was in being too sanguine in her calculations, but remember, a portion of the blame for concluding a bargain impossible of accomplishment cannot be confined to one only of the parties to it. The mountains which have proved our stumbling block were your own mountains, and within your own territory, and however deeply an impartial observer might sympathize with you in the miscarriage of the two time terms of the compact, one of which—namely as to the commencement of the line in two years from 1871—has failed, and the other of which, namely, its completion in ten, must fail, it is impossible to forget that yourselves are by no means without responsibility for such a result. It is quite true—in what I must admit to be a most generous spirit—you intimated in various ways that you did not desire to hold Canada too strictly to the letter of her engagements as to time. Your expectations in this respect were stated by your late Lieutenant-Governor, Mr. Trutch, very fairly and explicitly, although a very unfair use has been made of his words, and I have no doubt that if unforeseen circumstances had not intervened, you would have exhibited as much patience as could have been expected of you. But a serious crisis supervened in the political career of Canada. Sir John Macdonald resigned office, and Mr. Mackenzie acceded to power, and to all the responsibilities incurred by Canada in respect to you and your Province. Now it is asserted, and I imagine with truth, that Mr. Mackenzie and his political friends had always been opposed to many portions of Canada's bargain with British Columbia. It therefore came to be considered in this Province that the new Government was an enemy to the Pacific Railway. But I believe this to have been and to be a complete misapprehension. I believe the Pacific Railway has no better friend in Canada than Mr. Mackenzie, and that he was only opposed to the time terms in the bargain because he believed them impossible of accomplishment, and that a conscientious endeavour to fulfil them would unnecessarily and ruinously increase the financial expenditure of the country, and in both these opinions Mr. Mackenzie was undoubtedly right. With the experience we now possess, and of course it is easy to be wise after the event, no one would dream of saying that the railway could have been surveyed, located, and built within the period named, or that any company who might undertake to build the line within that period would not have required double or treble the bonus that would have been sufficient had construction been arranged for at a more leisurely rate, but surely it would be both ungenerous and unreasonable for British Columbia to entertain any hostile feelings towards Mr. Mackenzie on this account, nor is he to be blamed in my opinion if on entering office in so unexpected a manner he took time to consider the course which he would pursue in regard to his mode of dealing with a question of such enormous importance. His position was undoubtedly a very embarrassing one; his Government had inherited responsibilities which he knew, and which the country had cause to know, could not be discharged. Already British Columbia had begun to cry out for the fulfilment of the bargain, and that at the very time that Canada had come to the conclusion that the relaxation of some of its conditions was necessary. Out of such a condition of affairs it was almost impossible but that there should arise, in the first place, delay—for all changes of Government necessarily check the progress of public business—and in the next, friction, controversy, and coll………… Happily it is not necessary that I need dwell……………………… the various points which were……………………………………………… respect to the course my Ministers may have thought it to be……, nor would it be gracious upon my part to criticise the action of your Province during the painful period. Out of the altercation which then ensued there resulted, under the auspices of Lord Carnarvon, a settlement; and when an agreement has been arrived at, the sooner the incidents connected with the conflict which preceded it are forgotten, the better. Here then we have arrived at a new era; the former laches of Canada, if any such there had been, are condoned, and the two time terms of the treaty are relaxed on the one part, while on the other certain specific obligations were superadded to the main article in the original bargain: that is to say—again omitting minor items—the Province agreed to the Pacific Railway being completed in 16 years from 1874, and to its being begun "as soon as the surveys shall have been completed," instead of at a fixed date, while the Dominion Government undertook to construct at once a railway from Esquimalt to Nanaimo, to hurry forward the surveys with the utmost possible dispatch, and as soon as construction should have begun, to spend two millions a year in the prosecution of the work. I find that in this part of the world these arrangements have come to be known as the "Carnarvon Terms." It is a very convenient designation, and I am quite content to adopt it on one condition, namely, that Lord Carnarvon is not to be saddled with any of the original responsibility with regard to any of these terms but one. The main body of the terms are Mr. Mackenzie's; that is to say, Mr. Mackenzie proffered the Nanaimo and Esquimalt Railway, the telegraph line, the waggon road and the annual expenditure. All that Lord Carnarvon did was to suggest that the proposed expenditure should be two millions instead of one and a half millions, and that a time limit should be added. But, as you are well aware, this last condition was necessarily implied in the preceding one relating to the annual expenditure, for once committed to that expenditure Canada would in self defence be obliged to hasten the completion of the line in order to render reproductive the capital she sunk as quickly as possible. It is therefore but just to Lord Carnarvon that he should be relieved from the responsibility of having been in any way the inventor of what are known as the "Carnarvon Terms." Lord Carnarvon merely did what every arbitrator would do under the circumstances; he found the parties already agreed in respect to the principal items of the bargain and was consequently relieved from pronouncing on their intrinsic merits, and proceeded at once to suggest to Canada the further concession which would be necessary to bring her into final accord with her opponent. In pursuance of this agreement the Canadian Government organized a series of surveying parties upon a most extensive and costly scale. In fact, during the last two years two millions of money alone have been expended upon these operations. The Engineer himself has told me that Mr. Mackenzie had given him *carte blanche* in the matter, so anxious was he to have the route determined without delay; and that the mountains were already as full of as many theodolites and surveyors as they could hold. I am aware it is said—indeed as much has been hinted to me since I came here—that these surveys were merely multiplied in order to furnish an excuse for further delays. Well, that is rather a hard saying. But upon this point I can speak from my own personal knowledge, and I am sure that what I say on this head will be accepted as the absolute truth. During the whole of the period under review I was in constant personal communication with Mr. Fleming, and was kept acquainted by that gentleman with everything that was being done. I knew the position of every surveying party in the area under examination. Now Mr. Fleming is a gentleman in whose personal integrity, and in whose personal ability every one I address has the most perfect confidence. Mr. Fleming, of course, was the responsible engineer who planned those surveys and determined the lines along which they were to be carried, and over and over again Mr. Fleming has explained to me how unexpected were the difficulties he had to encounter, how repeatedly after following hopefully a particular route his engineers found themselves stopped by an impassable wall of mountain which blocked the way, and how trail after trail had to be examined and abandoned before he had hit on anything like a practicable route. Even now, after all that has been done, a glance at the map will show you how devious and erratic is the line which appears to afford the only tolerable exit from the labyrinthine ranges of the Cascades. Notwithstanding, therefore, whatever may have been bruited abroad in the sense to which I have alluded, I am sure it will be admitted, nay, I know it is admitted, that so far as the prosecution of the surveys is concerned, Canada has used due diligence, yes, more than due diligence, in her desire to comply with that section of the "Carnarvon Terms" relating to this particular. You must remember that it is a matter of the greatest moment, affecting the success of the entire scheme, and calculated permanently to affect the future destiny of the people of Canada, that a right decision should be arrived at in regard to the location of the western portion of the line, and a Minister would be a traitor to a most sacred trust if he allowed himself to be teased, intimidated or cajoled into any **percipitate decision** on such a momentous point until every possible route had been duly examined. When I left Ottawa the engineers seemed disposed to report that our ultimate choice would lie between two routes, both starting from Fort George, namely, that which leads to the head of Dean's Canal, and that which terminates in Bute Inlet. Of these two the line to Dean's Canal was the shortest by some 40 miles, and was considerably the cheaper by reason of its easier grades. The ultimate exit of this channel to the sea was also more direct than the tortuous navigation out of Bute Inlet; but Mr. Mackenzie added—though you must not take what I am now going to say as a definite conclusion on his part, or an authoritative communication upon mine—that provided the difference in expense was not so great as to forbid it, he would desire to adopt what might be the less advantageous route from the Dominion point of view in order to follow that line which would most aptly meet the requirements of the Province. Without pronouncing an opinion on the merits of either of the routes, which it is no part of my business to do, I may venture to say that in this principle I think Mr. Mackenzie is right, and that it would be wise and generous of Canada to consult the local interests of British Columbia by bringing the line and its terminus within reach of existing settlement, if it can be done without any undue sacrifice of public money. From a recent article in the *Globe* it would seem as though the Bute Inlet line had finally found favour with the Government, though I myself have no information on the point, and I am happy to see from the statistics furnished by that journal that not only has the entire line to the Pacific been at last surveyed, located, graded, and its profile taken out, but that the calculated expenses of construction though very great, and to be incurred only after careful consideration, are far less than were anticipated. Well, gentlemen, should the indications we have received of the intentions of the Government prove correct, you are very much to be congratulated, for I am well aware that the line to Bute Inlet is the one which you have always favoured, and I should hope that now at last you will be satisfied that the Canadian Government has used, as it undertook to do, all possible expedition in prosecuting the surveys of the line to the Pacific Coast. I only wish that Waddington Harbour, at the head of the Inlet, was a better port. I confess to having but a very poor opinion of it, and certainly the acquaintance I have made with Seymour Narrows and the intervening channels which will have to be bridged or ferried, did not seem to me to be very favourable to either operation. Well, then, we now come to the Esquimalt and Nanaimo Railway. I am well aware of the extraordinary importance you attach to this work, and of course I am perfectly ready to admit that its immediate execution was promised to you in the most definite and absolute manner under Lord Carnarvon's arbitration. I am not, therefore, surprised at the irritation and excitement occasioned in this city by the non-fulfilment of this item in the agreement—nay, I will go further, I think it extremely natural that the miscarriage of this part of the bargain should have been provocative of very strenuous language and deeply embittered feelings; nor am I surprised that as is almost certain to follow on such occasions, you should in your vexation put a very injurious construction on the conduct of those who had undertaken to realize your hopes; but still I know that I am addressing high-minded and reasonable men, and moreover that you are perfectly convinced that I would sooner cut my right hand off than utter a single word that I do not know to be an absolute truth. Two years have passed since the Canadian Government undertook to commence the construction of the Esquimalt and Nanaimo Railway, and the Nanaimo and Esquimalt Railway is not even commenced, and what is more there does not at present seem a prospect of its being commenced. What then is the history of the case, and who is answerable for your disappointment? I know you consider Mr. Mackenzie. I am not here to defend Mr. Mackenzie, his policy, his proceedings, or his utterances. I hope this will be clearly understood. In anything I have hitherto said I have done nothing of this sort, nor do I intend to do so. I have merely stated to you certain matters with which I thought it well for you to be acquainted, because they have been misapprehended, and what I now tell you are also matters of fact, within my own cognizance and which have no relation to Mr. Mackenzie as the head of a political party, and I tell them to you not only in your own interest, but in the interest of public morality and English honour. In accordance with his engagements to you in relation to the Nanaimo and Esquimalt Railway Mr. Mackenzie introduced as soon as it was possible a Bill into the Canadian House of Commons, the clauses of which were admitted by your Representatives in Parliament fully to discharge his obligation to yourselves and to Lord Carnarvon in respect to that undertaking, and carried it through the Lower House by a large majority. I have reason to think that many of his supporters voted for the Bill with very great misgivings both as to the policy of the measure, and the intrinsic merits of the Railway, but their leader had pledged himself to exercise his Parliamentary influence to pass it, and they very properly carried it through for him. It went up to the Senate and it was thrown out by that body by a majority of two. Well, I have learnt with regret that there is a very widespread conviction in this community that Mr. Mackenzie had surreptitiously procured the defeat of his own measure in the Upper House. Had Mr. Mackenzie dealt so treacherously by Lord Carnarvon, by the Representative of his Sovereign in this country, or by you, he would have been guilty of a most atrocious act, of which I trust no public man in Canada or in any other British Colony could be capable. I tell you in the most emphatic terms, and I pledge my honour on the point, that Mr. Mackenzie was not guilty of any such base and deceitful conduct—had I thought him guilty of it either he would have ceased to have been Prime Minister or I should have left the country. But the very contrary was the fact. While these events were passing I was in constant personal communication with Mr. Mackenzie. I naturally watched the progress of the Bill with the greatest anxiety, because I was aware of the eagerness with which the act was desired in Victoria, and because I had long felt the deepest sympathy with you in the succession of disappointments to which, by the force of circumstances you had been exposed. When the Bill passed the House of Commons by a large majority with the assent of the leader of the opposition, in common with everyone else, I concluded it was safe, and the adverse vote of the Senate took me as much by surprise as it did you and the rest of the world. I saw Mr. Mackenzie the next day and I have seldom seen a man more annoyed or disconcerted than he was; indeed he was driven at that interview to protest with more warmth than he has ever used against the decision of the English Government, which had refused, on the opinion of the law officers of the Crown, to allow him to add to the members of the Senate, when soon after his accession to office, Prince Edward Island had entered Confederation. "Had he been permitted," he said to me, "to have exercised his rights in that respect, "this would not have happened, but how can these mischances be prevented in a body, " the majority of which, having been nominated by my political opponent is naturally "hostile to me." Now, gentlemen, your acquaintance with Parliamentary Government must tell you that this last observation of Mr. Mackenzie's was a perfectly just one. But my attention has been drawn to the fact that two of Mr. Mackenzie's party supported his Conservative opponents in the rejection of the Bill, but surely you don't imagine that a Prime Minister can deal with his supporters in the Senate as if they were a regiment of soldiers. In the House of Commons he has a better chance of maintaining a party discipline, for the constituencies are very apt to resent any insubordination on the part of their members towards the leader of their choice. But a Senator is equally independent of the Crown, the Minister, or the people, and as in the House of Lords at Home, so in the second Chamber in Canada, gentlemen will run from time to time on the wrong side of the post. But it has been observed—granting that the two members in question did not vote as they did at Mr. Mackenzie's instigation—he has exhibited his perfidy in not sending in his resignation as soon as the Senate had pronounced against the Bill. Now, gentlemen, you cannot expect me to discuss Mr. Mackenzie's conduct in that respect. It would be very improper for me to do so, but though I cannot discuss Mr. Mackenzie's conduct, I am perfectly at liberty to tell you what I myself should have done had Mr. Mackenzie tendered to me his resignation. I should have tol him that, in my opinion such a course was quite unjustifiable, that as the House of Commons was then constituted I saw no prospect of the Queen's Government being advantageously carried on except under his leadership, and that were he to resign at that time the greates inconvenience and detriment would ensue to the public service. That is what I should have said to Mr. Mackenzie, in the event contemplated, and I have no doubt that the Parliament and the people of Canada would have confirmed my decision. But it has been furthermore urged that Mr. Mackenzie ought to have resigned to force the Bill. Well, that is again a point I cannot discuss, but I may tell you t is, there is Mr. Mackenzie had done so, I very much doubt whether he would have succeeded in carrying it a second time even in the House of Commons. The fact is that Canada at large, whether rightly or wrongly I do not say, has unmistakingly shown its approval of the vote in the Senate. An opinion has come to prevail from one end of the Dominion to the other, an opinion which I find is acquiesced in by a considerable proportion of the inhabitants of British Columbia, that the Nanaimo and

Esquimalt Railway cannot stand upon its own merits, and that its construction as a Government enterprise would be, at all events at present, a useless expenditure of the public money. Now again let me assure you that I am not presuming to convey to you any opinion of my own on this much contested point. Even did I entertain any misgivings on the subject it would be very ungracious for me to parade them in your presence and on such an occasion. I am merely communicating to you my conjecture why it is that Mr. Mackenzie has shown no signs of his intention to re-introduce the Nanaimo and Esquimalt Railway Bill into Parliament, viz.:—because he had no chance of getting it passed. Well, then, gentlemen, of whom and what have you to complain? Well, you have every right from your point of view to complain of the Canadian Senate. You have a right to say that after the Government of the day had promised that a measure upon which a majority of the inhabitants of an important Province had set their hearts should be passed, it was ill-advised and unhandsome of that body not to confirm the natural expectations which had thus been gendered in your breasts, especially when that work was itself offered as a solution to you for a previous injury. I fully admit that it is a very grave step for either House of the Legislature, and particularly for that which is not the popular branch, to disavow any agreement into which the Executive may have entered, except under a very absolute sense of public duty. Mind, I am not saying that this is not such a case, but I say that you have got a perfect right from your own point of view, so to regard it. But, gentlemen, that is all. You have got no right to go beyond that. You have got no right to describe yourselves as a second time the victims of a broken *agreement*. As I have shown you, the persons who had entered into an engagement in regard to this Railway with you and Lord Carnarvon had done their very best to discharge their obligations. But the Senate who counteracted their intention, had given no preliminary promises whatsoever either to you or to the Secretary of State. They rejected the Bill in the legitimate exercise of their constitutional functions, and there is nothing more to be said on this head, so far as that body is concerned, either by you or Lord Carnarvon, for I need not assure you that there is not the slightest chance that any Secretary of State in Downing street would attempt anything so unconstitutional, so likely to kindle a flame throughout the whole Dominion, as to coerce the free legislative action of her Legislature. But there is one thing I admit the Senate has done, it has revived in their integrity those original treaty obligations on the strength of which you were induced to enter Confederation, and it has re-imposed upon Mr. Mackenzie and his Government the obligation of offering you an equivalent for that stipulation in the "Carnarvon Terms" which he has not been able to make good. Now, from the very strong language which has been used in regard to the conduct of Mr. Mackenzie, a bystander would be led to imagine that as soon as his Railway Bill had miscarried, he had cynically refused to take any further action in the matter. Had my Government done this they would have exposed themselves to the severest reprehension, and such conduct would have been both faithless to you and disrespectful to Lord Carnarvon; but so far from having acted in this manner, Mr. Mackenzie has offered you a very considerable grant of money in consideration of your disappointment. Now here again I won't touch upon the irritating controversies which have circled round this particular step in these transactions. I am well aware that you consider this offer to have been made under conditions of which you have reason to complain. If this has been the case it is most unfortunate, but still whatever may have been the sinister incidents connected with the past, the one solid fact remains that the Canadian Government has offered you $750,000 in lieu of the railway. This sum has been represented to me as totally inadequate, and as very far short of an equivalent. It may be so or it may not be so. Neither upon that point will I offer an opinion, but still I may mention to you the principle upon which that sum has been arrived at. Under the Nanaimo and Esquimalt Railway Bill, whose rejection by the Senate we have been considering, Canada was to contribute a bonus of $10,000 a mile; the total distance of the line is about 75 miles, consequently the $750,000 is nothing more or less than this very bonus converted into a lump sum. Now since I have come here it has been represented to me by the friends of the railway that it is a line which is capable of standing on its own merits, and that a company had been almost induced to take it up some time ago as an unsubsidized enterprise. Nay, only yesterday the local paper which is the most strenuous champion for the line, asserted that it could be built for $2,000,000; that the lands—which, in lieu of $750,000, were to be replaced by Mr. Mackenzie at your disposal—were worth several millions more, and that the railway itself would prove a most paying concern. If this is so, and what better authority can I refer to, is it not obvious that the bonus proposal of the Dominion Government assumes at least the semblance of a fair offer, and even if you did not consider it absolutely up to the mark, it should not have been denounced in the very strong language which has been used. However, I do not wish to discuss the point whether the $750,000 was a sufficient offer or not. I certainly am not empowered to hold out to you any hopes of an advance—all that I would venture to submit is that Mr. Mackenzie having been thwarted in his *bonâ fide* endeavour to fulfil this special item in the "Carnarvon Terms" has adopted the only course left to him in proposing to discharge his obligations by a money payment. I confess I should have thought this would be the most natural solution of the problem, and that the payment of a sum of money equivalent to the measure of Mr. Mackenzie's original obligation, to be expended under whatever conditions would be most immediately advantageous to the Province, and ultimately beneficial to the Dominion, would not have been an unnatural remedy for the misadventure which has stultified the special stipulation in regard to the Nanaimo and Esquimalt Railway, but of course of these matters you yourselves are the best judges, and I certainly have not the slightest desire to suggest to you any course which you may think contrary to your interests. My only object in touching upon them at all is to disabuse your minds of the idea that there has been any intention upon the part of Mr. Mackenzie, his Government, or of Canada, to break their faith with you. Every single item of the "Carnarvon Terms" is at this moment in the course of fulfilment. At enormous expense the surveys have been pressed forward to completion; the fifty millions of land and the thirty millions of money to be provided for by Canada under the Bill are ready; the profiles of the main line have been taken out, and the most elaborate information has been sent over to Europe in regard to every section of country through which it passes; several thousand miles of the stipulated telegraph have been laid down, and now that the location of the western terminus seems to have been determined, though upon this point I have myself no information, tenders I imagine will be called for almost immediately. Whatever further steps may be necessary to float the undertaking as a commercial enterprise will be adopted and the promised waggon-road will necessarily follow *pari passu* with construction. Well, then, gentlemen, how will you stand under these circumstances? You will have got your line to Bute Inlet. Now I will communicate to you a conclusion I have arrived at from my visit to that locality. If the Pacific Railway once comes to Bute Inlet, it cannot stop there. It may pause there for a considerable time, until Canadian trans-Pacific traffic with Australia, China, and Japan shall have begun to expand, but such a traffic once set going, Waddington Harbour will no longer serve as a terminal port, in fact it is no harbour at all, and scarcely an anchorage,—the Railway must be prolonged under these circumstances to Esquimalt, that is to say if the deliberate opinion of the Engineers should pronounce the operation feasible, and Canada shall in the meantime have acquired the additional financial stability which would justify her undertaking what under any circumstances must prove one of the most gigantic achievements the world has ever witnessed. In that case of course the Nanaimo Railway springs into existence of its own accord, and you will then be in possession both of your money compensation and of the thing for which it was paid, and with this result I do not think you should be ill-satisfied. But should the contrary be the case, the prospect is indeed a gloomy one; should hasty counsels, and the exhibition of an impracticable spirit throw these arrangements into confusion, interrupt or change our present railway programme, and necessitate any re-arrangement of your political relations, I fear Victoria would be the chief sufferer. I scarcely like to allude to such a contingency, nor, gentlemen, are my observations directed immediately to you. Now I know very well that neither those whom I am addressing nor do the greater majority of the inhabitants of Vancouver Island or of Victoria, participate in the views to which I am about to refer, but still a certain number of your fellow citizens, gentlemen with whom I have had a great deal of pleasant and interesting conversation, and who have shown to me personally the greatest kindness and courtesy, have sought to impress me with the belief that if the Legislature of Canada is not compelled by some means or other, which however they do not specify, to make forthwith these 70 miles of railway, they will be strong enough, in the face of Mr. Mackenzie's offer of a money equivalent, to take British Columbia out of the Confederation. Well, they certainly won't be able to do that. I am now in a position to judge for myself as to what are the real sentiments of the community. I will even presume to say I know more about it than these gentlemen themselves. When once the main line of the Pacific Railway is under weigh, the whole population of the Mainland would be perfectly contented with the present situation of affairs, and will never dream of detaching their fortunes from those of Her Majesty's great Dominion. Nay, I don't believe that these gentlemen would be able to persuade their fellow citizens even of the Island of Vancouver to so violent a course; but granting for the moment that their influence should prevail,—what would be the result? British Columbia would be still part and parcel of Canada. The great work of Confederation would not be perceptibly affected. But the proposed line of the Pacific Railway might possibly be deflected south. New Westminster would certainly become the capital of the Province, the Dominion would naturally use its best endeavours to build it up into a flourishing and prosperous city. It would be the seat of Government, and the home of justice, as well as the chief social centre on the Pacific Coast. Burrard Inlet would become a great commercial port, and the miners of Cariboo with their stores of gold dust would spend their festive and open-handed winters there. Great Britain would of course retain Esquimalt as a naval station on this coast, as she has retained Halifax as a naval station on the other, and inasmuch as a constituency of some 1,500 persons would not be able to supply the material for a Parliamentary Government, Vancouver and its inhabitants, who are now influential by reason of their intelligence rather than their numbers, would be ruled as Jamaica, Malta, Gibraltar, Heligoland, and Ascension are ruled, through the instrumentality of some Naval or other Officer. Nanaimo would become the principal town of the Island, and Victoria would lapse for many a long year into the condition of a village, until the development of your coal fields, and the growth of a healthier sentiment had prepared the way for its re-incorporation with the rest of the Province; at least that is the horoscope I should draw for it in the contingency contemplated by these gentlemen. But God forbid that any such prophecy should be realized. I believe the gentlemen I have referred to are the very last who would desire to see the fulfilment of their menaces, and I hope they will forgive me if I am not intimidated by their formidable representations. When some pertinacious philosopher insisted on assailing the late King of the Belgians with a rhapsody on the beauties of a Republican Government His Majesty replied, "You forget, sir, I am a Royalist by profession." Well, a Governor General is a Federalist by profession, and you might as well expect the Sultan of Turkey to throw up his cap for the commune as the Viceroy of Canada to entertain a suggestion for the disintegration of the Dominion. I hope therefore they will not bear me any ill-will for having declined to bow my head beneath their " separation " arch. It was a very good humoured, and certainly not a disloyal bit of " bounce " which they had prepared for me. I suppose they wished me to know they were the "arch" enemies of Canada. Well, I have made an arch reply. But gentlemen, of course, I am not serious in discussing such a contingency as that to which I have referred. Your numerical weakness as a community is your real strength, for it is a consideration which appeals to every generous heart. Far be the day when on any acre of soil above which floats the flag of England, mere material power, brute political preponderance, should be permitted to decide such a controversy as that which we are discussing. It is to men like yourselves who, with unquailing fortitude and heroic energy have planted the laws and liberties and the blessed influences of English homes amidst the wilds and desert plains of savage lands, that England owes the enhancement of her prestige, the diffusion of her tongue, the increase of her commerce and her ever-widening renown, and woe betide the Government or Statesmen who, because its inhabitants are few in number and politically of small account, should disregard the wishes or carelessly dismiss the representations however bluff, boisterous or downright, of the feeblest of our distant colonies. No, gentlemen, neither England or Canada would be content or happy in any settlement that was not arrived at with your own hearty approval and consent, and equally satisfactory to every section of your Province; but we appeal to your moderation and practical good sense to assist us in resolving the present difficulty, —the genius of the English race has ever been too robust and sensible to admit the existence of an irreconcileable element in its midst. It is only among weak and hysterical populations that such a growth can flourish; however hard the blows given and taken during the contest, Britishers always find a means of making up the quarrel, and such I trust will be the case on the present occasion. My functions as a constitutional ruler are simply to superintend the working of the political machine, but not to intermeddle with its action. I trust that I have observed that rule on the present occasion and that, although I have addressed you at considerable length, I have not said a word which has not been strictly within my province to say or has intruded on those domains which are reserved for my responsible advisers. As I warned you would be the case, I have made no announcement, I have made no promise, I have hazarded no opinion upon any of the administrative questions now occupying the joint attention of yourselves and the Dominion. I have only endeavoured to correct some misapprehensions by which you have been possessed in regard to matters of historical fact, and I have testified to the kind feeling entertained for you by your fellow subjects in Canada, and to the desire of my Government for the re-establishment of the friendliest and kindest relations between you and themselves, and I trust that I may carry away with me the conviction that from henceforth a less angry and irritated feeling towards Canada will have been inaugurated than has hitherto subsisted. Of my own earnest desire to do anything I can to forward your views so far as they may be founded in justice and reason I need not speak. My presence here and the way in which I have spent my time will have convinced you of what has been the object nearest my heart. I cannot say how glad I am to have come, or how much I have profited by my visit, and I assure you none of the representations with which I have been favoured will escape my memory or fail to be duly submitted in the proper quarter.

And now, gentlemen, I must bid you good-bye; but before doing so there is one other topic upon which I am desirous of touching. From my first arrival in Canada I have been very much preoccupied with the condition of the Indian population in this Province. You must remember that the Indian population are not represented in Parliament, and consequently that the Governor-General is bound to watch over their welfare with especial solicitude. Now, we must all admit that the condition of the Indian question in British Columbia is not satisfactory. Most unfortunately, as I think, there has been an initial error ever since Sir James Douglas quitted office, in the Government of British Columbia neglecting to recognize what is known as the Indian title. In Canada this has always been done; no Government, whether provincial or central, has failed to acknowledge that the original title to the land existed in the Indian tribes and communities that hunted or wandered over them. Before we touch an acre we make a treaty with the chiefs representing the lands we are dealing with, and having agreed upon and paid the stipulated price, oftentimes arrived at after a great deal of haggling and difficulty, we enter into possession, but not until then do we consider that we are entitled to deal with an acre. The result has been that in Canada our Indians are contented, well affected to the white man, and amenable to the Laws and Government. At this very moment the Lieutenant-Governor of Manitoba has gone on a distant expedition in order to make a treaty with the tribes to the northward of the Saskatchewan. Last year he made two treaties with the Sioux and Crows; next year it has been arranged that he should make a treaty with the Blackfeet, and when this has been done the British Crown will have acquired a title to every acre that lies between Lake Superior and the top of the Rocky Mountains. But in British Columbia, except in a few cases where, under the jurisdiction of the Hudson Bay Company or under the auspices of Sir James Douglas, a similar practice has been adopted, the British Columbia Government has always assumed that the fee simple as well as the sovereignty resided in the Queen. Acting upon this principle they have granted extensive grazing leases and otherwise so dealt with various sections of the country as greatly to restrict or interfere with the prescriptive rights of the Queen's Indian subjects. As a consequence there has come to exist a very unsatisfactory feeling amongst the Indian population. Intimations of this reached me at Ottawa two or three years ago, and since I have come into the Province my misgivings on the subject have been confirmed. Now, I confess I consider that our Indian fellow-subjects are entitled to exactly the same civil rights under the law as are possessed by the white population, and that if an Indian can prove a prescriptive right of way to a fishing station, or a right of way of any other kind, that that right should no more be ignored than if it was the case of a white man. I am well aware that among the coast Indians the land question does not present the same characteristics as in other parts of Canada, or as it does in the grass countries of the interior North. I have also been able to understand that in these latter districts it may be even more necessary to deal justly and liberally with the Indian in regard to his land rights even than on the prairies of the North-West. I am very happy to think that the British Columbia Government should have recognized the necessity of assisting the Dominion Government in ameliorating the present condition of affairs in this respect, and that it has agreed to the creation of a joint commission for the purpose of putting the interests of the Indian population on a more satisfactory footing. Of course in what I have said I do not mean that, in our desire to be humane and to act justly, we should do anything unreasonable or Quixotic, or that rights already acquired by white men should be inconsiderately invaded or recalled; but I would venture to put the Government of British Columbia on its guard against the fatal eventualities which might arise should a sense of injustice provoke the Indian population to violence or into collision with our scattered settlers. Probably there has gone forth amongst them very incorrect and exaggerated information of the warlike achievements of their brethren in Dakotah, and their uneducated minds are incapable of calculating chances. Of course there is no danger of any serious or permanent revolt, but it must be remembered that even an accidental collision in which blood was shed might have a most disastrous effect upon our present satisfactory relations with the warlike tribes in the North-West, whose amity and adhesion to our system of government is so essential to the progress of the Pacific Railway; and I make this appeal, as I may call it, with all the more earnestness since I have convinced myself of the degree to which, if properly dealt with, the Indian population might be made to contribute to the development of the wealth and resources of the Province. I have now seen them in all phases of their existence, from the half naked savage, perched like a bird of prey, in a red blanket, upon a rock trying to catch his miserable dinner of fish, to the neat Indian maiden in Mr. Duncan's school at Metlakatlah, as modest and as well dressed as any clergyman's daughter in an English parish, or to the shrewd horse-riding Siwash of the Thompson Valley, with his racers in training for the Ashcroft stakes and as proud of his stackyard and turnip field as a British squire. In his first condition it is evident he is scarcely a producer or consumer; in his second he is eminently both; and in proportion as he can be raised to the higher level of civilization will be the degree to which he will contribute to the vital energies of the Province. What you want are not resources, but human beings to develop them and to consume them. Raise your 60,000 Indians to the level Mr. Duncan has taught us they can be brought and consider what an enormous amount of vital power you will have added to your present strength. But I must not keep you longer. I thank you most heartily for your patience and attention. Most earnestly do I desire the accomplishment of all your aspirations, and if ever I have the good fortune to come to British Columbia again I hope it may be by—Rail.

No. 166.

The Earl of Carnarvon to the Earl of Dufferin.

CANADA.
No. 362.

DOWNING STREET,
December 18th, 1876.

MY LORD,—I duly received Your Lordship's Despatch (No. 190 of the 30th June last, enclosing a Report of a Committee of the Executive Council of British Columbia, respecting the course taken by the Dominion Government in reference to the construction of the Canadian Pacific Railway. This report, together with the previous one of the 4th January, and the Petition to the Queen from the Legislative Assembly of the Province, have received my very careful consideration.

2. In my despatch (No. 113 of the 23rd May) I informed you that I proposed to postpone any reply to the Minutes of Council, which had previously reached me from British Columbia and Canada respectively, upon this subject; and that I should also defer laying before the Queen the Petition from the Provincial Assembly, until after your contemplated visit to British Columbia.

3. It has not yet been possible for you to complete and transmit to me your official report of this visit, but as I understand that the meeting of the British Columbia Legislature is now near at hand, I think I ought not any longer to withhold from the Governments of the Dominion and of the Province an expression of my opinion, so far as it has yet been possible for me to form one, on the principal questions now at issue.

4. Although, in visiting British Columbia, you were not charged to offer any explanations or to make any proposals, either on behalf of Her Majesty's Government or of your Ministers, to the Government and people of the Province, I naturally anticipated that the result of your communications with them would be to enlighten them as to the views and policy of the Dominion Government, and the difficulties with which that Government has had to contend in fulfilling the terms of the settlement which I proposed

in 1874; and consequently would tend to allay the irritation which had been felt in the Province on account of the failure of the Bill providing for the Nanaimo and Esquimalt Railway, as well as on other points in regard to which the people of British Columbia have been dissatisfied.

5. I have already learnt enough of your proceedings to feel assured that I do not misinterpret the result of your visit, in believing that my anticipations, as above expressed, have been to a great extent fulfilled, and that public opinion in British Columbia will at all events be prepared to concur with me in the opinion that the circumstances of the case are such as to render it not unreasonable that the Dominion Government should ask for time, and an indulgent consideration of their own difficulties, in order that they may fulfil, to the best of their ability, the obligations under which they find themselves placed.

6. If I do not at this moment comply with the representations of the Assembly and Council of the Province, that I should urge upon the Government of Canada the strict and immediate fulfilment of the obligations to which I have referred in the preceding paragraph, it is because I appreciate, more distinctly perhaps than it is possible for the people of the Province to do, the position in which the Dominion Government has been placed by the failure of the Island Railway Bill. I recognize, moreover, the fact that there are many considerations which require that the whole of this most important question of the Pacific Railway should be treated with the utmost deliberation consistent with the pressing requirements of the Province, and that no hasty action should be pressed upon the Canadian Government, whom, I need hardly say, I believe to be thoroughly sincere in their desire to construct the main line of railway with all the expedition of which the resources of the country and the engineering problems remaining yet unsolved will admit.

7. After much and anxious consideration, and with every sympathy for the sense of disappointment under which I see that the people of British Columbia are labouring, I cannot avoid the conclusion that the objections which have been made against the course taken by the Dominion Government have been couched in more severe and exaggerated language than a fair estimate of the peculiar embarrassments and the difficulties of the case would seem to justify.

8. The British Columbian Government must, I feel sure, be convinced (as I am) that the surveys of the line have been prosecuted with the greatest vigour and dispatch possible, that these surveys are now approaching completion, and that every effort has been made by the Government of Canada to hurry forward the antecedent preparations necessary to the construction of the railway.

9. It must, of course, be expected that, even after the completion of the surveys upon the spot, a great amount of work will remain to be done in the Engineer's office, and the Dominion Government will require time to consider fully, after sufficiently accurate data have been collected, not only the exact proportions and details of the undertaking, but also the calls which it will entail upon the resources of the country. Those, again, who may be disposed to contract for sections of the line, and some of whom may not improbably be resident in England, would presumably require to send their agents to the localities, in order to make such calculations as would enable them to tender for the work.

10. There is a further question of the greatest importance which has weighed much with me. Not only is it evident that the route inland must be laid down with sufficient precision for the purpose, but the question of the terminus is one in which the most serious consequences are obviously involved, and with regard to which, after having recourse to the information now in the possession of the Lords Commissioners of the Admiralty, I see clearly that we have not at present the materials for any definite conclusion.

11. The future success of the railway is, indeed, in so great a degree dependent upon a proper approach to the sea being selected, that it would be obviously improper for the Canadian Government to be hurried into a premature decision on this point by any untimely pressure. For example, grave objections, I understand, may be urged against the Bute Inlet route, which has been looked upon with much favour, on account of the inadequacy of its head waters as a safe anchorage; and unless the Railway could hereafter be practically prolonged to some point in Vancouver Island, such as Barclay Sound or Esquimalt, by means of steam ferry navigation across the intervening channels, it appears difficult to see how this route could be adopted.

12. The question of the terminus on the Pacific is in fact one which can only be decided after fuller and more conclusive reports have been procured from Marine Engineers or Naval Officers than have yet been obtained, and these considerations, coupled with other circumstances, make it now evident that with the best intentions and exertions, and under the most favourable circumstances, no serious commencement of the Railway within the Province can be at once made.

13. Between the coming spring, however, and the spring of 1878, it may fairly be expected that many points now surrounded with doubt will have become more clearly defined, and I fully hope and believe that after the very limited delay of a single summer the Province of British Columbia will find that there is no longer any obstacle to the active prosecution of the undertaking, and I trust that the Province will not fail to perceive with me that its case will be by no means strengthened if impatience (however natural) under other circumstances is displayed at the non-commencement of a line of a Railway the proper course and terminus of which are as yet altogether uncertain, while at the same time an independent observer must admit that the Canadian Government are using every exertion to carry out the work as rapidly as possible.

14. I will not now further notice the offer made to British Columbia, by Canada, of a money payment in lieu of the Esquimalt and Nanaimo Railway, and in compensation for delay, than by observing that I could not with advantage at the present moment enter into the question of the sufficiency or otherwise of the amount offered. The present condition of the whole question renders it, in my opinion, premature to discuss this particular point inasmuch as the duration of the delay in commencing the main line of Railway may become, equitably at all events, a material consideration in estimating the amount which should be paid to the Province. It would, however, be a source of much satisfaction to me to learn that the Province were willing to accept the principle of a money equivalent for the line in question, the construction of which I am bound to say does not appear to me likely to be the most judicious expenditure of capital.

15. To sum up, then, the considerations to which I have referred, I wish you to inform your advisers and the Provincial Government that, while I do not feel myself in a position to decline to entertain the representations pressed upon me by the Province, I am nevertheless at this moment unable to pronounce an opinion as to the course which should be taken, either with regard to the Esquimalt and Nanaimo Railway or with regard to the delays which have occurred, or which may yet occur, in the construction of the main line. Until it is known what is to be the route and terminus of that line and what offers may be made by contractors for its construction, I feel that it would be improper to come to any conclusions on the subject.

16. I sincerely regret the immense engineering difficulties which have presented themselves and which have necessarily rendered impracticable in some respects the settlements which I recommended in 1874, but I am satisfied that the Dominion Government has contended with them to the best of its ability; and while I trust that the Province will now wait patiently until the terminus can be settled and tenders for the work can be received, I shall be ready when in possession of this information to assist so far as I can, if both parties should desire it, in the settlement of the minor, though of course very important, question which has arisen as to the compensation offered in substitution for the Railway on the Island.

I have, &c.,
(Signed)   CARNARVON.

No. 167.

Telegram.

The Lieutenant-Governor to the Secretary of State for the Colonies.

VICTORIA, B.C., 8th January, 1877.

To Earl Carnarvon, Secretary of State, London.

My Ministers are anxious to convene Legislature directly and to place before House Her Majesty's decision on Petition of February, 1876, respecting Canadian Pacific Railway, and request me earnestly to beg your Lordship to telegraph at once to me the substance of the decision arrived at.

(Signed)   A. N. RICHARDS,
Lieutenant-Governor.

No. 168.

Telegram.

The Secretary of State to the Lieutenant-Governor.

LONDON, 17th January, 1877.

To *Lieutenant-Governor Richards.*

Pacific Railway. I write direct by mail, and trust no conclusions will be formed nor action taken pending receipt of Despatch.

(Signed)   CARNARVON.

No. 169.

The Governor-General's Secretary to Lieutenant-Governor Richards.

GOVERNOR-GENERAL'S OFFICE,
OTTAWA, 5th January, 1877.

SIR,—I have the honour, by desire of His Excellency the Governor-General, to forward to you, for the information of your Government, the accompanying copy of a Despatch (No. 362, Dec. 18th, 1876), from the Secretary of State for the Colonies, acknowledging the receipt of a despatch from His Excellency transmitting a Report of a Committee of the Executive Council of British Columbia, respecting the course taken by the Dominion Government in reference to the construction of the Canadian Pacific Railway.

I have, &c.,
(Signed)   E. G. P. LITTLETON,
Governor-General's Secretary.

No. 170.

Telegram.

The Lieutenant-Governor to the Secretary of State for the Colonies.

VICTORIA, B.C., 2nd February, 1877.

To *Earl Carnarvon, Secretary of State.*

Pacific Railway. Is Despatch of 18th December to Governor-General the same mentioned in your telegram?

(Signed)   A. N. RICHARDS.

No. 171.

Telegram.

The Secretary of State for the Colonies to Lieutenant-Governor.

6th February, 1877.

Lieutenant-Governor Richards, British Columbia.

My telegram of 17th January referred to Despatch dated 18th January, which was supplementary to that of 18th December, and should be read with it.

(Signed)   CARNARVON.

No. 172.

The Earl of Carnarvon to Lieutenant-Governor Richards.

BRITISH COLUMBIA.

DOWNING STREET,
18th January, 1877.

SIR,—I duly received your telegram informing me that your Ministers are anxious to convene the Legislature directly, and to place before the House Her Majesty's decision on the Petition of February, 1876, respecting the Canadian Pacific Railway, and requesting me to telegraph to you the substance of the decision arrived at.

2. I replied by my telegram of the 17th instant, informing you that I was about to write to you by the mail, and trusted that no conclusions would be arrived at nor action taken until the arrival of my Despatch.

3. I now wish to explain to you that on the 18th of December last, I addressed a Despatch to the Governor-General of Canada (No. 362), setting forth at length the views of Her Majesty's Government in regard to the Railway question.

4. A copy of that Despatch has, I am informed by Lord Dufferin, been transmitted to you, and it is my desire that it should be regarded as addressed as much to the Province of British Columbia in answer to the representations received from the Council and Assembly, as to the Government of the Dominion.

5. I feel assured that your Government and Legislature will give due weight to the recommendations therein contained, and that they will accept my assurance that after careful and anxious consideration of the subject, I feel that any attempt at this precise moment to come to a final decision would be inexpedient in the interest of any party, and would create fresh difficulties to the settlement of the question on that just and satisfactory footing which Her Majesty's Government so earnestly desire.

6. As you are well aware, it is not usual for the Secretary of State to correspond direct with a Provincial Government, the rules of the service requiring that all such communications should be made to the Governor General. As, however, I have been led to understand that in the present case your Government have expected a direct communication from Her Majesty's Government, I have addressed this Despatch to you, and have explained to the Governor-General the circumstances under which I have done so.

I have, &c.,
(Signed)   CARNARVON.

No. 173.

Report of the Executive Council, approved by the Lieutenant-Governor on the 26th day of March, 1877.

The Committee of Council, having had before them the Despatch of the Earl of Carnarvon to the Earl of Dufferin, dated 18th December 1876, and the Despatch of the Earl of Carnarvon to Lieutenant-Governor Richards, dated 18th January, 1877, in reply to the Petition of the Legislative Assembly of British Columbia to Her Most Gracious Majesty the Queen and to the Report of a Committee of the Executive Council of British Columbia, dated 3rd June, 1876, and having reference to the non-fulfilment by the Canadian Government of the modified Railway agreement recommended in 1874 by the Right Honourable the Earl of Carnarvon, in substitution for the 11th clause of the Terms of Union under which British Columbia entered the Canadian Confederation, report,—

1. That they desire to thank Lord Carnarvon, Her Majesty's Principal Secretary of State for the Colonies, for the careful attention he has devoted to the consideration of the complaint of the Province concerning the failure of the Dominion Government to commence Railway construction in British Columbia.

2. That they deeply regret that His Lordship should have been unable to feel himself in a position to urge upon Canada the necessity of carrying into effect at once the terms of the agreement entered into in 1874; inasmuch as the continued delay, deepening, as it naturally does, the sense of disappointment and injury under which the people of the Province have so long laboured, renders it difficult to sustain that feeling of confidence in the Canadian Government without which it will be impossible for the union to be productive of beneficial results, either to the Dominion or the Province.

3. That they, however, feel that they are bound to accept the recommendations of Lord Carnarvon to concede to the Dominion Government the short delay of another summer, which his Lordship informs them is still necessary to enable fuller and more conclusive reports to be procured from Marine Engineers and Naval Officers than have yet been obtained, and which His Lordship states are necessary for the determination of the question of the Railway terminus on the Pacific.

4. That with regard to the acceptance by the Province of a money equivalent in lieu of the Esquimalt and Nanaimo portion of the Railway, and in compensation for delay, they do not think it advisable to re-open the terms, and are, therefore, not prepared to enter upon the consideration of the question.

5. That they desire to reiterate in the most distinct and emphatic manner their earnest protest against the unwarrantable assumption by the Dominion Government that the Treaty obligation to construct the Canadian Pacific Railway has been limited or in any degree modified or affected by the Resolution of the 11th of April, 1871, passed by the House of Commons several days after the Terms of Union creating that obligation had been adopted and ratified by the Parliament of Canada.

6. That they desire particularly to report, that the succession of failures on the part of the Dominion Government to fulfil the several Railway agreements solemnly entered into with this Province, has produced a feeling of disappointment and distrust, so wide-spread and intense, as to severely and injuriously affect the commercial and industrial interests, and seriously retard the general prosperity of this portion of the Dominion.

7. The Committee request that Your Excellency will be pleased, if this Report be approved, to cause copies thereof to be severally forwarded to the Right Honourable the Secretary of State for the Colonies, and to the Honourable the Secretary of State for Canada.

Certified,
(Signed) W. SMITHE,
Minister of Finance and Clerk Executive Council.

No. 174.

Papers relating to the non-fulfilment by Canada of the Railway Clause of the Terms of Union, not published until 5th February, 1879.

The Governor-General of Canada to the Lieutenant-Governor.

GOVERNOR-GENERAL'S OFFICE,
Ottawa, 31st July, 1877.

SIR,—I am directed by His Excellency the Governor-General to transmit to you the accompanying copy of a despatch from the Secretary of State for the Colonies, acknowledging the receipt of a copy of a Report of a Committee of the Executive Council of the Province of British Columbia, relating to the Canadian Pacific Railway question.

I have, &c.,
(Signed) JOHN KIDD,
For Governor-General's Secretary.

The Earl of Carnarvon to the Earl of Dufferin.

CANADA.   DOWNING STREET,
No. 219.   19th July, 1877.

MY LORD,—I have the honour to acknowledge the receipt of your despatch, No. 165, of the 18th June, enclosing a Minute of your Privy Council, with a despatch from the Lieutenant-Governor of British Columbia covering a copy of a Report of a Committee of the Executive Council of the Province relating to the Canadian Pacific Railway.

I had already received this Report of the Executive Council in your despatch, No. 117, of the 19th of April.

As it has been agreed to allow a reasonable time for the settlement of certain necessary preliminaries, which I am confident will be industriously used, it is obviously desirable that I should now confine myself to a general expression of the satisfaction with which I have learnt the acquiescence of the Provincial Government in the proposal for a temporary suspension of the negotiations and discussions upon this matter.

I have, &c.,
(Signed) CARNARVON.

No. 175.

Report of the Executive Council approved by the Lieutenant-Governor on the 8th day of November, 1877.

The Committee of Council having had under consideration the subject of the construction of the Canadian Pacific Railway, report :—

That the year having nearly elapsed, which was represented by the Right Hon. the Secretary of State for the Colonies as being required by the Dominion Government to enable it to determine the route and terminus of the Canadian Pacific Railway, it is highly desirable that the Government of this Province should be advised at the earliest period possible of the result of the year's surveys, in order that they may be in a position to convene the Legislature at an early date, and lay before it definite information with reference to the intention of the Dominion Government to carry out its Railway obligations to this Province, under the terms of the settlement recommended in 1874 by the Earl of Carnarvon, and agreed to by the Dominion Government as well as that of this Province.

That having complied with the request of Lord Carnarvon to grant the delay he thought necessary, as represented in his despatches of dates the 18th of December, 1876, and 18th January, 1877, respectively, the people of British Columbia now feel that his Lordship will be careful to discountenance any further unnecessary delay in the commencement of railway construction within the Province; and they confidently expect that on or before the expiration of the year his Lordship will be able to give the Government an assurance that actual construction will be begun as soon as tenders can be received and contracts awarded; and that work thereon be prosecuted thereafter in a manner that will ensure the ultimate completion of the undertaking within such reasonable period as the interests of the Empire, the Dominion and the Province alike demand.

The Committee advise that the Report be approved, and that copies be forwarded by his Honour the Lieutenant-Governor to the Right Honourable the Secretary of State for the Colonies, and the Secretary of State for the Dominion of Canada.

Certified,
(Signed) WM. SMITHE,
Minister of Finance and Clerk Executive Council.

No. 176.

The Secretary of State to the Lieutenant-Governor.

OTTAWA, 29th December, 1877.

SIR,—With reference to your despatch of the 9th ultimo, and the accompanying Minute of your Executive Council of the 8th of that month, I have the honour to transmit to you herewith, for the information of your Government, a copy of an Order of his Excellency the Governor-General in Council on the subject of the construction of the Canadian Pacific Railway.

I have, &c.,
(Signed) R. W. SCOTT.

No. 177.

Report of the Privy Council, approved by the Governor-General on the 24th December, 1877.

The Committee have had under consideration the despatch from the Lieutenant-Governor of British Columbia of the 9th of November, 1877, enclosing copy of a Minute of his Executive Council of the 8th of that month, which had been forwarded to the Secretary of State for the Colonies, on the subject of the construction of the Canada Pacific Railway.

The Honourable the Minister of Public Works, to whom the above despatch and enclosure were referred, observes that the Minute in question calls the attention of the Secretary of State for the Colonies to the delay the Earl of Carnarvon thought necessary in commencing the construction of the Pacific Railway, in his despatches of December 18th, 1876, and January 18th, 1877, and states that the British Columbia Government are anxious to obtain a knowledge of the result of the year's surveys as early as possible, in order that they may be in a position to convene the Local Legislature at an early date, and lay before it "definite information as to the intentions of the Dominion Government to carry out its railway obligations."

The Minister reports that the delay deemed necessary before advertising for tenders was consequent upon the manifest necessity of making a careful instrumental survey of the Fraser valley route, upon which an exploratory survey only had been made in previous years.

That, as early as the season permitted, a large staff of engineers was sent to perform this work under the immediate charge of Mr. Cambie.

That the field work was finished about the beginning of November, and in the course of that month the engineers returned to Ottawa, where they are now engaged in plotting the results of the season's operations.

That it will take some time yet to accomplish this, and to report in such detail as will enable the Government to come to a decision as to the value of the route. That it is impossible to venture upon any decided opinion in advance of the complete report, maps, and profiles of the road, which are now in course of preparation.

That the Government also took necessary steps to obtain accurate information regarding the possibility of a route to the ocean at Port Essington, at the mouth of the Skeena river; as well as to ascertain the feasibility of a better pass through the Rocky Mountains in the vicinity of Pine river. That the information on both these points will be embraced in the Report of the Engineer, and will include the Reports of the Naval Officers upon the harbour at the mouth of the Skeena.

That, so far as can be seen at present, there would appear to be no necessity for any further explorations in British Columbia with the view of the determination of the best route from the summit of the Rocky Mountains to the sea.

That the conclusion reached will be duly communicated to the Secretary of State for the Colonies.

The Committee concur in the foregoing report, and advise that a copy of this Minute be transmitted to Lord Carnarvon and to the Lieutenant-Governor of British Columbia.

Certified.
(Signed) W. A. HIMSWORTH,
Clerk Privy Council, Canada.

No. 178.

Report of the Privy Council approved by the Governor-General on the 17th April, 1877.

On a Report, dated 16th April, 1877, from the Honourable the Minister of Public Works, stating that special efforts have been made during the past summer and autumn to procure information through the Officers of the Admiralty and Royal Navy, respecting the several harbours and roadways on the Coast of British Columbia, but that it would appear no surveys have yet been made of the coast adjacent to the mouth of the River Skeena, and that no decided opinion has been obtained regarding the waters in that quarter;

That, as the Dominion Government have no means of conducting an examination in that direction, he recommends that a request be forwarded to the Imperial Government that they will direct a nautical survey to be made during the coming season of the channels and approaches at the point indicated, and that surveys should be made of Frederick Arm, and the waters leading thereto, as decided information respecting this point should be obtained before a final decision is arrived at, fixing the seaport terminus of the Canada Pacific Railway.

The Committee concur in the foregoing recommendation, and submit the same for Your Excellency's approval.

Certified. (Signed) W. A. HIMSWORTH,
Clerk, Privy Council.

No. 179.

Admiral DeHorsey to Secretary of the Admiralty.

(No. 326.)   "Shah" at Esquimalt, 9th October, 1877.

Sir,—With reference to the directions of the Lords Commissioners of the Admiralty, contained in your letter, No. 86, of the 19th May last, (received 14th August), I have the honour to report that I sent the "Daring," Commander Hanmer, to make a general examination of the channels and approaches of the River Skeena.

From Commander Hanmer's report, and from such information as I have been able to obtain, I am of opinion that, whether in view of communication with the inhabited parts of British Columbia, or of through traffic across the Pacific, the vicinity of Skeena is totally unfit for the ocean terminus of the proposed Canadian Pacific Railway. The mere circumstance that the bars of the river are not navigable for ocean steamers, except at high water, is of itself condemnatory, in my opinion. Added to this are the difficulties of tortuous approaches on a very foggy and rainy coast, and that the land in the vicinity is reported to consist of mountains and swamps, offering little inducement to settlers.

I beg to transmit herewith a copy of my orders to Commander Hanmer, and of his report, accompanied by plans of the mouth of the Skeena and of Woodcock's Landing.

The lateness of the season and the almost constant rain, caused a service of this kind (necessarily performed in open boats) to be somewhat arduous. I submit Commander Hanmer's execution of it for their Lordship's approval.

I have forwarded a copy of this report and enclosures for the information of the Governor-General of Canada.

I have, &c.,
(Signed)   A. DeHorsey,
Rear Admiral and Commander-in-Chief.

No. 180.

Report of the examination of the River Skeena by Commander Hanmer.

H. M. S. "Daring" at Departure Bay,
4th October, 1877.

Sir,—I have the honour, in accordance with your directions, dated 22nd August, 1877, to report the result of my examination of the channels and approaches to the River Skeena, British Columbia.

1. As regards the channels and approaches of the three named respectively, Telegraph, Middle and North Channels, Telegraph Channel is available at high water for ships drawing 25 feet up to Port Essington, the deepest water being on the mainland side, abreast of Kennedy Island, and on the Island side abreast of DeHorsey Island (as will be seen by the plan annexed), heavy tide rips occur at springs. The passage between Kennedy and DeHorsey Islands I have designated as the "Middle;" it is between sand banks, which, I should think are liable to shift at different seasons of the year, and is only fit for small steamers. North Channel (or North Skeena Passage), has a passage for steamers of light draught, and is entered over a flat with about three fathoms low water springs, and has an outlet between DeHorsey Island and the mainland of only half a cable in width, at low water the ebb tide setting strongly through it. I do not recommend it for large vessels. Port Essington should therefore be reached from the Westward, either by the Browning Entrance, Ogden Channel and Cardena Bay, or by Dixon Entrance, Chatham Sound, Arthur Channel and Cardena Bay.

2. *Anchorages*—Skeena River has an extensive anchorage ground between Port Essington and the north end of DeHorsey Island; holding ground is good, being soft mud; at springs heavy tide rips occur, making boat or lighter work dangerous. Mr. Cunningham (a trader of many years experience at Port Essington), informed me that the river was never frozen at Port Essington, but great quantities of ice come down in the spring, as well as immense trees. During the winter months heavy gales from the north are frequent, and I should think, would completely suspend communication between the shore and vessels in the stream, as there is no shelter from their full force. High water approximate 1·0·0, F. & C. rise 24 feet springs.

Woodcock's Landing affords a fair anchorage, but is limited in extent (plan annexed), it is more sheltered than Port Essington, and is free from tide rips, although the ebb tide runs between four and five knots at springs; holding ground is good, being mud off the village, H. W. F. & C., 12 ʰ 15, rise springs 24 feet approximate, neaps 17 feet (vessels must moor).

Cardena Bay is the best anchorage in the vicinity, being sheltered from N. and S. E.; holding ground is good; tide sets fairly through the anchorage; H. W. F. & C., noon springs rise 24 feet; neaps, 17 feet approximate.

The prevailing winds in the vicinity of the Skeena are said to be westerly during the summer months, and during the remainder of the year S.E. and N. E., with heavy gales occasionally from the north. Fogs are frequent in August and September. Rain is prevalent in spring and autumn and during the stay of the "Daring." From 1st to 27th September, the prevailing winds were easterly and south-easterly, with almost constant rain and frequent squalls; during the same time the barometer's lowest was 28° 90′; highest, 30° 30′.

The land about the entrance of the Skeena is mountainous and densely wooded (chiefly cedar and hemlock) and shows signs of a remarkably wet climate, and, I should say, is quite unfit for settlement.

                    I have, &c.,
                        (Signed)   JOHN G. HANMER,
J. H. CLEVERTON,   *Commander.*
   Secretary.

181.

Report of Admiral DeHorsey respecting Canadian Pacific Railway Terminus.

                                         "SHAH" AT ESQUIMALT,
                                              26th October, 1877.

SIR,—I request you will bring under the consideration of the Lords Commissioners of the Admiralty the following observations, submitting my opinion relative to the best site for the ocean terminus of the Canadian Pacific Railway.

2. With a view to forming an opinion on this subject I have carefully perused the reports of exploration of 1874 and 1877, made by Mr. Sanford Fleming, the Engineer-in-Chief, and I have had the advantage of personal interviews with Mr. Marcus Smith, Mr. Cambie, and other Engineers of the Survey. An ascent of the Fraser River, as far as Yale, and on to Boston Bar by land, has enabled me to form some idea of the difficulty of penetrating the Cascade Range of mountains with a line of railway. I have further inspected Burrard Inlet, Haro and Georgia Straits (as well as the inner channels emerging at Active Pass), Discovery Passage and some of the channels in the vicinity of Valdes Island, including Seymour Narrows. An examination has also been made by their Lordships' direction of the approaches to the Skeena River, the result of which has been reported in my letter, No. 326, of the 9th instant.

3. The question of site of ocean terminus should, it appears to me, be determined by two main considerations (besides feasibility in an engineering point of view):—

   1st. Its suitability for the interests and traffic of the populated parts of British Columbia, that Province having joined the Dominion upon the promise of a railway.

   2nd. Its being situated at a convenient port for ocean steamers to take up, direct from wharf accommodation, the through traffic for Australia, China, Japan, and other places across the Pacific at all seasons of the year and in all weathers.

4. Bearing in mind these considerations, it appears desirable to reject all idea of a terminus on the coast between Vancouver and Queen Charlotte Islands. The navigation of that part of the coast, judging from the charts and from the reports of Admiral Richards and other naval officers, is decidedly unfavourable, and I should equally reject the vicinity of the River Skeena owing to the prevalence of fog, ice, and other climatic causes incident to a high latitude, as well as to the difficulties of approach from sea.

5. If the above views are correct, the question of site for the terminus is narrowed to a choice between Burrard Inlet and a port in Vancouver Island.

6. Burrard Inlet does not appear suitable for an ocean terminus on account of difficulties of navigation to seaward. The tortuous channel from Burrard Inlet to sea through Haro Strait will frequently be unsafe on account of the strength of the tide,

great prevalence of fog and absence of anchoring depth. Burrard Inlet itself also, although possessing a safe port in Coal Harbour, and a good anchorage in English Bay, has these objections, viz.: that the narrow entrance to Coal Harbour through the First Narrows is hardly safe for large steamers in consequence of the rapidity of the tide; and that English Bay, although affording good anchorage, would not, in my opinion, be smooth enough during north-westerly gales for ships to lie at wharves, there being a drift of forty miles to the north-west.

7. Another grave objection to Burrard Inlet as the final terminus, is the possession of San Juan and Stuart Islands by a foreign power. These Islands form the key of the navigation inside Vancouver Island. In case of war with the United States that power might readily stop our trade through Haro Strait. (San Juan was visited last month by General Sherman. I believe with a view to its fortification.)

8. Condemning Burrard Inlet for the above reasons, I conclude that the terminus should be in Vancouver Island, which may be reached in three ways:—

1st. By steam ferry carrying a train from Burrard Inlet to Nanaimo.
2nd. By bridging Seymour Narrows.
3rd. By steam ferry, carrying a train from Estero Basin (Frederick Arm) to Otter Cove.

9. The train once landed on Vancouver Island, can, I understand, be carried without much difficulty either to Esquimalt or to Quatsino Sound, or perhaps to Barclay Sound, where Uchucklesit Harbour forms an admirable port.

10. The first method of crossing the Strait, that of a steam ferry from Burrard Inlet to Nanaimo, has three objections,—1st. The drawbacks above mentioned to navigating the First Narrows, and to going alongside a wharf in English Bay; 2nd. The difficulty and certain frequent detention in mid-channel, owing to fog; 3rd. The heavy sea with north-westerly and south-easterly gales, which would be at least inconvenient for the conveyance of a train across the Strait of Georgia. Another, and I think a cardinal objection, to the route by the course of the Fraser River and Burrard Inlet, is its passing within six or eight miles of United States territory, and its consequent liability to destruction when most wanted in time of war.

11. The second method, that of a line of railway across Valdes Island, without water conveyance, would require very expensive bridging. Valdes is not one island as shown on the Admiralty Chart, but consists of three or four Islands.

The main difficulty, of course, exists in bridging Seymour Narrows, a distance of 2,575 feet, in two spans of respectively 1,200 and 1,350 feet. To execute this work the middle pier has to be erected on a rock, said to be eighteen feet under water at low tide, with a velocity of tide over it from five to eight knots. This would be a work of vast magnitude and expense, even if it be practicable to place a foundation on the rock, which I doubt, as there is hardly any slack tide. Nor must it be forgotten that bridging Seymour Narrows would, as regards large ships, obstruct the only practicable channel between Vancouver Island and the Main. This alone should, in my opinion, preclude its attempt.

12. The third method, and the one I recommend, that of ferrying a train from Estero Basin to Otter Cove, is, in my opinion, not only feasible, but perfectly simple. I have carefully examined this route, and find :—

1st. That Otter Cove is well adapted for a pile dock terminus for the steam ferry.
2nd. That the head of Frederick Arm, at the entrance to Estero Basin, is also well adapted for a pile dock terminus.
3rd. That the channel between the two is easy of navigation, being nearly straight, free from dangers, smooth as glass, sheltered from all winds, and having very little tidal stream.

13. The tide in this, the Nodales Channel, is noted on the chart as running from two to three knots, but I think it is much less.

I spent five hours in this channel during what should have been the strength of the tide, the day before the full moon, and found the tide scarcely perceptible.

The distance for steam ferry between the two ports is thirteen miles of still clear navigation, and I consider it may, with proper signals, be safely traversed in a fog.

14. In advocating the route by Frederick Arm, it will be observed that I am assuming that the railway can be brought to that point.

This assumption is borne out by Mr. Fleming's report of 1877, in which he states it to be "a feasible scheme," but one exacting a heavy expenditure, which expenditure would, I suppose, be in part compensated by the route No. 6, from Yellow Head Pass to the head of Bute Inlet, being estimated at two million dollars less than that by the Lower Fraser (No. 2) to Burrard Inlet.

15. From conversation with Mr. Marcus Smith (the principal officer of the survey, next to the Engineer-in-Chief) I am given to understand that the Rocky Mountains can be crossed at a comparatively low level, and that the line can be carried through a far less mountainous district by avoiding Yellow Head Pass altogether, and selecting a route by Lesser Slave Lake and Pine River Pass, and thence in a more or less direct line to Bute Inlet. Should this prove correct, it will be an additional reason for ending the main line route at Frederick Arm rather than at Burrard Inlet, omitting, as I do, all consideration of taking water conveyance from the head of Bute Inlet on account of its length and tortuous passages, which would be impracticable in foggy weather.

16. Having thus come to the conclusion that the line should pass by Frederick Arm, and that the train should be conveyed by steam ferry through Nodales Channel, to Otter Cove, the extension to one of the good ports of Vancouver Island remains to be considered.

17. In future years, I imagine for the sake of more direct through ocean traffic, a line will be extended to Quatsino Sound, by bridging Quatsino Narrows, and thence on to a terminus at Winter Harbour.

18. But for present wants, it seems that the line should be continued from Otter Cove past Baynes Sound and Nanaimo to Esquimalt, there to make the ocean terminus. This port is easy and safe of approach at all times; its dock (to take the largest ships) has been commenced, and there is reason to think that the line coming from the principal collieries and iron districts on Vancouver Island, ought to pay itself in great part by the conveyance of minerals to Esquimalt for shipment. Not only for trade, but for the supply of coal to Her Majesty's Squadron at Esquimalt, a line of rail from Nanaimo would be advantageous, as the possession of San Juan might enable the United States, in case of war, to cut off our supply from the mines by sea.

19. Assuming, therefore, that a line of rail between Esquimalt and Nanaimo will be constructed, not only for the reasons above detailed, but because its construction appears to have been virtually promised by the Dominion Government in accordance with Lord Carnarvon's suggestion (a large portion of the rails are actually lying at Esquimalt), the chief difficulty connected with the Vancouver part of the through line will be overcome, for I understand that the extension of the line from Nanaimo to Otter Cove presents comparatively few difficulties.

20. It will be observed that I have omitted consideration of a terminus in Howe Sound. This is because the same objections in respect to difficulties of navigation to sea through Haro Strait, apply to Howe Sound as to Burrard Inlet, and with greater force. The route to Howe Sound is also, I observe, estimated to cost six million dollars more than that to Bute Inlet.

21. Finally, whilst submitting the foregoing remarks in accordance with their Lordship's instructions to me, of the 23rd August, 1876, I beg to express much diffidence in respect to such as are not strictly within the scope of the Naval Service. Viewing the shortness of my stay in British Columbia waters, this Report cannot pretend to deserve much weight; but it has, I submit, one merit, that of coming from an officer who, from his position, must be totally disconnected from all local interests.

I have, &c.,

(Signed)   A. DeHorsey,
Rear Admiral and Commander-in-Chief.

The Secretary to the Admiralty.

No. 182.

Report of the Executive Council, approved by the Lieutenant-Governor on the 18th day of March, 1878.

On a memorandum from the Honourable Minister of Finance, dated 16th March, 1878, reporting that it is desirable that it be represented to the Dominion Government that definite information relative to the commencement of Railway construction in the Province should be communicated immediately to this Government, in order that, before the prorogation of the Provincial Legislature, an assurance may be given of the intention of the Dominion Government to carry out in good faith the intimation of Lord Carnarvon that the year which has now passed should terminate the delay in beginning actual construction of Railway, and recommending that His Excellency the Lieutenant-Governor be requested to forward, by telegraph, to the Secretary of State for the Dominion, the following despatch:—

"Pacific Railway. Government desire to be definitely informed immediately if construction will be commenced in this Province at an early period of present season."

The Committee advise that the recommendation be approved.

      Certified,
      (Signed) WM. SMITHE,
       Minister of Finance and Clerk Executive Council.

No. 183.

The Secretary of State to the Lieutenant-Governor.

No. 26.   OTTAWA, 15th March, 1878.
               [Received 5th April, 1878.]

SIR,—I have the honour to acquaint you, for the information of your Government, that a despatch has been received from the Right Honourable the Secretary of State for the Colonies, stating that the present position of the Canadian Pacific Railway question is under his consideration.

      I am, &c.,
      (Signed) R. W. SCOTT,
           Secretary of State.

No. 184.

The Secretary of State to the Lieutenant-Governor.

              OTTAWA, 27th March, 1878.
               [Received 16th April, 1878.]

SIR,—Your telegram of March 19th, stating that your Government desired to be definitely informed immediately if the construction of the Pacific Railroad will be commenced in British Columbia at an early period of the present season, was duly received.

I have to inform you that the Engineers have not yet completed the mapping and calculations of the last season's work. As soon as this is done, the Government will endeavour to finally decide upon the route to be taken through British Columbia, when tenders will be invited in accordance with the terms of the Railway Act of 1874.

No time has been lost by Government in promoting this enterprise, as they have pushed on the work as rapidly as possible, with a view to a commencement being made at the earliest practicable date.

      I have, &c.,
      (Signed) R. W. SCOTT,
           Secretary of State.

No. 185.

The Secretary of State to the Lieutenant-Governor.

              OTTAWA, 31st May, 1878.
               [Received 22nd June, 1878.]

SIR,—I am directed to transmit to you herewith, for the consideration of your Government, a copy of a letter from the Secretary of the Department of Public Works, in which it is requested that certain land therein described may be reserved for the purpose of the probable terminus of the Canadian Pacific Railway at Burrard Inlet.

      I have, &c.,
      (Signed) R. W. SCOTT,
           Secretary of State.

No. 186.

DEPARTMENT OF PUBLIC WORKS, CANADA,
Ottawa, May 29th, 1878.

SIR,—I am directed by the Honourable the Minister of Public Works to inform you that an Order in Council has passed, on the 23rd instant, cancelling that of the 7th June, 1873, which designated Esquimalt in Vancouver Island as the Terminus of the Canadian Pacific Railway, and required the conveyance to the Canadian Government of a strip of land twenty miles in width along the Eastern Coast of that Island, between Seymour Narrows and the Harbour of Esquimalt.

I am further directed to state that, as Burrard Inlet will in all probability be adopted as the Western Terminus of the Canadian Pacific Railway, it is deemed advisable that a strip of Land should be reserved, for the conveyance to the Dominion Government, in accordance with the eleventh paragraph of the Terms of Union, along said line of Railway, beginning at English Bay or Burrard Inlet, and following the Fraser River to Lytton; thence by the valley of the River Thompson to Kamloops; thence up the valley of the North Thompson, passing near to Lakes Albreda and Cranberry, to Tête Jaune Cache; thence up the valley of the Fraser River to the summit of Yellow Head or boundary between British Columbia and the North-West Territories.

The Honourable the Minister of Public Works desires me to request you to convey the foregoing information to the Government of British Columbia, in order that they may take the necessary steps to reserve the land in question.

I have, &c.,

(Signed) F. BRAUN,
Secretary.

No. 187.

Report of the Executive Council, approved by the Lieutenant-Governor on the 2nd day of July, 1878.

On a Memorandum dated 2nd July, 1878, from the Minister of Finance, reporting that an advertisement dated 14th June, 1878, appears in the Daily British *Colonist,* stating that tenders will be received at the C. P. Railway Office, Victoria, till 4 P. M. on the 8th July next, for the removal of 5,266 tons steel rails now lying at Esquimalt, to certain places on Fraser River, and recommending that his Honour the Lieutenant-Governor be requested to telegraph to the proper authorities at Ottawa, requesting that a contract be not awarded for removal nor the rails removed, and informing them that a despatch on the subject to the Dominion Government will follow by mail.

The Committee advise that the recommendation be approved.

Certified.

(Signed) T. B. HUMPHREYS,
Clerk Executive Council.

No. 188.

[TELEGRAM.]

The Lieutenant-Governor to the Secretary of State for Canada.

JULY 3RD, 1878.

Local Government request that steel rails at Esquimalt be not moved nor contract awarded for their removal. Despatch on the subject will follow by mail.

(Signed) A. N. RICHARDS.

No. 189.

Report of the Executive Council, approved by the Lieutenant-Governor on the 13th day of July, 1878.

On a Memorandum, dated the 9th day of July, 1878, from the Honourable the Attorney-General, reporting that the Dominion Government have, by current advertisements in the local newspapers, invited tenders for the removal of over 5,000 tons of steel rails from Esquimalt and Nanaimo to Yale and other distant places on the River Fraser. The Committee of Council would observe that, although no official intimation of the intentions of the Dominion Government with respect to the rails has reached this Government, yet the advertisements so strongly indicate a determination on the part of the Dominion Government to ignore one of their principal Railway engagements with the Province, that an expression of opinion by this Government upon the facts before them seems imperatively necessary. Besides, silence on a matter of such grave importance might hereafter be regarded as acquiescence in the course contemplated by the Dominion Government, and possibly be injuriously interpreted as a passive surrender by British Columbia of one, at least, of its railway rights. For these reasons the Provincial Government sent the following telegram on the 3rd instant to the Secretary of State at Ottawa:—

"Local Government request that the steel rails at Esquimalt be not removed, nor "contract be awarded for their removal. Despatch on the subject will follow by mail."

The rails alluded to were landed by the Dominion Government, at Esquimalt and Nanaimo in 1875, ostensibly for the purpose of carrying into effect that condition of the Railway Settlement of 1874 which expressly bound the Dominion to establish immediate Railway communication between Esquimalt and Nanaimo—an obligation that still exists and that has not been, even partially, observed though the necessary surveys of the route have long since been completed.

The proposed transport of the rails (if carried out) must be regarded as a deliberate infraction, by the Dominion Government, of the above obligation, as their removal will, of necessity, indefinitely postpone the construction of a work which, in 1874, they undertook, after much deliberation, to press to completion "with all practicable "dispatch."

The Committee therefore protest against the rails being removed or used except for the purpose for which they were manifestly intended, and they would strongly but respectfully urge the Dominion Government to adhere to their Railway engagements with the Province.

The Committee also deem it advisable that the Dominion Government should be respectfully requested to immediately inform this Government of their intentions with respect to Railway construction both on the Mainland and Island, in order that the information may be imparted to the House of Assembly early in August next.

The Committee advise that, if this Minute be approved, a copy thereof be sent to the Dominion Government with a request that the information asked for be forwarded as desired. Certified.

(Signed) T. BASIL HUMPHREYS,
Provincial Secretary and Clerk Executive Council.

No. 190.

The Lieutenant-Governor to the Secretary of State.

GOVERNMENT HOUSE,
VICTORIA, B. C., July 16th, 1878.

SIR,—Referring to my telegram to you of the 3rd instant, requesting that certain steel rails lying at Esquimalt be not removed, nor contract awarded for their removal, as advertised for in the local newspapers, I have now the honour to enclose you a copy of a Minute of my Executive Council, giving the views of my Government on this subject. I have, &c.,

(Signed) A. N. RICHARDS.

No. 191.

Report of the Executive Council, approved by the Lieutenant-Governor on the 3rd day of August, 1878.

The Committee of Council recommend that a Reservation, in accordance with the request of the Dominion Government, as expressed in their despatch of the 31st of May, 1878, be made of all lands lying within the limits mentioned in the said despatch, save such lands as have been applied for under the 61st and 62nd Sections of the Land Act of 1875, and lands that have been alienated under the provisions of the said Act, or that are held or occupied by settlers on the date hereof.

The Committee would remark that the reservation of the land is not required by or in accordance with the Terms of Union, but that they consider it advisable in order to facilitate and, if possible, hasten railway construction on the Mainland.

The Committee advise that the recommendation be approved, and that the Dominion Government be furnished with a copy hereof, and also be informed that the Reservation has been made.

Certified.
(Signed)   T. BASIL HUMPHREYS,
Provincial Secretary and Clerk Executive Council.

No. 192.

Public Notice.

Whereas by an Order in Council, dated the 23rd day of May, 1878, of the Honourable the Privy Council of Canada, it has been decided that "Burrard Inlet will, in all probability, be adopted as the Western Terminus of the Canadian Pacific Railway, it is deemed advisable that a strip of land should be reserved, for the conveyance to the Dominion Government, in accordance with the eleventh paragraph of the Terms of Union, along said line of Railway, beginning at English Bay on Burrard Inlet, and following the Fraser River to Lytton; thence by the valley of the River Thompson to Kamloops; thence up the valley of the North Thompson, passing near the Lakes Albreda and Cranberry, to Tête Jaune Cache; thence up the Valley of the Fraser River to the summit of Yellow Head or boundary between British Columbia and the North-West Territories."

And whereas it has been deemed advisable that the land within the limits, and in the direction aforesaid, should be reserved prior to a conveyance being made thereof.

Public Notice is, therefore, hereby given, that from and after this date the land above-mentioned is reserved accordingly for Railway purposes.

By Command.
T. B. HUMPHREYS,
Provincial Secretary's Office, 3rd August, 1878.   *Provincial Secretary.*

No. 193.

The Secretary of State to the Lieutenant-Governor.

OTTAWA, 5th August, 1878.
Received 20th August, 1878.

SIR,—Adverting to your telegram of the 3rd ultimo, and to your despatch, No. 71, of the 16th ultimo, and its accompanying copy of a Minute of your Executive Council, requesting that certain steel rails, now lying at Esquimalt and Nanaimo, may not be removed, I have the honour to acquaint you, for the information of your Government, that the rails in question are being removed to the neighbourhood of Yale, where it is the intention of the Government to commence the construction of the Canada Pacific Railway, under the Act of 1874.

I may remark that it will be seen by the advertisement, that this Government advertised for tenders for the removal of these rails with the above object in view.

I have, &c.,
(Signed)   R. W. SCOTT,
Secretary of State.

No. 194.

The Secretary of State for Canada to the Lieutenant-Governor.

OTTAWA, 9th September, 1878.

SIR,—Referring to my letter of the 31st May last, enclosing a copy of a letter from the Secretary of the Department of Public Works, in which your Government was requested to reserve for conveyance to the Dominion Government, in accordance with the 11th paragraph of the Terms of the Union, lands in certain localities therein set forth, for the purposes of the Canadian Pacific Railway, I have the honour to transmit to you herewith, a copy of an Order of his Excellency the Governor-General in Council in further relation to the subject.

I have to request that this Order in Council may be brought under the early notice of your Government, with particular reference to the concluding portion thereof.

I have, &c.,
(Signed)   R. W. SCOTT,
Secretary of State.

No. 195.

Report of the Privy Council, approved by the Governor-General on the 3rd September, 1878.

On a Report, dated 31st August, 1878, from the Honourable the Minister of Public Works, stating that by the eleventh clause of the agreement under the Terms of which the Province of British Columbia entered the Dominion of Canada, the Government of British Columbia engaged to convey to the Dominion Government in trust, to be appropriated in such manner as the Dominion Government might deem advisable, in furtherance of the construction of the Canadian Pacific Railway, an extent of public lands along the line of Railway throughout its entire length in British Columbia, (not, however, exceeding twenty (20) miles on each side of the said line), equal to the area which might be appropriated for the same purpose by the Dominion Government from the public lands of the North-West Territories and the Province of Manitoba, the conditions of the agreement further providing that the quantity of land held under pre-emption right or by Crown Grant, within the limits of the tract of land in British Columbia to be so conveyed to the Dominion Government, should be made good to the Dominion from contiguous public lands.

That by several Orders in Council in that behalf, the necessary public lands in the North-West Territories and Province of Manitoba, along the line of the said Railway have been withdrawn from sale and settlement, pending the appropriation thereof for the purposes of the said Railway, and the route of the line of Railway through Manitoba, the North-West Territories, and British Columbia, having been now defined by Orders in Council, it is advisable that the necessary appropriation should be made and that the Government of British Columbia should be called upon to convey to the Dominion Government such extent of public lands in British Columbia as has been above specified.

The Minister therefore recommends that all public lands in the Province of Manitoba, and in the North-West Territories, within twenty miles on each side of the said line of Railway be set apart for the purposes of the Canadian Pacific Railway, and be appropriated in such manner as the Dominion Government may deem advisable in furtherance of the construction of the said Railway.

The Minister further recommends that the Secretary of State be authorized, on behalf of this Government, to inform the Government of British Columbia as to the route of the line of Railway, notifying them that all public lands in the Province of Manitoba and in the North-West Territories, within twenty miles on each side of the line, have been set apart as above-mentioned; and to request that Government, in accordance with their agreement in that behalf, to convey to the Dominion Government in trust, to be appropriated in such manner as the Dominion Government may deem advisable in furtherance of the construction of the said Railway, a similar extent of public lands along the line of Railway, throughout its entire length in British Columbia, and to make good to the Dominion, from contiguous public lands, the quantity of land (if any) which may be held under pre-emption right or by Crown grant within the limits of the tract of land in British Columbia to be so conveyed to the Dominion Government.

The Committee submit the foregoing recommendations for Your Excellency's approval.
Certified.
(Signed)   W. A. HIMSWORTH,
Clerk, Privy Council.

No. 196.

The Secretary of State for Canada to the Lieutenant-Governor.

OTTAWA, 23rd September, 1878.

SIR,—Adverting to my letter of the 9th instant, and its accompanying copy of an Order of His Excellency the Governor-General in Council of the 3rd instant, on the subject of the land in the Province of British Columbia to be reserved for the purposes of the Canadian Pacific Railway, I have the honour to transmit to you herewith, for the information of your Government, a copy of a letter from the Secretary of the Department of Public Works, together with plan therein referred to, showing the line of the said Railway through that Province as now defined.

I have to request that a conveyance may be obtained from your Government to that of the Dominion, in trust, of the extent of public lands mentioned in the Order in Council of the 3rd instant.

I have, &c.,
(Signed)   R. W. SCOTT.

No. 197.

Mr. Braun to the Secretary of State for Canada.

OTTAWA, September 20th, 1878.

SIR,—I have the honour to transmit two copies of the plan showing the line of the Canadian Pacific Railway through British Columbia, as now defined, together with a copy of the Order in Council of the 3rd instant (copy sent with letter of 9th September) setting apart a certain area of land on either side of the line throughout the Province for the purposes of the Railway; and I am directed to request you to obtain from the Government of British Columbia a conveyance to the Dominion Government, in trust, of the extent of public lands mentioned in the said Order in Council.

I have, &c.,
(Signed)   F. BRAUN, *Secretary.*

No. 198.

Extract from the Journals of the Legislative Assembly, 29th August, 1878.

The Honourable Mr. *Walkem* moved, seconded by the Honourable Mr. *Beaven*,—
That in the opinion of this House an humble Address, to the following or to the like effect, respecting the violation by Canada of her Railway engagements with this Province, be presented to Her Majesty:—

To the Queen's Most Excellent Majesty.

MOST GRACIOUS SOVEREIGN:—

We, Your Majesty's most dutiful and loyal subjects, the Members of the Legislative Assembly of the Province of British Columbia, in the First Session of the Third Parliament assembled, humbly approach Your Majesty for the purpose of representing—

1. That, on the 31st day of July, 1874, the Government of this Province humbly presented a Petition to Your Majesty, alleging (amongst other matters) that the main inducement which led British Columbia to enter the Dominion of Canada, on the 20th day of July, 1871, was the Agreement by the latter to commence in two and complete

in ten years from that date the construction of the Canadian Pacific Railway; and that this Agreement has been violated by Canada. The Petitioners, therefore, prayed that Your Majesty would, under the circumstances set forth in the Petition, be graciously pleased to cause justice to be done to British Columbia. To this Petition your present Petitioners (the Legislative Assembly) beg leave to refer Your Majesty.

2. That after protracted negotiations on the subject between Your Majesty's Right Honourable Secretary of State for the Colonies (the Earl of Carnarvon) and the Dominion Government, his Lordship was pleased to signify his conclusions upon the question in dispute, in the following language, addressed to His Excellency the Governor-General of the Dominion of Canada :—

"(1.) That the Railway from Esquimalt to Nanaimo shall be commenced as soon as " possible, and completed with all practicable dispatch.

" That the surveys on the Mainland shall be pushed on with the utmost vigour.

* * * * * * * *

" It would be distasteful to me, if, indeed, it were not impossible, to prescribe strictly " any minimum of time or expenditure with regard to work of so uncertain a nature; " but, happily, it is equally impossible for me to doubt that your Government will loyally " do its best in every way to accelerate the completion of a duty left freely to its sense " of honour and justice.

"(3.) That the waggon road and telegraph line shall be immediately constructed. " There seems here to be some difference of opinion as to the special value to the " Province of the undertaking to complete these two works; but after considering what " has been said, I am of opinion that they should both be proceeded with at once, as, " indeed, is suggested by your Ministers.

"(4.) That 2,000,000 dollars a year, and not 1,500,000 dollars, shall be the minimum " expenditure on railway works within the Province from the date at which the surveys " are sufficiently completed to enable that amount to be expended on construction. In " naming this amount, I understand that, it being alike the interest and the wish of the " Dominion Government to urge on with all speed the completion of the works now to " be undertaken, the annual expenditure will be as much in excess of the minimum of " 2,000,000 dollars as in any year may be found practicable.

"(5.) Lastly, that on or before the 31st December, 1890, the railway shall be com-" pleted and open for traffic from the Pacific seaboard to a point at the western end of " Lake Superior, at which it will fall into connection with the existing lines of railway " through a portion of the United States, and also with the navigation on Canadian " waters. To proceed, at present, with the remainder of the railway extending, by the " country northward of Lake Superior, to the existing Canadian lines, ought not, in my " opinion, to be required, and the time for undertaking that work must be determined " by the development of settlement and the changing circumstances of the country. " The day is, however, I hope not very distant when a continuous line of railway " through Canadian territory will be practicable, and I therefore look upon this portion " of the scheme as postponed rather than abandoned." [*Vide* despatch, Lord Carnarvon to Lord Dufferin, 17th November, 1874.]

3. That the Dominion Government, one month later, assented to these proposals, and stated, in effect, that they would be carried out, as they upheld in the main their own policy on the question, and violated neither the letter nor the spirit of any parliamentary provision. The Settlement thus effected was intended and supposed to be final and conclusive. [*Vide* despatch, Lord Dufferin to Lord Carnarvon, 18th December, 1874.]

4. That, owing to the almost total disregard of the above Settlement by the Dominion, and the consequent serious and recurring loss inflicted upon the Province, the Legislative Assembly, early in the Session of 1876, unanimously passed an humble Address to Your Majesty, setting forth the several grounds upon which their complaint was based, and praying that Your Majesty would be graciously pleased to cause the Dominion Government to be moved to carry out the terms above mentioned. To this Address, Your Petitioners humbly beg leave to refer Your Majesty.

5. That, in December of the same year, Your Majesty's Secretary of State for the Colonies (Lord Carnarvon) was pleased to inform the Province that it might fairly be expected that, between the Spring of 1877 and that of 1878, many doubtful points connected with the route of the Railway would be more clearly defined; and his Lordship

further intimated that, as it was his belief that "after the delay of a single summer * * "British Columbia" would experience no "obstacle to the active prosecution of the "undertaking," the Province should not refuse to submit to the work of construction being deferred for that period. [*Vide* despatch, Lord Carnarvon to Lord Dufferin, 18th December, 1876.]

6. That the Provincial Government, on the 26th March, 1877, without prejudice to any of the rights of the Province, conceded the delay mentioned, in deference to his Lordship's wishes.

7. That, although the time so conceded expired some months ago, the Dominion Government have not carried out their agreement, nor have they fulfilled any of the conditions of the Settlement of 1874 with respect to the active prosecution of railway construction in the Province.

8. To repeat the language of the Minute of the Provincial Government, approved of on the 26th March, 1877, Your Petitioners exceedingly regret to state " that the succes-" sion of failures on the part of the Dominion Government to fulfil the several railway " agreements solemnly entered into with this Province, has produced a feeling of dis-" appointment and distrust so widespread and intense as to severely and injuriously " affect the commercial and industrial interests" of the Province, "and seriously retard " its general prosperity."

9. Under these circumstances, and with a view to prevent, if possible, the repetition in the future of the disasters of the past, Your Petitioners, with great regret, feel compelled, in defence of the interests of the people of the Province at large, to resort to the unavoidable alternative forced upon them by the conduct of the Dominion Government in this matter, and to therefore humbly pray that, in the event of the Dominion Government failing to carry into effect the terms of the Settlement of 1874, on or before the 1st day of May next, Your Majesty will be graciously pleased to see fit to order and direct—

That British Columbia shall thereafter have the right to exclusively collect and retain her Customs and Excise duties and to withdraw from the Union; and shall also, in any event, be entitled to be compensated by the Dominion for losses sustained by reason of past delays and the failure of the Dominion Government to carry out their railway and other obligations to the Province.

And Your Petitioners, as in duty bound, will ever pray, &c., &c., &c.

FRED'CK. WILLIAMS,
Speaker of the Legislative Assembly.

Victoria, British Columbia,
September, 1878.

[The Resolution was carried on division, 14 to 9, on the 30th August, 1878.]

No. 199.

Report of the Executive Council approved by the Lieutenant-Governor on the 24th Sept., 1878.

The Committee of Council recommend that the Petition of the House of Assembly to Her Majesty the Queen, respecting the violation by the Dominion of her Railway engagements with this Province, be forwarded to the Right Honourable the Secretary of State for the Colonies, through the usual and proper channel; that extra printed copies be also enclosed to the Colonial Office, as well as to the Dominion Government.

The Committee advise that the recommendation be approved.

Certified,
(Signed)   T. B. Humphreys,
Provincial Secretary and Clerk Executive Council.

200.

The Lieutenant-Governor to the Secretary of State for Canada.

GOVERNMENT HOUSE,
VICTORIA, B.C., 26th September, 1878.

SIR,—I have the honour to enclose you, herewith, a Petition from the Legislative Assembly of this Province (*see* No. 198, p. 278), adopted at the last Session thereof, to Her Majesty the Queen, praying, in a certain event, that the Province may be allowed to collect the Customs and Excise duties, and withdraw from the Union with the Dominion; also twenty-four printed copies of the Petition.

I have further the honour to request that the original Petition, with a number of the printed copies, be forwarded, through the proper channel, to the Right Honourable the Secretary of State for the Colonies, and that the remaining copies be retained by you for the consideration of the Dominion Government.

I have, &c.,
(Signed) A. N. RICHARDS.

No. 201.

The Lieutenant-Governor to the Secretary of State for Canada.

GOVERNMENT HOUSE,
Victoria, November 9th, 1878.

SIR,—I have the honour to enclose to you, herewith, a copy of a Minute of my Executive Council, dated 5th instant, calling the attention of the Dominion Government to despatches of the 31st May, 9th and 23rd September, 1878, respectively, having reference to the reservation and conveyance, for the purpose of the Canadian Pacific Railway, of land on the Mainland of British Columbia, and requesting that the present Dominion Government will be good enough to communicate their views on said despatches to the present Government of this Province as soon as possible.

I have, &c.,
(Signed) A. N. RICHARDS.

No. 202.

Report of the Executive Council, approved by the Lieutenant-Governor on the 5th day of November, 1878.

The Committee of Council consider it advisable to respectfully invite the attention of the Dominion Government to their predecessor's despatches of the 31st May, 9th of September, and 23rd of September, 1878, respectively, referring to the reservation and conveyance, for the purposes of the Canadian Pacific Railway, of land on the Mainland of British Columbia, and to request the present Dominion Government to be good enough to communicate their views on said despatches to this Government as soon as possible.

The Committee would observe that the land mentioned has been fully reserved for railway purposes, and that every facility should and will be given to the Dominion Government to enable them to commence railway construction in the Province at the earliest practicable moment.

The Committee advise that this Minute be approved, and that a copy thereof be forwarded to the Dominion Government.

Certified.
(Signed) T. B. HUMPHREYS,
Provincial Secretary and Clerk Executive Council.

No. 203.

Report of the Executive Council, approved by the Lieutenant-Governor on the 16th day of January, 1879.

The Committee of Council recommend that his Honour the Lieutenant-Governor be respectfully requested to forward the following telegrams, which explain themselves, to the Honourable the Secretary of State:—

"VICTORIA, January 15th, 1879.

"*To the Secretary of State, Ottawa:*

"Expected reply to my despatch of 9th November not having been received, please acquaint Government by telegram with your railway policy, as Legislature meets Twenty-ninth January. Ministry, anticipating a reply, have deferred troubling your Government until latest moment. Also please forward accompanying telegram to Imperial Government, if their reply to Province not received."

BRITISH COLUMBIA, January 15th, 1879.

"*To the Secretary of State, Colonies, London:*

"No reply to Petition of Legislative Assembly, which meets twenty-ninth. Has it been forwarded?"

The Committee recommend that copies of this Minute be sent to the Imperial and Dominion Governments.

Certified.

(Signed) T. B. HUMPHREYS,
Provincial Secretary and Clerk Executive Council.

No. 204.

GOVERNMENT HOUSE
Victoria, January 16th, 1879.

The above Telegrams were sent this day at 3.30 p. m.

(Signed) A. N. RICHARDS.

No. 205.

Telegram.

OTTAWA, ONTARIO,
January 24th, 1879.

To the Hon. Geo. A. Walkem, Attorney-General:

Railway matters are now under consideration, and your representations and claims will receive our best attention.

(Signed) JOHN A. MACDONALD.

No. 206.

Extract from the Journals of the Legislative Assembly of British Columbia.

WEDNESDAY, 19th March, 1879.

Mr. Speaker stated he had received an answer to his Telegram to the Dominion Government referring to the Railway Petition; which was read, and *Ordered* to be placed on the Journals of the House, and is as follows:—

"OTTAWA, ONTARIO, March 19th, 1879.
[Received at Victoria March 19th, 1879.]

" *To the Speaker of the Legislative Assembly:*

"The Petition of Legislative Assembly of British Columbia to the Queen, passed
"last Session, was received here on eleventh of October last. At that time Ministry
"had resigned, and only held office till successors appointed. The attention of the
"present Ministry on taking office was not called to this Petition, and it remained
"unnoticed. On its being discovered it was transmitted to England. This will account
"for the Petition not being answered by Colonial Minister. The Government here
"greatly regret the oversight.

(Signed) " J. C. AIKINS."

No. 207.

*Report of the Executive Council, approved by the Lieutenant-Governor
on the 22nd March, 1879.*

The Committee of Council advise that his Honour the Lieutenant-Governor be
respectfully requested to cause the following telegram to be forwarded to the Dominion
Government:—

"VICTORIA, March 22, 1879.

"*Hon. Secretary of State, Ottawa:*

"When was Petition to Queen forwarded to London? Be good enough to answer
"Speaker's messages about Railway despatch of June, seventy-six."

Certified.
(Signed) T. B. HUMPHREYS,
Clerk Executive Council.

No. 208.

Telegram.

OTTAWA, Ont., March 24th, 1879.
[VICTORIA, March 25th, 1.30 p. m.]

To the Lieutenant-Governor of British Columbia:

Petition to the Queen forwarded to London twenty-fourth (24th) February.
Speaker's message about railway despatch of June, seventy-six, answered by telegraph
twenty-second inst.

(Signed) J. C. AIKINS.

No. 209.

*Report of the Executive Council, approved by the Lieutenant-Governor
on the 12th April, 1879.*

The Committee of Council beg leave to recommend that the following telegram be
forwarded to the Dominion Government:—

"VICTORIA, 14th April, 1879.

"*The Hon. the Secretary of State, Ottawa:*

"Assembly adjourned awaiting information as to your Railway policy. Please
"reply immediately."

Certified.
(Signed) T. B. HUMPHREYS,
Clerk Executive Council

No. 210.

Extract from Journals, Legislative Assembly, British Columbia.

16th April, 1879.

Mr. Speaker stated that he had received two despatches from the Secretary of State for Canada, which were read, and are as follows:—

"OTTAWA, 21st March, 1879.

"SIR,—Adverting to your telegram of the—instant, addressed to the Right Honourable Sir John A. Macdonald, and to my message in reply thereto, of the 19th instant, I have the honour to inform you that the Petition of the Legislative Assembly of British Columbia to the Queen, to which you refer, passed during the last Session of the Provincial Legislature, was received here on the 11th October last.

"At that time the Ministry had resigned, and only held office until the appointment of their successors, and the attention of the present Ministry not having been called to the Petition, it remained unnoticed. Upon its being discovered, however, it was at once transmitted to the Right Honourable the Secretary of State for the Colonies.

"This will account for the Petition not having been answered by the Colonial Secretary.

"I may add, that this Government greatly regret the oversight.

"I have, &c.,
(Signed) "J. C. AIKINS,
"The Hon. the Speaker of the Legislative Assembly, "Secretary of State.
"Victoria, British Columbia."

"OTTAWA, 24th March, 1879.

"SIR,—With reference to your telegrams of the 19th ultimo and the 18th instant, and to my replies thereto of the 6th and 22nd instant, on the subject of the line of the Canadian Pacific Railway, I have the honour to inform you that, as regards the Order of His Excellency the Governor-General in Council of the 9th June, 1876, a copy of which was enclosed in the letter from this Department of the 13th of that month,—that Order in Council was superseded by a subsequent Order, in so far as the route to be followed is concerned, defining that route from Tête Jaune Cache to Burrard Inlet.

"I have to add, that by an Order in Council of the 3rd September last, a copy of which was enclosed to the Lieutenant-Governor on the 9th of that month, the British Columbia Government was requested to convey to the Dominion Government certain lands along the line of railway, as shown on a plan, which plan was enclosed to the Lieutenant-Governor on the 23rd of the same month.

"I have, &c.,
(Signed) "J. C. AIKINS,
"To the Speaker, Legislative Assembly, "Secretary of State.
"Victoria, British Columbia."

No. 211.

Extract from Journals, Legislative Assembly, British Columbia.

Monday, 28th April, 1879.

Mr. Speaker stated that, on Thursday, the 24th instant, he dispatched the following Telegrams:—

"VICTORIA, 24th April, 1879.

"To Sir John A Macdonald, Ottawa.

"House regret delay of your Railway Policy, and unanimously request to be informed of policy immediately, and whether construction and vigorous prosecution will take place in Province this year.

(Signed) "SPEAKER."

"*From Speaker to Secretary of State, Ottawa.*

"Please forward the following Telegram to Colonial Office:"—

"BRITISH COLUMBIA.
"Hon. Secretary of State, Colonies, London.   "24th April, 1879.

"No action yet taken on Railway by Dominion Government. This Legislature in Session awaiting answer to Petition, unanimously and respectfully request immediate reply to its prayer.

(Signed)   "SPEAKER."

And had received from the Secretary of State for Canada, the following reply:—

"OTTAWA, April 26th, 1879.
"*To Mr. Speaker Williams, Legislative Assembly.*

"Canadian Government is determined to commence work of construction in British Columbia this season, and to press it vigorously.

(Signed)   "J. C. AIKINS,
                  "*Secretary of State.*"

The Honourable Mr. *Walkem* presented, by command of His Honour the Lieutenant-Governor, a copy of a Despatch from the Right Honourable Sir *M. E. Hicks Beach*, respecting the Railway Petition forwarded last Session by this House.

No. 212.

The Under Secretary of State for Canada to the Lieutenant-Governor.

OTTAWA, 4th April, 1879.

SIR,—I have the honour to transmit to you herewith, for the information of your Government, a copy of a despatch from the Right Honourable the Secretary of State for the Colonies, in reference to the Canadian Pacific Railway and other outstanding matters relating to British Columbia.

I have, &c.,
(Signed)   EDOUARD J. LANGEVIN,
             Under Secretary of State.

No. 213.

Sir Michael Hicks Beach to the Marquis of Lorne.

DOWNING STREET,
26th February, 1879.

MY LORD,—I have the honour to acknowledge the receipt of your despatch, No. 22, of the 4th instant, transmitting, with other papers, a Minute of the Executive Council of British Columbia, embodying a telegram addressed to the Secretary of State for Canada, and making an enquiry of myself as to whether any reply has been forwarded to a petition of the Legislative Assembly of the Province relating to the Canadian Pacific Railway.

2. The date of the petition is not given in the Minute of Council, and I shall be obliged if you will give by telegraph such information as may enable me to ascertain, without doubt, the document referred to.

3. If the enquiry relates to the petition dated in February, 1876, which was forwarded to my predecessor direct by the Lieutenant-Governor of the Province, and subsequently formed the subject of the Governor General's despatch, No. 75, of the 17th March, 1876, I find some difficulty at the present moment in giving a definite reply to the Assembly, as your despatch does not contain any allusion to the action which your present Ministers may propose to take on the subject of the Canadian Pacific Railway, or in regard to the settlement of the outstanding questions with British Columbia.

4. I should be glad, therefore, to receive, as soon as convenient, some explanation as to the course which your Government may propose to adopt with reference to the representations made from time to time by the Provincial Government and Legislature in relation to this matter.

5. You will be so good as to communicate a copy of this despatch to the Lieutenant-Governor of British Columbia.

I have, &c.,
(Signed) M. E. HICKS BEACH.

POSTSCRIPT, 27th February, 1879.—Since the above was written I have received a telegram from the Speaker of the Assembly of British Columbia, asking whether the petition of the Assembly sent in September last had reached my hands, and requesting a reply thereto. As this petition has not been received at the Colonial Office, I telegraphed to you this day requesting you to forward it to me and to inform the Speaker.

No. 214.

Report of the Executive Council, approved by the Lieutenant-Governor in Council on the 11th May, 1879.

The Committee of Council advise that the despatch of the 24th of April, 1879, recently received from the Honourable the Secretary of State, relating to the adoption of Esquimalt as the Western terminus of the Canadian Pacific Railway, be published for the information of the public.

Certified.
(Signed) T. B. HUMPHREYS,
Clerk Executive Council.

No. 215.

The Secretary of State to Lieutenant-Governor.

OTTAWA, 24th April, 1879.

SIR,—I have the honour to transmit to you herewith for the information of your Government a copy of an Order of His Excellency the Governor-General in Council on the subject of the terminus of the Canadian Pacific Railway in the Province of British Columbia.

I have, &c.,
(Signed) J. C. AIKINS,
Secretary of State.

No. 216.

Report of the Privy Council, approved by the Governor-General on the 22nd April, 1879.

On a memorandum dated 16th April, 1879, from the Hon. the Minister of Public Works, representing that on a memorandum from the Chief Engineer of the Canadian Pacific Railway, dated 23rd May, 1873, an Order in Council was passed June 7th, 1873, fixing Esquimalt on Vancouver Island as the terminus of that railway in British Columbia. That subsequently—March 25th, 1875—an Order in Council was passed authorizing the Dominion Government to notify the Government of British Columbia that it would be necessary that the Legislature of that Province, then in session, should pass an Act setting apart such extent of public lands along the line of the Railway in Vancouver Island in the manner set forth by the 11th paragraph of the terms of agreement of the Union.

That on the 23rd May, 1878, the late Government had another Order in Council passed cancelling that of June 7th, 1873, which fixed the terminus at Esquimalt; but no reason appears to have been given for their action in the matter, nor is there any mention made of the Order in Council of March, 25th, 1875, which **provides for the appropriation of the necessary lands in Vancouver Island.**

The Minister, therefore, recommends that in the absence of satisfactory reasons having been given for cancelling the Order in Council of June 7th, 1873, that the Order in Council (of May 23rd, 1878,) cancelling it be annulled, and that of June 7th, 1873, be revived.

He also recommends that a copy of his report to Council, if approved, be furnished to the Hon. Secretary of State for transmission to the Government of British Columbia for their information.

The Committee submit the above recommendations for Your Excellency's approval.

Certified.

(Signed)   W. A. HIMSWORTH,
Clerk Privy Council, Canada.

No. 217.

Report of the Executive Council, approved by the Lieutenant-Governor on the 14th May, 1879.

The Committee of Council have had under consideration Despatch No. 29, of the 24th of April, 1879, from the Hon. the Secretary of State, informing this Government that the Privy Council had, by Minute of the 22nd of April, 1879, cancelled their Order of the 23rd of May, 1878, and revived their Order of the 7th June, 1873, which fixed the Western terminus of the Canadian Pacific Railway at Esquimalt, and they advise that the Dominion Government be at once requested to inform the Provincial Government whether the following reserve made for railway purposes at the instance of the Dominion Government, under the said Order of May, 1878, shall be cancelled or retained, as it is highly undesirable that the land should longer be withdrawn from settlement, if not to be used, that is to say:—A tract of land, beginning at English Bay, on Burrard Inlet, and following Fraser River to Lytton; thence by the Thompson River Valley to Kamloops; thence up the Valley of the North Thompson, passing near Lakes Albreda and Cranberry to Tête Jaune Cache; thence up the Fraser River Valley to the summit of Yellowhead Pass, or the boundary between British Columbia and the North-West Territories.

The Committee further advise that a copy of this Minute be forwarded to the Dominion Government.

Certified.

(Signed)   T. BASIL HUMPHREYS,
Clerk, Executive Council.

No. 218.

The Secretary of State for Canada to Lieutenant-Governor.

OTTAWA, 18th June, 1879.

SIR,—With reference to your Despatch, No. 42 of the 19th ultimo, and its accompanying Minute of your Executive Council, I have the honour to transmit to you herewith, for the information of your Government, a copy of an Order of His Excellency the Governor-General in Council, relative to the reservation of certain land on the mainland of British Columbia, for the purpose of the Canadian Pacific Railway.

I have, &c.,

(Signed)   J. C. AIKINS,
Secretary of State.

No. 219.

Report of the Privy Council approved by the Governor-General on the 12th June, 1879.

On a memorandum dated 10th June, 1879, from the Honourable the Minister of Railways and Canals, stating that he had under consideration a communication, dated 14th May, 1879, from the Lieutenant Governor of British Columbia, enclosing a Minute of His Executive Council, of the 14th May, 1879, in reference to the reservation of land on the Mainland of British Columbia, between Burrard Inlet and Yellow Head Pass.

The Minister recommends that the Government of British Columbia be informed that the object of the Order in Council of the 22nd April, 1879, was simply to rescind the Order in Council of the 23rd May, 1878, so as to leave the General Government free to adopt which ever route might appear in the public interest the most eligible. That it is not proposed to release the reservation of land on either route, and it is felt that this will result in no serious inconvenience for the short period which will now elapse before the location of the Railway will be finally established.

The Committee submit the above recommendation for Your Excellency's approval.

       Certified.
        (Signed) W. A. HIMSWORTH,
                Clerk Privy Council.

No. 220.

Telegram.

             VICTORIA, B.C., October 2nd, 1879.

Sir John A. Macdonald, Ottawa:

Delay in commencing Railway construction causes great dissatisfaction. We strongly urge you not to overlook your assurances to our Legislature, prior to its prorogation last Spring.

        (Signed) GEO. A. WALKEM.

No. 221.

Telegram.

             OTTAWA, Oct. 6th, 1879.

Hon. G. A. Walkem, Victoria.

One hundred and twenty-seven (127) miles from Yale to Kamloops to be constructed forthwith. Tenders to be received till seventeenth (17) November. Work to be vigorously prosecuted.

        (Signed) JOHN A. MACDONALD.

No. 222.

The Under Secretary of State to the Lieutenant-Governor.

             OTTAWA, 11th October, 1879.

SIR,—I am directed to transmit to you herewith, copy of an Order in Council, dated 4th instant, confirming the Order in Council of the 13th July, 1878, defining the line of route of the Canadian Pacific Railway through British Columbia to a point on or near Burrard Inlet.

        I have, &c.,
       (Signed) EDOUARD J. LANGEVIN,
               Under Secretary of State.

No. 223.

Report of the Privy Council, approved by the Governor-General on the 4th October, 1879.

On the recommendation of the Honourable the Minister of Railways and Canals, the Committee advise that the Order in Council of the 13th July, 1878, defining the line of route of the Canadian Pacific Railway through British Columbia to a point on or near Burrard Inlet, be confirmed.

        Certified.
       (Signed) W. A. HIMSWORTH,
               Clerk Privy Council, Canada.

No. 224.

Report of the Executive Council approved by the Lieutenant-Governor on the 11th day of October, 1879.

The Committee of Council have had under consideration the possibility that the Dominion Government might omit to provide, in the contracts for Railway construction in this Province, that the Contractors are not to employ Chinese.

The Committee consider that it is of great importance to the Dominion and the Province that Railway construction should be carried on in such a manner as to employ and permanently settle in the Province as many families of our own and kindred races as possible.

That the Chinese, in the Australias, New Zealand, California, and British Columbia, are an alien, non-assimilating race, whose presence in large numbers is injurious to settlement as their system of Coolie labour defies competition, and seriously discourages immigrants from coming.

That there is no necessity to employ Chinese labour on Railway construction in this Province, and that the employment of such labour on works of magnitude simply means a large importation and employment of slave labour, the profits from which wil only enrich Chinese companies resident in a foreign country.

The Committee remark that the Legislative Assembly, by Resolution, have prohibited the employment of Chinese upon Provincial Public Works, and that, in accordance therewith, the Specifications for the Graving Dock at Esquimalt provide that the Contractor shall not directly or indirectly employ Chinese upon, about, or in connection with the works; and that, in the event of his doing so, the Government will not be responsible for payment of the Contract.

The Committee therefore recommend that, if this Minute be approved, the following telegram be forwarded to the Secretary of State, Canada:—

"VICTORIA, B. C., 11th October, 1879.

"To the Secretary of State for Canada :

"This Government respectfully suggest that a condition be inserted in Contracts prohibiting the employment of Chinese on Railway construction in this Province. Will forward Minute of Council by mail."

The Committee further advise that a copy of this Minute be forwarded to the Government of Canada through the usual channel.

Certified, (Signed) T. BASIL HUMPHREYS,
Clerk Executive Council.

No. 225.

Telegram.

VICTORIA, 28th October 1879.

Sir John A. Macdonald, Ottawa:

Council consider disallowance Road Tolls Act will increase contract price for Railway construction, as Act exempted Railway material and plant from toll, whereas Tolls Act, 1876, now revived makes no such exemption. Can you remedy this? Government anxious to facilitate construction.

(Signed) GEO. A. WALKEM.

No. 226.

Report of the Executive Council, approved by the Lieutenant-Governor 31st October, 1879.

On a memorandum from the Honourable the Provincial Secretary, dated 30th October, 1879, recommending that the following telegram be forwarded to the Hon. Secretary of State, Canada :—

"Please forward copy Order in Council 13th July, seventy-eight, referred to in despatch 11th instant, as defining route Pacific Railway, British Columbia."

The Committee advise that the recommendation be approved.

Certified,
(Signed) T. B. HUMPHREYS,
Clerk, Executive Council.

No. 227.

The Secretary of State to the Lieutenant-Governor.

OTTAWA, 13th November, 1879.

SIR,—In compliance with the request contained in your telegram of the 31st ultimo, I have the honour to transmit to you herewith a copy of an Order of His Excellency the Governor-General in Council, referred to in my letter of the 11th ultimo, on the subject of the route of the Canadian Pacific Railway.

I have, &c.,
(Signed)   J. C. AIKINS,
Secretary of State.

No. 228.

Report of the Privy Council approved by the Governor-General on the 13th July, 1878.

On a memorandum dated 11th July, 1878, from the Honourable the Minister of Public Works, reporting that on the 1st June, 1877, an Order in Council was passed in accordance with the provisions of the Canadian Pacific Railway Act of 1874, defining the route of the Railway between Fort William on the Kaministiquia and Jasper House and Tête Jaune Cache.

That the same Order in Council also defined the route from the last named point to the Pacific Ocean, in the event of the Bute Inlet or Dean Inlet routes being ultimately adopted, these being routes through British Columbia, one of which, at that time, it seemed probable would be adopted.

That later information has shown that it would be in the public interest that the route of the railway, from the neighbourhood of the Tête Jaune Cache, should be towards Burrard Inlet.

The Minister therefore recommends that the route of the railroad shall be defined generally, as passing from the neighbourhood of the Tête Jaune Cache, by the Albreda, to the North Thompson River, towards Kamloops Lake, to the Fraser Valley at Lytton, and thence descending the valley of the Fraser, by Yale and New Westminster, to Port Moody, or such other point on or near Burrard Inlet as may be found most convenient for the purpose of harbour accommodation.

The Committee submit the above recommendation for Your Excellency's approval.

Certified.   (Signed)   W. A. HIMSWORTH,
Clerk Privy Council

No. 229.

The Under Secretary of State for Canada to the Lieutenant-Governor.

OTTAWA, 27th November, 1879.

SIR,—I have the honour to transmit to you herewith, for the information of your Government, a copy of a Despatch from the Right Honourable the Secretary of State for the Colonies on the subject of the line of route of the Canadian Pacific Railway.

I request that a copy of this Despatch may be communicated to the Speaker of the Legislative Assembly in accordance with Sir M. E. Hicks-Beach's request.

I have, &c.,
(Signed)   EDOUARD J. LANGEVIN,
Under-Secretary of State.

No. 230.

The Secretary of State for the Colonies to the Governor-General.

DOWNING STREET, 29th October, 1879.

MY LORD,—I have the honour to acknowledge the receipt of your Despatch of the 7th inst., No. 276, transmitting an approved report of a Committee of the Privy Council confirming one of the 13th July, 1878, which defines the line of route of the Canada Pacific Railway through British Columbia, to a point on or near Burrard Inlet.

I request that you will now inform the Speaker of the Legislative Assembly of British Columbia with reference to the Address to the Queen enclosed in your Despatch No. 44, of the 24th February, that I deemed it inexpedient to tender any advice to Her Majesty on the subject of this Address until I had received full and authoritative explanations of the policy of the Dominion Government.

Your Lordship will be good enough further to inform the Speaker that I am glad to learn that the action of the Dominion Parliament, during its recent session, and the course since taken by the Government, have generally been considered in British Columbia as a sufficient fulfilment of the obligations of the Dominion towards the Province in respect of the Canadian Pacific Railway, and that I do not now propose to tender to Her Majesty any specific advice on the subject of the Address bearing his signature.

I have, &c.,
(Signed)   M. E. HICKS-BEACH.

No. 231.

Report of a Committee of the Executive Council, approved by the Lieutenant-Governor on the 27th day of December, 1879.

The Committee of Council have had under consideration the recent unexpected and additional conditions attached by the Dominion Government to their agreement to pay $250,000 in aid of the construction of the Esquimalt Graving Dock, and they deem it advisable, in order to expedite the letting of the work and to secure its speedy completion, that the leader of the Provincial Government be authorized to proceed immediately to Ottawa to confer with and make such arrangements with the Dominion Government as are within the powers of the Provincial Government.

They are also of opinion in view of the approaching Sessions of both the Dominion and Local Legislatures, that some satisfactory understanding between the two Governments should be arrived at with respect to railway matters as affecting the Island, Indian Affairs, the Administration of Justice, Chinese Immigration, the Cariboo Main Trunk Road, the subsidizing of a line of vessels for the encouragement of Trade between the Eastern Provinces and this Province, and also to minor matters of unsettled accounts between the two Governments.

The Committee therefore advise that the leader of the Government (Mr. Walkem) be authorized to proceed to Ottawa immediately and confer with the Dominion Government upon the matters above mentioned.

Certified.
(Signed)   T. B. HUMPHREYS,
Clerk of Executive Council.

No. 232.

The Secretary of State for Canada to the Lieutenant-Governor.

OTTAWA, 9th January, 1880.

SIR,—Referring to previous correspondence upon the subject of the line of route of the Canada Pacific Railway through British Columbia, I have the honour to request that steps may be taken by your Government, without unnecessary delay, to convey to the Dominion Government the lands for twenty miles on each side of the Railway line in the said Province, pursuant to the eleventh section of the Terms of Union between British Columbia and the Dominion, and in accordance with the location of the Railway as described in the Order in Council .... , a copy of which was transmitted to you with Mr. Under Secretary Lee's letter of the 11th of that month.

I have, &c.,
(Signed)   J. C. AIKINS,
Secretary of State.

No. 233.

Extract from Journals, Legislative Assembly, British Columbia.

Tuesday, 6th April, 1880.

Mr. Speaker stated that he had received during the recess, several despatches, which were read and *Ordered* to be placed on the Journals of the House:—

"GOVERNMENT HOUSE, VICTORIA,
"December 17th, 1879.

"SIR,—I am directed by the Lieutenant-Governor to transmit to you herewith, a copy of a Despatch from the Under Secretary of State for Canada, with its enclosure therein referred to, on the subject of the line of route of the Canadian Pacific Railway.

"I have, &c.,
(Signed) "W. L. BOYLE,
"*Private Secretary.*

"Hon. F. Williams,
"*Speaker of the Legislative Assembly.*"

"OTTAWA, 26th April, 1879.

"SIR,—I am directed to acknowledge the receipt, on the 25th inst., of your telegram of the 24th inst., on the subject of the Petition to the Queen of the Legislative Assembly of the Province of British Columbia relative to the Canadian Pacific Railway, which you request may be forwarded to the Right Honourable the Secretary of State for the Colonies.

"Your telegram has been duly submitted to His Excellency the Governor-General.

"I have, &c.,
(Signed) "EDOUARD J. LANGEVIN,
"*Under-Secretary of State.*

"*The Hon. the Speaker of the Legislative Assembly,*
"*Victoria.*"

No. 234.

The Secretary of State for Canada to the Lieutenant-Governor.

OTTAWA, 3rd March, 1880.

SIR,—I have the honour to inform you that so far as this Government is aware no action has been taken by the Government of British Columbia towards conveying to the Dominion the lands for railway purposes agreed to be transferred by that Province to Canada under Section 11 of the "Terms and Conditions of Union," in compliance with the request contained in my letter of the 9th ultimo.

I have therefore to request that the early attention of your Government may be called to the subject with a view to a compliance with the terms of my letter, above cited, and to the necessary legislation to that end being obtained during the ensuing session of the Legislative Assembly.

I have further to inform you in connection with this subject that the Honourable J. W. Trutch, C.M.G., has been appointed a Confidential Agent of the Dominion in the Province of British Columbia, and is fully authorized to represent the Dominion Government in all communications, verbal or otherwise, with the Government of that Province on the subject of the adjustment and transfer of the land granted for Railway purposes set forth in the "Terms and Conditions of Union," and that Mr. Trutch is accordingly duly accredited to the Government of British Columbia with that view.

I have, &c.,
(Signed) J. C. AIKINS,
Secretary of State.

No. 235.

Report of the Executive Council, approved by the Lieutenant-Governor on the 27th day of March, 1880.

The Committee of Council advise that the Dominion Government be informed that the legislation necessary to transfer the railway lands on the Mainland alluded to in the despatch of the Hon. the Secretary of State, dated the 3rd day of March, 1880, will be undertaken at the ensuing session of the Legislature.

Certified.

(Signed)   T. BASIL HUMPHREYS,
Clerk Executive Council.

No. 236.

The Lieutenant-Governor to the Secretary of State for Canada.

VICTORIA, B.C., 1st April, 1880

SIR,—I have the honour to enclose a copy of a Minute of my Executive Council, date 27th ultimo, by which you will see that the necessary steps will be taken at the ensuing session of the Legislature to convey to the Dominion Government the Railway lands on the Mainland alluded to in your despatch of the 3rd ultimo.

I have, &c.,
(Signed)   A. N. RICHARDS.

No. 237.

Extract from the Report, by Hon. Mr. Walkem, of his mission to Ottawa, with respect to Railway, Dry Dock, and other matters.

ATTORNEY GENERAL'S OFFICE,
Victoria, March 29th, 1880.

MAY IT PLEASE YOUR HONOUR:

I have the honour to report the result of the negotiations which I was deputed to enter into with the Dominion Government, at Ottawa, upon the subjects mentioned in a Minute of Council approved of by Your Honour on the 27th of December last.

Leaving Victoria on the last day of December, I reached Ottawa on the evening of the 15th of January, and on the following day had preliminary business interviews with the Leader of the Government and some of his colleagues.

Learning that arrangements with the Government were pending for transfers to third parties of the contracts which had been awarded for railway work on the Mainland, I considered it prudent to defer negotiations respecting railway work on the Island until the transfers had been settled, lest any action on my part with respect to the Island Section should unsettle the plans of the Government, and possibly lead to the postponement, for the season at least, of construction on the Mainland. It also appeared advisable in presenting the Railway and Dock Questions to completely sever them, and leave the consideration of one to await the settlement of the other. As Your Honour is aware, the earliest possible settlement of dock matters was very desirable, as the tenders which had been received for its construction could not be safely dealt with until the final intentions of the Dominion Government respecting the aid to be given by them to the work should be ascertained.

CANADIAN PACIFIC RAILWAY.

Esquimalt-Nanaimo Section.

As the construction of this section of the Railway was one of the subjects referred to in the Order of Your Honour in Council of the 27th December, it was naturally alluded to from time to time by members of the Government when conversing with me on British Columbia matters. I, however, refrained, for the reasons already assigned, from entangling or embarrassing its consideration with unsettled questions regarding the Mainland Railway contracts or the Dock Subsidy. Immediately, however, after these questions had been disposed of, I arranged and had a meeting with Senator Macdonald and Messrs. DeCosmos, Bunster and Thompson, for the purpose of deciding upon the best means to secure the construction of the work. After considerable discussion, it was unanimously agreed that all present should, as a deputation, wait upon the Premier and press the claims of the Province in this respect upon him. I accordingly wrote the following note to him, and received the following reply:—

"OTTAWA, Feb. 14th, 1880.

"*The Right Hon. Sir John A. Macdonald:*

"SIR,—In conjunction with some of the Members from British Columbia, I am desirous to have a conference with you respecting Railway matters affecting the Province. Will you be good enough to name a time and place which will be convenient to you for meeting us.

"I have, &c.,
(Signed)   "GEO. A. WALKEM."

"OTTAWA, Feb. 16th, 1880.

"*The Hon. G. A. Walkem:*

"DEAR SIR.—I shall be very glad to see you and the other gentlemen at my house to-morrow, Tuesday, at 11 o'clock, a.m.

"Yours, very truly,
(Signed)   "JOHN A. MACDONALD."

Accordingly, a meeting was held, which lasted some time. While credit was given to the Government for placing 127 miles of the Mainland portion of the line under contract, and active prosecution of the work advocated, the members of the deputation forcibly represented the loss and injury which would be inflicted on the Southern portion of the Province by longer delaying construction of the Esquimalt-Nanaimo section. I feel that I would be doing injustice to the subject, as well as to the members of the deputation, were I to attempt a recital at any length of their various arguments against further delay of the work. In supporting their views, all the main points of the official correspondence were referred to. The offer of the Dominion Government in 1874 to construct the work as a "portion of the Railway," and their solemn engagement made with England and the Province in January, 1875, to commence it "as soon as possible," and complete it "with all practicable dispatch," were specially dwelt upon. English public opinion, as expressed in leading journals, was quoted; figures showing the advantages of the line (if constructed) were produced; much stress was laid on the facts that the surveys had been made, that valuable lands on the Island had, as far back as 1875, been ceded by Statute to the Dominion, at its special request, and solely for Canadian Pacific Railway purposes; that up to the present moment these lands had been retained, and the policy of retaining them in aid of the same Railway been re-affirmed by the present Dominion Government. A well-drawn document on the same subject from the Victoria Chamber of Commerce' was also referred to, and I can safely state that no favourable circumstance or argument which an intimate knowledge of the case could suggest, was omitted on the occasion. The Minister replied, in substance, that he and his colleagues had undertaken as much Railway work in the Province as they felt they could safely carry through, and that he could not, therefore, pledge his Government to do more at present. His attention was thereupon called to the fact that the expense of the work would be comparatively trifling, as its actual cost to the Dominion for years to come would merely be interest on the construction outlay, which would necessarily be gradual; that under all the circumstances of the case, the commencement and active prosecution of work were obligations which should have been fulfilled, and should therefore be carried out now. The Minister then remarked that the whole subject had been well considered before the contracts for the Mainland work had been let, and that the views of the Government were that all had been done that could be done at present. After some further observations of the same character as the above, the deputation withdrew.

Mainland Sections.

As a matter of information obtained from the Department of the Minister of Railways, I may add that the contracts let for the Mainland Section are as follows:—

Sub-Section A, Emory's Bar to Boston Bar, 29 miles, to be completed 1st December, 1883...	$2,727,300 00
Sub-Section B, Boston Bar to Lytton, 29¼ miles, to be completed 30th June, 1884..	2,573,640 00
Sub-Section C, Lytton to Junction Flat, 29 miles, to be completed 31st December, 1884..	2,056,950 00
Sub-Section D, Junction Flat to Savona, 40½ miles, to be completed 30th June, 1885..	1,809,150 00
Total......................	$9,167,040 00

A deposit of five per cent. on this amount has been lodged in cash with the Receiver-General, and the contracts, excepting an interest in that for Sub-Section B, transferred to A. Onderdonk, Esq., a gentleman who has an excellent reputation in California as an Engineer and Contractor. He represents the following wealthy gentlemen who are partners with him in the contract, viz.:— D. O. Mills, Esq., Banker of San Francisco, S. G. Reid, Esq., of Oregon, H. B. Laidlaw, Esq., Banker of New York, and L. P. Morton, Esq., Banker of New York (a member of the banking firms of Morton, Bliss & Co., and Morton, Rose & Co., of New York and London respectively). The manifest advantages of dealing with one firm of unquestionable means and ability, instead of with three or four firms, in the construction of the work, influenced the Government, as I learned, to consent to the transfer of the contracts mentioned. I should not omit to state that shortly after my arrival in Ottawa I was informed by one of the Ministers that a despatch (9th January, 1880,) had been forwarded to Your Honour requesting that the Mainland Railway lands should be transferred this Session by an Act of our Legislature. In reply to a question as to whether it would be done, I assured him that the policy of the Government was to give every assistance to the Railway, and that I had no doubt the legislation referred to would be introduced by the Government as requested. I was also assured by the Engineer-in-Chief, that engineering parties would at once be organized and sent to the Province to prepare the work for the contractor. Four parties are now on their way hither, and I have received a telegram from Mr. Onderdonk that he will also reach the Province in a few days.

*　　　　*　　　　*　　　　*　　　　*　　　　*　　　　*

I have the honour to be,
Sir,
Your obedient, humble servant,

GEO. A. WALKEM,
Attorney-General.

No. 238.

Telegram.

VICTORIA, March 29th, 1880.

Sir John A. Macdonald, Ottawa:

Awarding of Mainland contracts give satisfaction, but your refusal to give definite assurance of construction on Island creates dissatisfaction. A promise from you to commence and prosecute active construction of Island Railway next year would satisfy all. Can you give it? Please reply immediately, as House meets in a few days.

(Signed)　　GEO. A. WALKEM.

No. 239.

Telegram.

VICTORIA, April 7th, 1880.

Sir John A. Macdonald, Ottawa:

Please reply to my telegram of 29th March respecting construction Island Railway. Want to use reply at once.

GEO. A. WALKEM.

No. 240.

Mr. Trutch to the Attorney-General.

VICTORIA, B. C., April 14th, 1880.

SIR,—His Honour the Lieutenant-Governor having referred me to you as authorized to receive, on behalf of the Government of British Columbia, communications from me, as Agent of the Dominion Government, on the subject of the adjustment and transfer to the Dominion of the lands granted by the Province of British Columbia, under the "Terms and Conditions" of Union, in aid of the construction of 'the Canadian Pacific Railroad, I beg to lay before you the following statement of the views of the Dominion Government on this matter, and more particularly in regard to the selection of the lands to be transferred, which views I had the opportunity of verbally submitting more fully for your consideration at the interview I had the honour of having with you this morning.

There is reason to believe that the character of the land for a very considerable distance along the line of the Canadian Pacific Railway, as located in British Columbia, is such as to be altogether unsuited for agricultural purposes, and, therefore, valueless for the object contemplated at the time the Province was admitted into the Confederation, which was, that the lands proposed to be transferred to the Dominion should be laid out and sold to aid in the construction of the road.

The portion of Section 11 of the "Terms and Conditions," on which the Province became a part of the Dominion, which refers to the grant of land to be made by the Province for the purpose of the railway, is as follows:—

"And the Government of British Columbia agree to convey to the Dominion "Government, in trust, to be appropriated in such manner as the Dominion Government "may deem advisable, in furtherance of the construction of the said Railway, a similar "extent of Public Lands along the line of Railway throughout its entire length in British "Columbia, not to exceed, however, Twenty (20) Miles on each side of said line, as may "be appropriated for the same purpose by the Dominion Government from the public "lands in the North-West Territories and the Province of Manitoba. Provided that "the quantity of land which may be held under Pre-emption right or by Crown grant "within the limits of the tract of land in British Columbia to be so conveyed to the "Dominion Government, shall be made good to the Dominion from contiguous Public "Lands; and, provided further, that until the commencement, within two years, as "aforesaid, from the date of the Union, of the construction of the said Railway, the "Government of British Columbia shall not sell or alienate any further portions of the "Public Lands of British Columbia in any other way than under right of Pre-emption, "requiring actual residence of the Pre-emptor on the land claimed by him. In con-"sideration of the land to be so conveyed in aid of the construction of the said Railway, "the Dominion Government agree to pay to British Columbia, from the date of the "Union, the sum of 100,000 dollars per annum, in half-yearly payments in advance."

In view of the statement made in the preceding paragraph, it now becomes necessary that an understanding be arrived at with the Government of the Province by which the Dominion may receive an equal area of lands available for farming or economical purposes in lieu of those which, on investigation, may be found to be unavailable within the forty-mile belt. and the Dominion Government urgently request the concurrence of the Government of British Columbia in the following arrangements: *i. e.*, That such territory situate within the forty-mile belt referred to in the section of the "Terms and Conditions" above quoted as may be found on a thorough examination and investigation useless for farming or other valuable purposes, may not be regarded as properly forming part of the land consideration to be received by the Dominion, but that the same be eliminated from the area in the belt described, and that an equal area of land suitable for farming or other valuable purposes be selected elsewhere in the Province in lieu thereof. The area to be selected outside of the belt mentioned should, in addition, include a quantity of land to represent that in the Fraser River Valley and elsewhere along or in the vicinity of the Railway line which may be found to have been already disposed of by the Province, or with regard to which valid claims may be preferred as also to cover the deficiency caused by the International Boundary on the Mainland and the coast line on Vancouver Island respectively falling within the forty-mile belt.

The Dominion Government cannot doubt that the Provincial Government will consider itself pledged in good faith in view of the whole circumstances, and of the actual money consideration stipulated for in the section of the "Terms and Conditions" above cited, and which has been regularly paid, to place the Dominion Government in possession of land elsewhere in lieu of the corresponding area within the railway belt, which may be found to be useless for agricultural or other valuable purposes.

In accordance with these views, and acting as the Agent of the Dominion Government, duly accredited to the Government of British Columbia under authority of the Order in Council, dated the 25th February last, a copy of which has been received by His Honour the Lieutenant-Governor, I have the honour to prefer the request that the right above defined of selecting lands outside of the forty-mile belt in lieu of lands within that limit which, on investigation, shall be found to be valueless, and to supply the deficiency caused by the International Boundary on the Mainland and the coast line on Vancouver Island respectively falling within the forty-mile belt, be specifically conveyed to the Dominion by the insertion of provisions to that effect in the "Railway Lands Reservation Bill," now under consideration in the Legislative Assembly.

I have, &c.,
(Signed) JOSEPH W. TRUTCH.

No. 241.
Mr. Trutch to the Attorney-General.

VICTORIA, 24th April, 1880.

SIR,—I beg to solicit your attention to my letter to you of the 14th instant, as yet unacknowledged, and as to the subject matter of which I have not received any communication from you, either written or oral, since my letter was handed to you.

The views and requests conveyed in that letter to you are held by the Dominion Government to be of great moment to the public interests. I therefore take this opportunity of again urging their favourable consideration by the Government of the Province with a view to the requisite legislation being sought for during the current session, now apparently approaching its close.

I also venture to remind you of the fact, mentioned by me when I last had an interview with you, that business arrangements of pressing importance, which are entrusted to me in connection with the commencement of railway construction in the Province, urgently require my presence in the upper country, and that I am precluded from attending to this duty until the negotiation with the Government of the Province in relation to Railway Lands, with which I am specially charged by the Dominion Government, shall have reached some conclusion.

I have, &c.,
(Signed) JOSEPH W. TRUTCH.

No. 242.
The Attorney-General to Mr. Trutch.

VICTORIA, April 26th, 1880.

SIR,—In acknowledging the receipt of your two letters of the 14th and 24th inst., respecting the Dominion Railway Lands, I beg to state that a reply to your question will, in all probability, be communicated to you this week.

I have, &c.,
(Signed) GEO. A. WALKEM,
Attorney-General.

No. 243.

Mr. Trutch to the Attorney-General.

Victoria, B. C., 27th April, 1880.

Sir,—With reference to your's of yesterday's date, stating that a reply to the application which I, on behalf of the Dominion Government, addressed to you on the 14th inst., will probably be communicated to me this week, I beg to inform you that I have this morning received a telegram from Ottawa conveying directions which pressingly require my presence at and above Yale, and render it most desirable that I should leave Victoria for that locality on Friday next.

I would, therefore, earnestly request that, as far as you may judge it to be not incompatible with the public interests, the conclusions of the Provincial Government in regard to the application in question may be conveyed to me at as early a moment as practicable, and, if possible, in time to allow of my proceeding up the Fraser on Friday upon the public service with which I am charged in connection with the commencement of railway construction.

I have, &c.,
(Signed) J. W. Trutch.

No. 244.

The Attorney-General to Mr. Trutch.

Victoria, May 4th, 1880.

Sir,—I have the honour to enclose a copy of an Order in Council of this date, which expresses the views of the Provincial Government upon the proposals made in your letter of the 14th ult., on behalf of the Dominion Government, respecting Canadian Pacific Railway lands in this Province.

I have, &c.,
(Signed) Geo. A. Walkem,
Attorney-General.

No. 245.

Report of the Executive Council, approved by the Lieutenant Governor on the 4th day of May, 1880.

The Committee of Council have had under consideration the application of the Dominion Government for the transfer, according to the Terms of Union, of a twenty mile tract or belt of land along each side of the portion of the Canadian Pacific Railway line located on the Mainland; and also a further application made through their duly accredited Agent, the Honourable Joseph W. Trutch, C.M.G., for the privilege of eliminating from the said belt such lands as they may deem valueless for agricultural or other economic purposes, and selecting an equal area of land, in lieu thereof, from the public lands of the Province.

The Committee consider that although the obligations of the Dominion Government have not been complied with, yet in view of the railway locations made on the Mainland and the contracts let for construction there, it is advisable that a transfer by Statute be made to the Dominion of the belt of land above referred to, under and subject to the Terms of Union.

With reference to the application made through Mr. Trutch, the Committee would observe that, without conceding the principle involved in it, viz., that the Province is pledged under the Terms of Union to grant to the Dominion tracts of valuable lands outside, in lieu of valueless lands inside of the belt mentioned, the application should, in the event of railway work being actively prosecuted, receive a liberal consideration. It is, however, a request of much too indefinite a character, for one of such magnitude, to be immediately disposed of.

It is, therefore, suggested that the Dominion Government be requested—

1st, To define the lands which they might consider valueless for agricultural or other economic purposes;

2nd, To indicate the lands which they might desire to secure in lieu thereof;

3rd, To state how they propose to deal with such lands if ceded to them, the Committee deeming it essential that this should be done in order to prevent, as far as possible, an extension of the serious injury and loss already sustained by the Province by the withdrawal from settlement since June, 1873, by special request of the Dominion, of a valuable tract of 3,200 square miles of land on Vancouver Island for railway purposes ;

4th, To inform the Provincial Government of the nature of the guarantees that they are willing to give that railway work on the Mainland will be continuously and actively prosecuted, and that within an early definite period the promise to construct the Island section of the Trunk line will be fulfilled.

The Committee advise that a copy of this Minute (if approved) be sent to Mr. Trutch, and a further copy thereof, together with copies of any other papers on the subject, be laid before the House of Assembly.

Certified.

(Signed)   T. B. HUMPHREYS,
Clerk Executive Council.

No. 246.

No. 11, Statutes of British Columbia, 1880.

A.D. 1880.

An Act to authorize the grant of certain Public Lands on the Mainland of British Columbia to the Government of the Dominion of Canada for Canadian Pacific Railway purposes.

[*Assented to 8th of May,* 1880.]

HER MAJESTY, by and with the advice and consent of the Legislative Assembly of the Province of British Columbia, enacts as follows:

1. From and after the passing of this Act, there shall be, and there is hereby, granted to the Dominion Government for the purpose of constructing and to aid in the construction of the portion of the Canadian Pacific Railway Line located between Burrard Inlet and Yellow Head summit, in trust, to be appropriated in such manner as the Dominion Government may deem advisable, a similar extent of public lands along the line of railway before mentioned (not to exceed twenty miles on each side of the said line), as may be appropriated for the same purpose by the Dominion from the public lands of the North-West Territories and the Province of Manitoba, as provided in the Order in Council, section 11, admitting the Province of British Columbia into Confederation. The land intended to be hereby conveyed is more particularly described in a despatch to the Lieutenant-Governor from the Honourable the Secretary of State, dated the 31st day of May, 1878, as a tract of land lying along the line of said railway, beginning at English Bay or Burrard Inlet and following the Fraser River to Lytton; thence by the Valley of the River Thompson to Kamloops; thence up the Valley of the North Thompson, passing near to Lakes Albreda and Cranberry, to Tête Jaune Cache; thence up the Valley of the Fraser River to the summit of Yellow Head, or boundary between British Columbia and the North-West Territories, and is also defined on a plan accompanying a further despatch to the Lieutenant-Governor from the said Secretary of State, dated the 23rd day of September, 1878. The grant of the said land shall be subject otherwise to the conditions contained in the said 11th section of the Terms of Union. *Grant of lands to Dominion Government in aid of Canadian Pacific Railway line. Description of land granted.*

2. This Act shall not affect or prejudice the rights of the public with respect to common and public highways existing at the date hereof within the limits of the lands hereby intended to be conveyed. *Not to affect existing common and public highways.*

3. This Act may be cited as " An Act to grant public lands on the Mainland to the Dominion in aid of the Canadian Pacific Railway, 1880." *Short title.*

No. 247.

The Lieutenant-Governor to the Secretary of State for Canada.

VICTORIA, BRITISH COLUMBIA,
17th May, 1880.

SIR,—I have the honour to enclose a copy of a Minute of my Executive Council dated the 12th instant, embodying a resolution unanimously passed by the Legislative Assembly of this Province on the 7th instant, respecting the construction of the Island section of the Canada Pacific Railway, and strongly recommending that the request therein contained should be complied with.

I have, &c.,
(Signed)   A. N. RICHARDS.

No. 248.

Report of the Executive Council approved by the Lieutenant-Governor on the 12th day of May, 1880.

The Committee of Council advise that the enclosed Resolution, unanimously passed by the Legislative Assembly on the 7th day of May instant, respecting the construction of the Island section of the Canadian Pacific Railway, be forwarded to the Dominion Government, with a strong recommendation and respectful request that it be complied with.

Certified,
(Signed)   T. B. HUMPHREYS,
Provincial Secretary and Clerk Executive Council.

Resolved—

That, whereas this House freely concedes to the Dominion Government due credit for the steps lately taken by them towards commencing construction of the Canadian Pacific Railway on the Mainland, and is moreover desirous that the work should be actively prosecuted:

It is, nevertheless, of opinion that the Dominion Government should be respectfully informed that the fulfilment of the obligations assumed by them in 1874 to immediately commence and finish the portion of the main line lying between *Esquimalt* and *Nanaimo* should not, in justice to the Province, be deferred beyond the Spring of 1881:

Be it therefore resolved, That an humble Address be presented to His Honour the Lieutenant-Governor, praying that he will be pleased to communicate the views of the House, as above expressed, to the Dominion Government, and recommend them for favourable consideration.

No. 249.

The Under Secretary of State for Canada to the Lieutenant-Governor.

OTTAWA, 2nd June, 1880.

SIR,—I am directed to acknowledge the receipt of your Despatch of the 17th ultimo, enclosing a copy of a Minute of your Executive Council embodying a Resolution passed by the Legislative Assembly of British Columbia on the 7th ultimo, on the subject of the construction of the Island section of the Canadian Pacific Railway.

I have, &c.,
(Signed)   EDOUARD J. LANGEVIN,
Under Secretary of State.

No. 250.

Report of the Executive Council, approved by the Lieutenant-Governor on the 4th day of October, 1880.

The Committee of Council deem it advisable that the attention of the Dominion Government be earnestly invited to the official representations made by this Government respecting the expediency of the Island section of the Canadian Pacific Railway being commenced not later than next spring, and that the Dominion be respectfully urged to make such arrangements as may be required to commence and vigorously prosecute the work in the early part of the coming year.

The Committee advise that the Dominion Government be also respectfully requested to inform this Government of their arrangements for carrying out the above object, and that a copy of this Order, if approved, be forwarded to the Honourable the Secretary of State.

Certified,
(Signed) T. BASIL HUMPHREYS,
Provincial Secretary and Clerk Executive Council.

No. 251.

The Lieutenant-Governor to the Secretary of State for Canada.

VICTORIA, BRITISH COLUMBIA,
11th October, 1880.

SIR,—I have the honour to enclose to you, herewith, a copy of a Minute of my Executive Council, dated 4th day of October instant, inviting the attention of the Dominion Government to the representations made by this Government regarding the commencement of the Island section of Canada Pacific Railway not later than next spring, and also respectfully requesting that this Government be informed of the arrangements made by the Dominion Government for the carrying out of this object.

I have, &c.,
(Signed) A. N. RICHARDS.

No. 252.

The Secretary of State for Canada to the Lieutenant-Governor.

OTTAWA, 25th October, 1880.

SIR,—I have the honour to acknowledge the receipt of your despatch of the 11th instant, enclosing a copy of a Minute of your Executive Council, dated the 4th of that month, inviting the attention of the Dominion Government to the representations made by your Government regarding the commencement of the Island section of the Canada Pacific Railway not later than next spring, and also requesting that your Government may be informed of the arrangements made by the Dominion Government for carrying out that object.

I am, &c.,
(Signed) J. C. AIKINS,
Secretary of State.

No. 253.

Report of the Executive Council, approved by the Lieutenant-Governor on the 14th day of October, 1880.

The Committee of Council are of opinion that the interests of the Province require that some person resident at Ottawa should be authorized, on behalf of this Government, to press upon the Dominion Government the importance of their carrying out their agreement to construct the Island section of the Canadian Pacific Railway, and at the same time to point out the commercial and economic value of the work, as well as the serious injury sustained by the Province, by the withdrawal from sale and settlement for the past seven years, at the instance of the Dominion Government, of the extensive area of valuable lands along the East Coast of Vancouver Island, without even the compensating advantages of railway construction, aside from the larger questions of wealth and prosperity involved in its completion.

That such authority should be given at once, so as to afford ample time and opportunity to the Dominion Government to make their arrangements for proceeding actively with the work and without further delay.

The Committee therefore advise that the Honourable A. DeCosmos, M. P., who is now, it is believed, in Ottawa, receive such authority, and that he be requested, upon his accepting the same, to report the result of his proceedings to this Government from time to time.

It is further advised that copies hereof, if approved, be forwarded to the Honourable the Secretary of State and to the Honourable Mr. DeCosmos.

Certified.
(Signed)   T. B. HUMPHREYS,
Clerk, Executive Council.

No. 254.

The Lieutenant-Governor to the Secretary of State for Canada.

VICTORIA, B.C., October 16th, 1880.

SIR,—I have the honour to enclose to you herewith a copy of a Minute of my Executive Council, dated the 14th day of October inst., authorizing the Hon. A. De Cosmos, M.P., to press upon the Dominion Government the importance of their carrying out their agreement to construct the Island section of the Canadian Pacific Railway; to point out the advantages to be gained therefrom, as well as the serious injuries sustained by the Province in consequence of the withdrawal from sale and settlement of the extensive area of valuable lands along the East Coast of Vancouver Island.

I have, &c.,
(Signed)   A. N. RICHARDS.

No. 255.

The Private Secretary to Mr. DeCosmos.

VICTORIA, October 16th, 1880.

SIR,—I am directed by His Honour to enclose to you copies of two Minutes of the Executive Council dated the 14th inst., one, authorising you to press upon the Dominion Government the importance of their carrying out their agreement to construct the Island section of the Canada Pacific Railway; to point out the advantages to be gained therefrom, as well as the serious injury the Province has sustained by the withdrawal from sale and settlement for the past seven years of the extensive area of valuable lands along the East Coast of Vancouver Island. The other, authorizing the Provincial Secretary to inform you that any expenses necessarily incurred by you in acting under the foregoing Minute will be reimbursed.

I have, &c.,
(Signed)   R. G. TATLOW,
Private Secretary.

No. 256.

The Secretary of State for Canada to the Lieutenant-Governor.

OTTAWA, 4th November, 1880.

SIR,—I have the honour to acknowledge the receipt of your despatch of the 16th ult., enclosing copy of a Minute of your Executive Council of the 14th ult., authorizing the Hon. A. DeCosmos, M.P., to press upon the Dominion Government the importance of their carrying out their agreement to construct the Island section of the Canada Pacific Railway; to point out the advantages to be gained therefrom, as well as the serious injuries sustained by the Province in consequence of the withdrawal from sale and settlement for the past seven years of the extensive area of valuable lands along the East Coast of Vancouver Island. I have, &c.,

(Signed) J. C. AIKINS,
Secretary of State.

No. 257.

The Missing Railway Despatch (No. 164), 13th June, 1876. Report of Select Committee, with Minute of Evidence, &c.

Report of Select Committee to inquire into all the circumstances connected with the suppression or non-production of a Despatch from Ottawa, bearing date 13th June, 1876, referring to Railway matters, with power to call for persons and papers; said Committee consisting of Messrs. Ash, Wilson, Abrams, Harris, and Bennett.

Your Committee report that they have obtained the evidence of every person resident in the City of Victoria whom they considered likely to be able to afford information on the subject of the enquiry:

That they telegraphed, through Mr. Speaker, to Mr. Trutch, in Europe, and have received a telegraphic reply from him, and also an explanatory letter:

That they telegraphed, through Mr. Speaker, to the Secretary of State of Canada, and have received a telegraphic reply, which showed that their telegram had been misunderstood.

That they have sent a second telegram to the Secretary of State of Canada, to which a reply has not yet been received:

That, pending a reply to their second telegram to the Secretary of State, your Committee are unable to make a final Report, but deeming that the evidence now before them should be submitted to the consideration of the House, they submit it herewith in order that it may be printed.

Your Committee will submit a final Report when they shall have received a reply to the telegram last sent to the Secretary of State of Canada.

(Signed) JOHN ASH,
Chairman.

21st *March*, 1879.

MINUTES OF EVIDENCE.

CAPT. G. R. LAYTON examined.

Do you remember anything of a despatch on Railway matters, received about 13th June, 1876?

Ans.—I saw a copy of a despatch in the newspaper this morning. I remember something about it, but I cannot say precisely without seeing the original. The original may bear some mark which might recall the matter to my memory.

The Committee, with Capt. Layton, here went to the office of the Private Secretary, and inspected the original document.

By Dr. Ash—Have you seen anything recalling this despatch to your mind?

Ans.—On looking at Schedule Book I found an entry, made by myself, dated 4th July, stating that a despatch was transmitted informing Secretary of State that a copy of their despatch of the 13th June was laid before the Executive Council, and copy of an Order of His Excellency the Governor-General in Council and Memorandum of Minister of Public Works, in relation to a conveyance, 20 miles in width, from this Government to that of the Dominion, on each side of the line surveyed and located by Canada Pacific Railroad in this Province.

Did you make a copy of the despatch?

Ans.—I made a copy. It is so long since that I cannot say whether I gave it to the Messenger or to the Lieutenant Governor.

Are you quite sure that you transmitted it in the usual way?

A.—It is so long since I cannot remember.

By Mr. Larn—Do you try or wish to suppress this despatch?

A.—None whatever.

Had any such order been received by the Lieutenant-Governor would you have known of it?

Ans.—Yes.

By Mr. Wilson—Are copies of despatches sent down from the Lieutenant-Governor to the Executive numbered consecutively?

Ans.—Yes, they are numbered according to the Schedule Book, so that if any miscarried the Executive would know it.

Are you aware of the Lieutenant-Governor having been in the habit of consulting with his Executive on important railway matters?

Ans.—Yes, he was in the habit of doing so.

By Dr. Ash—Can you suppose it possible that the Lieutenant-Governor would have received so important a despatch as this, without consulting with his Executive?

Ans.—I cannot suppose it possible.

(Signed) GEORGE RICHARD LAYTON.

COPY OF SCHEDULE, 1876.

"No. Date Received.
" 44. 13th June. 4th July.—Trans. copy of an Order of H. E. Govr. Genl. in Council, and Memorandum of Hon. Minister of Public Works, representing expediency of obtaining from the Government of B. C. a conveyance of land, 20 miles in width, on each side of the portion of the Canadian Pacific Railway line surveyed and located in B.C."

SCHEDULE OF DESPATCHES TRANSMITTED BY LIEUT.-GOVERNOR TRUTCH TO THE SECRETARY OF STATE, 1876.

"No. Date. Trans.
" 47. 4th July. 6th July.—Stating that despatch of 13th ulto was laid before Executive Council and copy of an Order of H. E. Gov. Genl. in Council and Memo. of Min. of Public Works, in relation to a conveyance, 20 miles in width, from this Government to that of the Dominion, on each side of the line surveyed and located by Canadian Pacific R. in this Province.

J. JUDSON YOUNG examined.

By Dr. Ash—You were Deputy Clerk of Executive Council in 1876?

Ans.—Yes.

Do you know anything of these Railway documents?

Ans.—No, I never saw them before; I never heard of them; know nothing whatever about them.

What was the practice respecting the transmission of documents from the Lieut.-Governor to the Executive Council?

Ans.—Such papers were always addressed to the President of the Executive Council. I never opened them; I should not have charge of them until after they had been submitted to the Executive Council.

(Signed) JAS. JUDSON YOUNG.

MR. ELLIOTT examined.

Being interrogated as to whether he knew anything of the despatch dated 13th June, 1876, with memorandum by Mr. Trutch, stating that said despatch had been referred to the Executive Council the 4th day of July, respecting location of railway route by Yellow Head Pass and Fort George, and asking for a reservation of a 20 mile belt of land along that route, said—I have no recollection of ever having seen it, nor did I ever hear of it until yesterday evening when informed by Mr. William Wilson.

By Mr. Wilson—Did ever Mr. Trutch speak to you respecting this despatch?

Ans. He never did.

Was Mr. Trutch in the habit of speaking to you on railway matters?

Ans. Yes, he was.

By Mr. Abrams—What was the practice at that time with regard to documents that were referred by the Lieut.-Governor to the Executive Council?

Ans.—They were invariably sent to the Clerk of the Executive Council; I remember no instance to the contrary.

By Mr. Harris.—Were documents of that character ever handed to you directly by the Lieutenant-Governor?

Ans.—No, unless it might be that being at the Government House documents might have been put into my hand to carry down to the Council, but in all cases they would be addressed to the Clerk of Executive Council, and would be handed by me to him.

By Dr. Ash—Then you were entirely in ignorance, until yesterday, that the Dominion Government had located the Canadian Pacific Railroad between Yellow Head Pass and Fort George?

Ans.—I never knew. I should have been only too pleased to have known.

By Mr. Wilson—Was ever a despatch received, subsequently, calling your attention to the fact that no action had been taken by the British Columbia Government upon this despatch of 13th June, calling for a reservation to be made?

Ans.—There was none. There was never any despatch to me from the Dominion Government unless it came officially through the Governor. (Signed) A. C. ELLIOTT.

F. G. VERNON examined.

I was a member of the Government in June and July, 1876.

By Mr. Wilson—Do you know anything of the Railway despatch calling for a reserve of a belt of land at Fort George?

Ans.—No; I never heard anything of it until it was read in the House a few days since.

Was Governor Trutch in the habit of consulting with his Executive?

Ans.—Yes, on all important matters, particularly those connected with the Railway question; he invariably was present at the meetings of the Council.

Were you absent from any of the meetings of the Council in June and July?

Ans.—No, I believe I was always present.

Did the existence of any such despatch as this ever come indirectly to your knowledge?

Ans.—No. It could not have come to my knowledge, either directly or indirectly, without my remembering it. I never heard of it either from Lord Dufferin or Mr. Trutch.

Then the statement of Mr. Trutch, in his despatch of 4th July, 1876, to the Secretary of State for Canada, that he had that day laid before his Executive Council, the Despatch of 13th of June, is incorrect?

Ans.—Yes, it is incorrect. The minutes of every meeting were entered in the minute book, and had there been a meeting it would have been entered.

By Mr. Abrams—Did you notice, yesterday, the entry in the Private Secretary's Schedule book referring to this despatch?

Ans.—Yes.

Have your ever before looked over that Schedule book?

Ans.—No; I never saw the Schedule book before.

By Mr. Wilson—What was the usual procedure on the part of the Lieutenant-Governor in transmitting despatches to his Executive Council?

Ans.—Sometimes he would bring them down himself and read them to the Council. In such cases they would be addressed to no person, or if addressed would not be delivered to the address; on other occasions he would hand them to the President of the Council, Mr. Brown, who would open them and hand them back to the Governor who would then read them to the Council; at other times he would hand them to the messenger, addressed to the President of the Council, or the Clerk of the Council, I forget which.

I wish to state that I never upon any occasion opened any documents transmitted by the Lieutenant-Governor to the Executive Council. Such documents were of course never addressed to me. I never saw any such documents until they were produced in the Executive Council.

(Signed) F. GEO. VERNON.

MR. EBENEZER BROWN.

I was President of the Council in July, 1876.

Do you know anything about this despatch of 13th June, 1876?

Ans.—I know nothing about it, directly or indirectly; never saw it, or heard of it, until it was read in the House a few days since. (Signed) EBENEZER BROWN.

Hon. T. B. HUMPHREYS.
I was Clerk of the Executive Council in June and early part of July, 1876.
Do you know anything of this Railway Despatch of 13th June, 1876?
Ans.—I know nothing about it, and never heard of it until Mr. Beaven showed it to me in his office, a few days before Mr. Walkem produced it in the House last Tuesday. I wish to state that the Minute Book of the Executive Council shows that there was no meeting of the Council between the 28th June, 1876, and the 22nd July, 1876. I may, also, state that I never received documents of this character at first hand. They were always brought down by Mr. Trutch personally, or addressed, under cover, to the President of the Council.

         (Signed) THOS. BASIL HUMPHREYS.

Hon. ROBERT BEAVEN.
By Dr. Ash—How did this despatch come to be found?
Ans.—A reported statement of Mr. Mackenzie in the House of Commons, and a telegram from Mr. Roscoe, to the effect that Railway line had been located to Fort George, called my attention to the subject. No despatch on this subject having been published in British Columbia, when I came into office I sought for it, but could not find it. Mr. DeCosmos subsequently telegraphed to me its date, and I then had enquiry made among the papers in the Lieutenant-Governor's office, and there the despatch was found. A copy was made and sent down to the House.
By Dr. Ash—Did Mr. DeCosmos take action in the matter in consequence of anything you had said to him?
Ans.—I cannot say.
By Mr. Wilson—What was the course pursued by Governor Trutch, at the time you were a member of the Cabinet, in bringing before his Executive important despatches received by him from the Dominion Government?
Ans.—He frequently came down personally with despatches in his pocket, if the Council were in session, when an entry of the fact would appear in the minute book. At other times he would refer them to the Council, through the Premier or President of the Council.   (Signed) ROBERT BEAVEN.

            LEGISLATIVE ASSEMBLY,
Dr. *John Ash, M.P.P.*   Victoria, 6th February, 1879.
Chairman of Railway Despatch Committee.

SIR,—I desire to state in evidence before your Committee, that, during the time I was a member of the Executive Council under Lieutenant-Governor Trutch, that he was always singularly particular and careful about all public documents and the order of conducting business; that he held firmly to the view "that the only proper medium of "communication between the Sovereign and the Administration was the Prime Minister, "not merely on account of his position as head of the Government, but especially because "he is the Minister who had been personally selected by the Sovereign as the one in "whom the Crown reposes its entire confidence."

I desire, also, to state that the discovery of the despatch at the present time is, as far as I am aware, due to the exertions of the Hon A. DeCosmos.
           I am, &c.,
        (Signed) ROBERT BEAVEN.

     Telegram from Mr. Speaker to Hon. J. W. Trutch.
            VICTORIA, 7th February, 1879.

Your letter to Dominion Government, fourth July, seventy-six, states you laid Railway Despatch received that day before Executive Council. All your Ministers deny all knowledge of despatch until found among your office papers. Telegraph explanation.
         (Signed) WILLIAMS, *Speaker.*
    Reply.
         Received at Victoria, Feb. 15th, 1879.
To Speaker, British Columbia.
Doubtless usual copy sent Council, original retained office. I write.
         (Signed) TRUTCH.

VICTORIA, 18th February, 1879.

To the Secretary of State, Canada.

Please acquaint me by telegraph, for information of Committee Legislative Assembly, if despatch of Dominion Government, thirteenth June seventy-six, locating Railway, was rescinded or withdrawn, with date and mode of such withdrawal, by telegraph or letter.

(Signed) FREDERICK WILLIAMS,
Speaker Legislative Assembly.

FOLKESTONE, 12th February, 1879.

The Honourable the Speaker of the Legislative Assembly, British Columbia:

SIR,—Your telegraphic message, addressed to me in care of the Bank of British Columbia, was forwarded to me here on the 8th instant.

The message read as follows:—

"Your letter to Dominion Government, fourth July, seventy-six, states you laid Railway despatch, received that day, before Executive Council; all your ministers deny all knowledge of despatch, until found among your office papers. Telegraph explanation.

"WILLIAMS, *Speaker.*"

I have to-day returned the following reply:—

"*Speaker, British Columbia:*

"Doubtless usual copy sent Council. Original retained Office. I write.

"TRUTCH."

I deferred telegraphing in answer to your message until I had obtained from London the Sessional Papers of the Legislative Assembly of British Columbia for the Session of 1877, from which I hoped to obtain some clue to the identification of the despatches referred to. To-day I have searched those papers, but without finding any mention of the despatch in question, from me to the Dominion Government, or of that Railway despatch the receipt of which would seem to be acknowledged by it; nor is there any allusion to any such despatches in the House of Commons, Canada, Sessional Papers, 1877.

I am thus without information as to the precise subject matter of the despatch you allude to, and I cannot recall to mind any despatch on the Railway question which was received by me at or about the date you name, except that from the Governor-General's Secretary, forwarding a copy of a despatch from the Secretary of State for the Colonies to the Governor-General, in relation to Lord Dufferin's then approaching visit to British Columbia, which despatch was discussed in Executive Council, and of which a copy is printed in the British Columbia Sessional Papers, 1877.

No doubt however, a copy of any such despatch as may, in the despatch which you state I addressed to the Dominion Government on the 4th July, 1876, have been acknowledged to have been on that day received and laid before the Executive Council would have been sent by me to the Clerk of the Council in the usual course, whilst the original despatch would have been retained in the Lieutenant-Governor's Office. This would be in accordance with the course pursued invariably (certainly without any exception that I am aware of) up to the expiration of my term of office for the two years, or thereabouts, preceding, with respect to all despatches received by me which were of a character to render advisable their being laid before Executive Council, and which accordingly were so laid before the Council. Previous to the adoption of this course, that is to say, previous to a period extending back two years, or thereabouts, from the expiration of my term of office, all such despatches were laid before Council in the original as received, but this practice was discontinued in consideration of the risk of such original documents being mislaid. On relinquishing office I carefully looked through the records of correspondence in the Lieutenant-Governor's Office, and observed that all such original despatches were complete in their proper places and order in the office, and in accordance with the office schedule of despatches received.

I should be glad if I could add any other information which might aid in accounting for the apparent miscarriage of the despatch you call my attention to, and should any further facts or observations likely to tend to this result occur to me, after I have ascertained definitely what particular despatch is referred to, I shall not fail to communicate them to you.

I have, &c.,

(Signed) JOSEPH W. TRUTCH.

No. 258.

Second Report of Select Committee to enquire into all the circumstances connected with the suppression or non-production of a Despatch from Ottawa, bearing date 13th June, 1876, referring to Railway matters.

MR. SPEAKER;

The Committee appointed to enquire into the circumstances attending the non-publication of a despatch relating to the reservation of Railway lands, dated Ottawa, 13th June, 1876, have the honour to further report as follows:—

That a despatch dated Ottawa, 13th June, 1876, relating to the conveyance of a tract of land on each side of the portion of the Canadian Pacific Railway surveyed and located in this Province, from Yellow Head Pass, turning the north end of the Cariboo range, to a point near the confluence of the Rivers Stewart and Chilacoh, was duly received on the 4th day of July, 1876, by Mr. J. W. Trutch, then Lieutenant-Governor of this Province.

That Lieutenant-Governor Trutch informed the Dominion Government, by letter, that he had laid the said despatch before his Executive Council.

That Messrs. A. C. Elliott, F. G. Vernon, E. Brown, and T. B. Humphreys, who at the time of the receipt of the said despatch were the members of the Executive Council of the Province, have stated to the Committee that they knew nothing of the said despatch until the time when a copy thereof was read in the Legislative Assembly, on the 4th of February of the current year.

That there is no evidence to show that either the Dominion Government or Lieutenant Governor Trutch made inquiry into the cause of the non-reservation of the lands asked for, by the Provincial Government, in the said despatch.

That Mr. Trutch, according to his letter dated Folkestone, 12th February, 1879, " cannot recall to mind any despatch on the railway question which was received by him " at or about the date of the said despatch."

That the Dominion Government have informed Mr. Speaker that the Order in Council of the 9th June, 1876, was superseded by a subsequent Order in Council of the 3rd September last.

(Signed)   JOHN ASH, *Chairman.*

No. 259.

Extract from Journals, Legislative Assembly, British Columbia.

Wednesday, 23rd April, 1879.

Mr. Speaker stated he had received a letter from the Honourable J. W. Trutch, which was read, and is as follows:—

" FOLKESTONE, March 25th 1879.

" SIR,—Having recently received from Victoria a printed copy of the despatch to which I understand your telegram to me had reference, namely, a despatch dated 13th June, 1876, from the Dominion Government, applying for the conveyance of certain lands along a proposed line for the Canadian Pacific Railway from Tête Jaune Pass to the confluence of the Stewart and Chilacoh Rivers, I now beg to state, in connection with my letter to you of the 12th ultimo, that I recollect having received such a communication shortly before the expiration of my term of office.

" I do not remember any particular circumstances attending the receipt of that despatch, or its transmission to the Ministry, but I have no doubt that, as noted on the margin of the original, a copy of the despatch was sent to the Executive Council in the usual course, namely, in an envelope addressed to the Clerk of the Executive Council.

" I know no reason—nor can I suggest any—why such copy of this despatch should not have reached its proper destination, and I am, therefore, unable to afford any explanation of the miscarriage, which, from the statement contained in your telegram, would appear to have occurred.

                           " I have, &c.,

" The Hon. the Speaker of the   (Signed)   " JOSEPH W. TRUTCH.
   " Legislative Assembly, British Columbia."

No. 260.

Report of Select Committee appointed re Railway despatch of 13th June, 1876.

MR. SPEAKER:

Your Committee submit a copy of the evidence given by the Hon. Mr. Trutch, which does not show that a copy of the despatch of the Dominion Government, dated 13th June, 1876, reached the Executive Council.

Your Committee recommend that the evidence in question be published with this report in the Journals of the House.

(Signed)   JOHN ASH,
Chairman.

Copy of the Minutes of the evidence given by the Hon. Joseph William Trutch, C. M. G., before the Committee " On the suppression or non-production of the Railway Despatch, 13th June, 1876 " :—

The HON. MR. TRUTCH says that he is happy to have the opportunity of meeting the Committee, and can only regret that he is unable to thrown any light on the subject of the inquiry, other than that contained in his letters to the Speaker, which are printed in the minutes of evidence taken in 1879.

The fact is, I do not remember mentioning or speaking about that despatch either to Mr. Elliott or any one else. I had no communication with the Dominion Government upon the matter, either by letter or telegram, otherwise than through my despatch to the Secretary of State. The expression "laid before my Executive Council," which occurs in my letter to the Dominion Government in connection with this despatch, is an official phrase, and does not necessarily imply that I personally placed the document in the hands of my Ministers or any one of them.

After I had acknowledged the receipt of the despatch, and had placed a copy thereof in an envelope addressed to the Executive Council, I suppose that I threw the matter off my mind. It was only a fortnight before my term of office expired. I may have regarded it in this way:—that it was not a matter demanding immediate action, and that it would be better that it should be dealt with by my successor in office. I do not affirm that these were my ideas at the time, because I recollect nothing about it; but on thinking the matter over, I can suggest no other explanation of my not having spoken with my Ministers on the subject. I had no knowledge at that time, or since, that the copy of the despatch had never reached the hands of my Council.

I was in the habit of talking with Mr. Elliott on railway matters. I am sure now that I never mentioned this despatch, because he has stated that I did not; and I have no recollection of having done so. I know no reason why I should not have done so.

Question by Dr. Ash.—Were you not a strong advocate of the Fraser River route? *Ans.*—Not an advocate, but I consistently held a decided professional opinion, which I expressed publicly at Ottawa in 1874, that the Fraser River route, being the natural outlet from the interior to the sea coast of British Columbia, was the most available line for the Canadian Pacific Railway. In regard to that opinion, I wish to state that with the exception of two lots at New Westminster which I purchased in 1859 for about $800 and sold in 1877 for about $1,000, and two lots at Hope, I have never possessed any pecuniary interest, direct or indirect, in any real estate on the mainland of British Columbia. My toll charter right in the Alexandra bridge ceased in 1870.

(Signed)   JOSEPH W. TRUTCH.

12th April, 1880.

4th May, 1880.

Members present:—Messrs. Abrams, Harris, Ash and Bennett.

MR. ALEX. WILSON says:—

Some time in the month of July, 1876, I saw Mr. Elliott pass down Fort street. A few minutes afterwards I had occasion to go down town, when I saw Mr. Elliott and Mr. McLean in conversation at one of the counters. Upon my return, in less than a quarter of an hour, I met Mr. Elliott at the corner of Fort and Government streets. On passing Mr. McLean's door, Mr. McLean hailed me and then came out. I cannot give the exact words, but he used words to this effect:—" That the railway route was fixed; that Mr. Elliott told him that he had got word that the route was fixed by Chilcotin." Upon that information I told someone connected with the *Standard* newspaper to feel for the news,—that there was something in connection with railway in town. I also told the same thing to Mr. Pearse,—that the route had been defined, and he told me afterwards that he had the same information, almost word for word, from one in authority.

              (Signed) ALEX. WILSON.

ALEX. MCLEAN examined:—

Question by Dr. Ash.—Do you know anything at all about this missing despatch? *Ans.*—I never had any conversation with Mr. Elliott on the subject of the contents of this despatch. I have no recollection of ever speaking to Mr. Alex. Wilson on the subject.

Having heard Mr. Alex. Wilson's evidence read by the Secretary, I beg to state that I have no recollection of anything of the kind taking place, and I believe his statement to be untrue.

              (Signed) A. MCLEAN.

May 4th, 1880.

www.ingramcontent.com/pod-product-compliance
Lightning Source LLC
Chambersburg PA
CBHW022112160426
43197CB00009B/988